Narrative and Poetry

Teaching Guide

Year 3
P4

Heinemann is an imprint of Pearson Education Limited, a company incorporated in England and Wales, having its registered office: Edinburgh Gate, Harlow, Essex, CM20 2JE. Registered company number: 872828

www.pearsonschools.co.uk

Heinemann is the registered trademark of Pearson Education Limited.

Text © Pearson Education Limited 2009

First published 2009

12 11 10

10 9 8 7 6 5 4 3 2

British Library Cataloguing in Publication Data
A catalogue record for this book is available from the British Library.

Literacy Evolve Year 3 Teaching Guide

ISBN 978-0435035600

Authors: Lorna Morris, Michael Lockwood, Carol Matchett

Series editor: Janice Pimm

Series Consultant: Michael Rosen

Illustrated by Luke Finlayson

Typeset by Phoenix Photosetting, Chatham, Kent

Printed in the UK by Ashford Colour Press

Acknowledgements

The publisher gratefully acknowledges permission to reproduce copyright material in this book:
'The Sound Collector' reprinted from PILLOW TALK (Viking 1990) copyright © Roger McGough

The publisher would like to thank the following for allowing us to reuse their artwork: Egmont UK Limited for illustrations by Alan Marks, from 'Storm'; Macmillan Children's Books Ltd for illustrations by Chris Riddell from 'Ottoline and the Yellow Cat' and Penguin Books Ltd for illustrations by Tony Ross from 'The Legend of Spud Murphy'.

We would like to thank Coppetts Wood Primary School, Winchcombe Abbey Primary, St Mary Magdalen's Catholic Primary, Dorridge Junior School, Fourlanesend CP School, Brookside Primary School, Archbishop of York's CE Jnr School, Lady Modiford's CofE School, Hursthead Jnr School, The Deans Primary School and St Peter's CE Primary School for their invaluable help in the development and trialling of this programme.

Every effort has been made to contact copyright holders of material reproduced in this book. Any omissions will be rectified in subsequent printings if notice is given to the publishers.

To find the latest information about *Literacy Evolve* visit:

www.pearsonschools.co.uk/literacyevolve

Contents

Welcome to *Literacy Evolve*

"If all we mean by literacy is just being able to read one word after another, we're living in a terrible, impoverished world."

Michael Rosen

Sometimes literacy can feel like little more than reading one word after another. *Literacy Evolve* offers a more inspiring way to approach the subject. It is a whole-class resource for narrative and poetry with enjoyment at its heart. It has been influenced by the ideas of former Children's Laureate Michael Rosen and uses whole, 'real' novels, powerful short films and 'single-voice' poetry collections to ignite children's interest in communication and language. If this passion and enjoyment can be inspired at school, then children are likely to read more for pleasure in their own time which in turn will lead to a greater facility with language, increased vocabulary, critical-thinking, personal development and other benefits across the curriculum (UNESCO PISA Report, 2000).

The teaching support has been designed to help you teach literacy in a creative and exciting way. The notes are written by teachers who are passionate about literacy and are packed with ideas that will spark children's creativity and provide imaginative contexts in which to apply their developing literacy skills. The sessions aim to be lively and interactive with an emphasis on speaking and listening, talk for writing and drama. 'Open-ended' questions are used frequently to stimulate meaningful discussion and develop children's confidence in talking about books and ideas. Additionally, its use of film and highly visual books allows great scope for developing children's visual literacy skills.

The units seek to immerse the children in the stimulus piece and move from reading and analysing through to responding and writing. Word and sentence level skills are covered along the way as appropriate to the unit, though the expectation is that a separate spelling programme will also be in place. Assessment for learning practices are embedded throughout, content is matched to Assessment Focuses to help you with Assessing Pupils' Progress, and our interactive planner (I-Planner Online) allows you to track progress.

Welcome to *Literacy Evolve*

Literacy Evolve is correlated to all UK curricula including the new Proposed Primary Curriculum and the Renewed Primary Framework. At Year 3 (P4) there are 23 weeks of teaching divided into units of between 1 and 4 weeks. The teaching sessions are intended to last around 1 hour to 1 ½ hours, but they can be extended or contracted as appropriate to the needs of individual classes and timetables.

Progression is built in across the units and therefore, within the narrative or poetry section it is advisable to use the units in the numbered order. However, I-Planner Online allows you to reorder the units and customise them if you so wish.

Literacy Evolve is not a one-size-fits-all programme. I-Planner allows you to teach your way and according to the needs of your class. You can customise the lesson plans as you wish, including moving units around, changing the day-to-day detail of the weekly plans, allocating different independent tasks, evaluating children and changing your future plans according to assessments.

Read on to find out more about what *Literacy Evolve* has to offer.

Literacy Evolve components

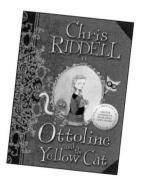

Meet the team

Michael Rosen (Series Consultant)

When I ask myself how I got into this world of children's books it all goes back to my mum and dad, who were teachers. One of the most amazing memories I have from my childhood was of when we were on a camping holiday in Yorkshire. Every night we gathered in the tent, my dad pumped up a little lamp and he read us the whole of *Great Expectations* with all the voices and actions. The voices and gestures live with me even now. It's this kind of power - literature in action - that I believe in. It's these 'Golden Moments' that teachers cherish. Every child is entitled to that level of engagement and delight that my father gave us.

A real 'Golden Moment' for me was when I was reading the story of Persephone to my 8 year-old daughter, when we came across the word 'pity'. Here is a difficult, abstract idea but when enacted in the Persephone myth it becomes accessible and concrete. Suddenly we were able to think of other examples of pity from her life and mine and also to juggle it with other abstract words like sympathy, compassion or callousness.

Literature is the most pleasurable way we have access to these difficult ideas, but we will never reach them if we quiz children too closely with closed-ended questions. Literature is a way of opening up a conversation between equals: there is no difference between my daughter's right to talk about 'pity' and mine. So here we have this enormous treasure house of literature stretching back thousands of years, giving us the greatest wisdom that the human race can put together, accessible to all.

Literacy Evolve has evolved out of the ideas that I'm expressing here, so I'm delighted to be a part of the project and hope that teachers and children will enjoy finding their way through its stories and poems. No-one involved in the project is claiming that this is an end in itself - what matters with reading and young people is that we get them hooked, and *Literacy Evolve* strikes me as a great way to do just that. It reaches out into that vast world of books that can never exhaust.

Lorna Morris

I was an English Coordinator until 1998 when I became a Literacy Consultant, working in the West Midlands. One of my real interests is the use of film and visual stimulus as a means of engaging and motivating children to write.

That's why I wanted to get involved with *Literacy Evolve*. When I saw the *Dragon Slayer* film, I thought it was just fantastic. It had visual literacy, emotion, humour, excitement - it had it all! It was so good that I used it for two units.

Golden Moment
I was working with a Year 4 class on a three-week unit based around a film. Four boys in the class were very reluctant writers. They rarely managed more than half a page and found every opportunity to avoid writing. The use of film totally transformed their attitude to writing - so much so that they begged to stay in at playtime to finish their work. Their finished stories exceeded all expectations.

Meet the team

Michael Lockwood

I was a teacher for nearly 10 years, specialising in KS2 and literacy. I've always believed in the power of whole texts read aloud to hook children into books, with or without the special effects. Since leaving the classroom, I've lectured in teacher training, working with the next generation of teachers to develop their strategies for bringing children and texts together. I've also been able to research and write about the teaching of English. In my most recent book, *Promoting Reading for Pleasure in the Primary School* (Sage 2008), I try to show teachers how they can inspire the reading habit and just how important that is. Poetry has always been a special interest of mine and the chance to work on this strand of *Literacy Evolve* was too good to miss.

Golden Moment

I was reading aloud Mildred Taylor's *Roll of Thunder, Hear My Cry* to a Year 6 class. I'd reached the climax of the novel where the storm in the title happens – and lo and behold the heavens opened outside and a real thunderstorm broke out. I've never had a more spellbound audience. Even the caretaker who was passing by stayed to listen!

Carol Matchett

During my 17 years as a class teacher, engaging children with reading and writing was always a particular interest. I carried out classroom research projects in this area and shared classroom practice with other teachers. I began to write and create my own materials and that's how I eventually became a full-time writer.

I liked to put 'whole books' and stories at the centre of my literacy teaching. I loved that whole sense of sharing a story with a class – laughing together, sharing the edge-of-seat excitement, feeling moved or uplifted by a story… The shared experience is then such a great starting point for discussion, drama, reading and writing. And working on *Literacy Evolve* has given me the chance to explore a whole new set of exciting books.

Golden Moment

I was reading Bernard Ashley stories to a class. A boy – not really an enthusiastic reader – asked if he could borrow the book to read instead of his 'reading book'. It was actually rather more difficult than his usual 'reading book' so I thought he would soon give up. But he didn't. He read the book to me, he read it in quiet reading time; he even took it home to read. As a young teacher I think I learned more from the experience than he did. It showed me the power of books and what really motivates children to read.

Novels

"When a book is written, it's written whole. The point of a book is that it should be fun, it should be exciting, it should tell you more about the world around you, it should open your eyes and open your heart, it should make you joyful, it should make you sad — and you can't get this from just taking little snippets from it."

Michael Morpurgo

The joy of reading whole novels aloud to children is central to *Literacy Evolve*. As the stories spark their imagination and interest, children will feel more confident about reading for themselves – another book by the same author, or a story with a similar theme. As they listen to the story unfold and see characters develop, children are encouraged to ask questions and explore the answers for themselves. This is 'comprehension' in its truest sense.

The novels in *Literacy Evolve* have been selected by children's literature experts and trialled in classrooms across the country. They have been selected for their quality, power and teaching potential.

Literacy Evolve assumes that you will read the book to the children in the first instance and has time built in for reading during the sessions. (It is also recommended that teachers read the novel themselves before sharing in class.) If timetable restrictions occasionally mean that a book has to be read independently, simply written chapter summaries in I-Planner Online have been included for children who may have difficulty accessing the text for themselves.

Year 3 (P4) novels

Storm by Kevin Crossley-Holland

Annie's sister is in labour and urgently needs a doctor. Cut off in a remote village in the middle of a violent storm, Annie and her family are helpless, until a mysterious stranger appears…

Kevin Crossley Holland's atmospheric Carnegie Medal winner is a thrilling story, but simply told and perfect for young juniors.

Winner of the Carnegie Medal, 1986.

Ottoline and the Yellow Cat by Chris Riddell

A string of daring burglaries have taken place in Big City and precious lapdogs are disappearing all over town. Enter a small girl named Ottoline and a mute Norwegian bog creature. Who better to solve the mystery and put an end to the Yellow Cat's reign of crime?

The stimulus materials

This strikingly original mystery novel is written and illustrated by Chris Riddell. The detailed illustrations are packed with small intricacies to intrigue even the most reluctant reader.

Winner of the 2007 Nestle Children's Book Prize Gold Award, shortlisted for the 2008 Red House Children's Book Award (Books for Younger Readers), and shortlisted for the 2008 Kate Greenaway Medal.

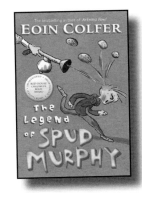

The Legend of Spud Murphy by Eoin Colfer

A comic, fast-paced, quirky novel by the author of Artemis Fowl, but scratch the surface and you find a surprisingly serious message...

Two brothers are sentenced to spend their holiday in the library, in a bid by their parents to keep them out of trouble. But the library is ruled by the tyrannical Ms Spud Murphy, with her gas-powered spud gun and long list of library rules. Yet through their ordeal, the brothers discover a surprising love for reading.

Shortlisted for the 2005 Red House Children's Book Award.

Poetry Collections

"With the Literacy Evolve project, what we've got are poets talking about why they wrote a poem, how they wrote a poem and where they come from. So we get the possibility of the child engaging with the poet and the poem and that's very, very important."

Michael Rosen

Literacy Evolve doesn't offer just another yearly anthology of poetry. Instead, the whole collection is dedicated to the voice of one poet, such as Benjamin Zephaniah, Grace Nichols or Ted Hughes.

This 'single voice' collection approach means that children get to know the poets as individuals: they understand their views and their style. Additionally, the collections have a 'personal journal' feel to them, with the poets giving insights into their backgrounds and the inspiration behind their poems. All this helps to bring poetry to life for children and increases their understanding and enjoyment.

There are two poetry collections a year (both contained in a single 'flipover' volume).

"I think it's important that children look at and enjoy a volume of poetry by one poet; then they get the voice and they get the point of view. Rather than, you know, a hundred poems about hedgehogs..."

Roger McGough

Films

Literacy Evolve harnesses the power of film to engage children. Research (UKLA/PNS Report Raising Boys' Achievement in Writing, 2004) has shown that film can inspire even reluctant readers and writers to perform well. Short, whole films have been expertly sourced for *Literacy Evolve*. They have been chosen for their quality and teaching potential. They are all supplied on our Interactive Teaching Resource, meaning that they benefit from clear display, a whole range of annotation tools, the ability to create markers, and a saving facility.

Year 3 (P4) films

Dragon Slayer

A seasoned dragon slayer is just notching up another kill, when the baby dragon he has orphaned emerges from the undergrowth. Can this plaintive little creature melt the heart of the fearsome dragon slayer?

This computer animated short film is both funny and poignant and, without the use of dialogue to tell the story, allows great scope for visual literacy and imaginative writing.

The stimulus materials

Unit stimuli

This chart shows the main stimulus pieces across *Literacy Evolve* Key Stage 2 (P4-P7) and how they are matched to units.

Year 3/P4

 Narrative Unit 1: *Storm* – novel (Settings)

 Narrative Unit 2: *Dragon Slayer* – film (Myths and legends)

 Narrative Unit 3: *Ottoline and the Yellow Cat* – novel (Mystery)

 Narrative Unit 4: *The Legend of Spud Murphy* – novel (Author study)

 Narrative Unit 5: *Dragon Slayer* – film (Play and film scripts)

 Poetry Units 1, 2 and 3: Gina Douthwaite, Roger McGough

Year 4/P5

 Narrative Unit 1: *Invasion* – novel (Historical settings)

 Narrative Unit 2: *The Spiderwick Chronicles* – novel (Fantasy)

 Narrative Unit 3: *Christophe's Story* – novel (Other cultures)

 Narrative Unit 4: *Lard* – film (Issues)

 Narrative Unit 5: *Bicho* – film (Play and film scripts)

 Poetry Units 1 and 2: Grace Nichols, James Carter

Year 5/P6

 Narrative Unit 1: *Friend or Foe* – novel (Author study)

 Narrative Unit 2: *The Book* – film (Traditional stories)

 Narrative Unit 3: *Oranges in No Man's Land* – novel (Other cultures)

 Narrative Unit 4: *Tales of the Family from One End Street* – novel (Classic literature)

 Narrative Unit 5: *Magik Circus* – film (Film narrative)

 Narrative Unit 6: *News and adverts* – film (Media scripts)

Poetry Units 1, 2 and 3: Michael Rosen, Charles Causley

Year 6/P7

 Narrative Unit 1: *Fantastic, Funny, Frightening!* – stories (Genres)

 Narrative Unit 2: *Planet Prision* – multi-media text (Multi-modal reading)

 Narrative Unit 3: *Millions* – novel (Author study)

 Narrative Unit 4: *Eye of the Wolf* – novel (Narrative technique)

 Narrative Unit 5: *Fantastic, Funny, Frightening!* – stories (Revision)

Poetry Units 1, 2 and 3: Benjamin Zephaniah, Ted Hughes

The teaching approach

Visual literacy
A focus on visual literacy skills gives children another access point to understanding and responding to the texts.

Open questions
Open-ended questions stimulate meaningful discussion and develop children's confidence in talking about books and ideas.

Active strategies and talk for writing
Talk for writing, speaking, listening and drama strategies mean that the children are active and engaged all through the lesson and are continually preparing for writing. The strategies are highlighted and a glossary is provided on page xvii.

Differentiation
Where appropriate, tasks are differentiated three ways, with three dots indicating tasks for the more able. Often the differentiation ideas are offered in the supporting T/TA notes on I-Planner Online.

Session 12

We are learning to …	Resources
• use drama to explore characters	*Lard* (film)
• understand different points of view and how this affects characters' behaviour (PNS Strands 4.1, 7.2)	PCM: 4.11
Assessment Focuses AF (R): 3	

Shared teaching
- Share the learning objectives.
- Review Thought Tracking from Session 11 to recap Jake's thoughts and motives in *Lard*.
- Recap the thinking point from Session 11. Take feedback.
- Organise a Forum Theatre activity to show how the other characters in the film felt. Explain that the film follows the main character Jake, but the children will focus on the viewpoint of the other characters.
- Watch the film again. Ask the children to nominate peers to act out the roles of the characters in the film: the two boys, Jake's mum, the neighbour, the old man, the young girl and the shopkeepers. The rest of the children act as directors and explain to the characters what they should do. Use props if appropriate.
- Guide the children while the Forum Theatre takes shape and remind them of the ground rules for large group work. If possible, film the activity to review in the plenary.
- After the Forum Theatre, use Hot-Seating to focus on the two boys. Show 'Quality questions' (PCM 4.11) as a prompt to ask the children playing those characters to explain how they felt and what they thought about what Jake did.

Independent and Guided
- In small groups, Hot-Seat the rest of the characters in *Lard*: Jake's mum, the shopkeepers, the young girl, the neighbour and the old man.
- 🔵🔵🔵 Take turns to play a character and answer questions from the rest of the group to explain what they saw and what they thought about it.
- 🔵🔵 As above. Focus on Jake's mum and the shopkeepers first. (TA+)
- 🔵 As above. Use PCM 4.11 as a prompt. (T)

Plenary
- Remind the children that their actions can be perceived differently by different people, depending on their point of view.
- Recap the learning objectives.
- If you filmed the Forum Theatre activity, show the highlights.
- Discuss the viewpoints of the other characters in the film. *Were you surprised by what they thought? Have you changed your view of what happened in the film? How did the hot-seating help you explore the characters?*
- Explain that in Session 13, the children will look more closely at the other characters and what they know about them.

Assessment pointers
- S&L: drama activities will show how far the children can sustain roles and understand the characters.
- AF3 (R): the forum theatre and hot-seating activities show how well the children can interpret information and events from different viewpoints.

Session 13

We are learning to …	Resources
• explore shots, music, words and images in film	*Lard* (film)
• explore how film directors use film techniques	ITP: 4.10, 4.11, 4.12
• choose words and images for particular effects (PNS Strands 2.2, 8.3, 9.5)	PCM: 4.12
Assessment Focuses AF (R): 5, 6, AF (W): 1, 7	

Shared teaching
- Show 'Film shots' (ITP 4.10) to recap film vocabulary learned in Year 3.
- Share the learning objectives. Explain that this session will focus on how the director made the film in order to convey meaning to the viewer, e.g. the choices made about what camera shots and music to use, how the characters should speak and look, etc.
- Watch *Lard* from the beginning to Marker 1. *What do you notice about the way the clip is filmed? How does the director portray the tall boy playing football?* Focus on the way the director films the ball rolling across the road. *Why is the ball rolling filmed at ground level? What effect does this have? What is the effect of the colour of the ball?*
- *As an author how might you write about the ball rolling?* Reflect on work from Phase 1 about expressive and figurative language. Encourage the children to suggest adverbs.
- Watch *Lard* from Marker 1 to Marker 2. Note the camera angles, the close-up of the boy's face and the way he walks towards Jake. *What is the effect of these shots?*
- Show 'How does Jake feel?' (ITP 4.11). Ask for words to describe how Jake felt about the ball while he watched the other boys playing. *Jake obviously wanted to play with the ball. Why? How does he feel when he is bouncing the ball? How does he feel after the ball is flattened?*

- Explain that you're going to put the film sequence into written words. Use Modelled Writing to create a model text or show 'The golden ball' (ITP 4.12) example text.
- Use Think Alouds to show your thought processes while developing the model text, e.g. *Jake was very excited about the ball … how can I convey that? How could I describe the ball? What does it look like? Sound like?* Show or create your own model text.

Independent and Guided
- The children watch *Lard* from Marker 3 to Marker 4 and describe the scene in written words.
- 🔵🔵🔵 Write a description of the incident in the shop from the moment Jake enters until he leaves.
- 🔵🔵 As above. Use prompts from 'Jake's dilemma in the shop' (PCM 4.12) to structure writing. (T)
- 🔵 As above. Use PCM 4.12 as a writing frame (TA)

Plenary
- Take feedback and ask for volunteers to share their writing.
- Recap the learning objectives and explain that just like a film director, an author makes choices to get the reader to think and feel certain things. *What tools can an author use?* (E.g. powerful vocabulary, suspense, descriptive and expressive language, etc.)
- Discuss the tools a film director has to work with. *How do music, sound, images and different camera shots change how you feel when watching a film?*

Assessment pointers
- AF5, 6 (R): shared discussions will indicate how far the children understand the effect an author's choice of language has on a reader.
- AF1, 7 (W): written outcomes show how far the children can write imaginatively and use effective vocabulary.

The teaching approach

Objectives
Clear objectives for sharing with the class and evaluating against. Assessment Focuses are also clearly flagged.

Reference to the Interactive Teaching Resource
Interactive teaching pages which support and enliven your shared teaching are clearly referenced.

Teaching Assistant or Teacher notes
(T) or (TA) indicates the recommended support for each Independent Activity. A + sign indicates that additional notes are available on I-Planner Online.

Assessment for Learning
Assessment for learning is embedded throughout, including peer review, self-review, marking ladders and success criteria.

Assessment Pointers
Assessment pointers identify relevant evidence for each Assessment Focus, including Speaking and Listening, and help with APP.

PHASE 3: PLANNING AND WRITING A STORY WITH A DILEMMA (7 DAYS)

Session 14

We are learning to …	Resources
• plan writing using planning tools	ITP: (4.1)
• work together to plan writing (PNS Strands 9.1)	PCM: (4.1, 4.2)
Assessment Focuses	
AF (W): 3	

Shared teaching
- Recall annotated 'Story mind map' (ITP 4.1). Remind the children of the work they did when they planned their oral stories. *How did the storymaker cards help you to plan?*
- Share the learning objectives. Explain that the children are going to write a story with issues based on a structure like *Lord*, so that the ending opens up another issue or dilemma and leaves the main character on a cliffhanger.
- Discuss what the story should include, e.g. a beginning, middle, end and twist.
- Discuss the audience for the children's stories, e.g. their peer group, and the purpose of a story with a dilemma, e.g. to make people think carefully about the issues raised as well as to entertain.
- As a starting point for ideas, read through the dilemmas collected on the Learning Wall and recall dilemmas in films and stories from earlier sessions.

Independent and Guided
- The children plan in groups, pairs or individually, using a technique of their own choice, e.g. Mind Mapping, Improvisation, etc. Give the children time to explore dilemmas and solutions and provide support according to their needs.

Use 'Storymaker cards 1' (PCM 4.1) and 'Storymaker cards 2' (PCM 4.2) to plan a new dilemma story.
As above. (TA+)
As above. (T+)

Plenary
- Play *Just a Minute*. Talk Partners take turns to tell the rough sequence of their story.
- Encourage the children to give positive verbal feedback about what they liked in each other's story and why.
- Ask the children to give peer assessment, using thumbs up, down, or half way. *Has your partner got a clear idea of their own story with a dilemma?* Make a note of any thumbs down and support these children in Session 15.
- Recap the learning objectives. *How did you plan your story? Did anyone help you develop your ideas? How?*

Assessment pointers
- S&L: group or pair work will show how far the children can adopt group roles, drawing ideas together and promoting effective discussion.
- AF3 (W): peer assessment and independent planning work will show how far the children can generate imaginative ideas and structure their stories.

Session 15

We are learning to …	Resources
• plan writing using planning tools	ITP: 4.13
• choose words and images for particular effects (PNS Strands 9.1, 9.5)	PCM: (4.1, 4.2), 4.13, 4.14
Assessment Focuses	
AF (W): 3, 4, 7	

Shared teaching (1)
- Share the learning objectives. Explain that in this session, the children will continue to develop plans for their stories with a dilemma. Explain that they will need to have a clear plan for your story and know the order in which things happen in the plot before you start writing.
- Recap the notes made in the independent and guided activity in Session 14 and explain that the children are going to take these notes and develop a story plan.

Independent and Guided (1)
- The children work independently to complete 'Dilemma story planner' (PCM 4.13), using notes from 'Storymaker cards 1' (PCM 4.1) and 'Storymaker cards 2' (PCM 4.2). Encourage the children to add figurative and expressive language and adverbs to the plan, that they can use in their story.
Use PCM 4.13. Complete all sections, including the final 'Twist'.
As above. Provide support with the "Vocabulary" column. (TA+)
As above. If necessary, allow the children to draw scenes from their story plan instead of writing. (T+)

Shared teaching (2)
- Remind the children of the work they did on story structure in Session 10. *How did the director structure the film to make it interesting?*

- Show 'Story plan' (ITP 4.13). Ask for a volunteer to share their ideas from PCM 4.13. Model how to transfer these ideas onto the first screen of ITP 4.13, thinking about the order in which events happen. *What comes next, after I have opened my story and set the scene?*
- Discuss chapters in a story and how they are used. Explain that each step on ITP 4.13 could form a chapter.
- Model completing the second screen of ITP 4.13. Show the children how to use the Learning Wall and other sources to find interesting opening sentences and connectives to use.

Independent and Guided (2)
- The children use annotated PCM 4.13 to complete their 'Story plan' (PCM 4.14).
Complete PCM 4.14 and start thinking about openings and connectives to use in their story. (T)
As above, thinking about openings to use in their story.
As above, concentrating on completing their story plans. (TA+)

Plenary
- Talk Partners peer review each other's plans using thumbs up, down or half way. *Does the story build up to the most exciting part?* Allow the children time to respond to the feedback.
- Recap the learning objectives. *What opening sentences and connectives have you made a note of?*

Assessment pointers
- S&L: pair work will show how well the children can express and respond to opinions.
- AF3, 4, 7 (W): story plans will show how far the children can sequence and structure their stories.

Narrative Unit 4: *Lord* · 81

Interactive Teaching Resource

The Interactive Teaching Resource (ITR) is the one-stop shop for all the supporting materials you will need to use *Literacy Evolve*. All resources are accessed using a 'player' which provides a range of annotation and editing tools.

The ITR contains:

- Films (up to three per year for Key Stage 2 (P4–P7))
- Videos of author interviews
- Videos of poetry performances by the original poet
- Additional stimulus materials (short stories, extracts, photos, artwork, audio, etc.)
- PDF versions of PCMs (editable versions can be found on I-Planner)
- A wealth of interactive teaching pages which structure and support your lesson in an engaging and interactive way

Navigating the DVD

The ITR is very simple to navigate. You will find references to the pages you require in the teaching notes. These are the Interactive Teaching Pages (ITPs).

To access your desired electronic resource:

1) Simply choose the unit that you are studying. This screen is broken down into columns, one for narrative units and one for poetry.

2) Once you have opened your chosen unit, you can then select the resource type that you require (as indicated in the lesson plans). From this screen you can access video resources, ITPs and electronic versions of PCMs. (Please note that the Storybooks option is only available for Key Stage 1 units.)

3) When you have clicked on the type of resource that you need, you can then select the specific ITP, film or PCM that you require by checking the relevant number and name of the resource against the lesson plan. Once clicked, the resource will load automatically and is ready to use. You can then navigate to the previous menus via the 'breadcrumb' navigation toolbar at the bottom of the screen.

Interactive Teaching Resource

Toolbar

At the bottom of any activity or video, you will find a toolbar full of features for you to use to annotate the screen.

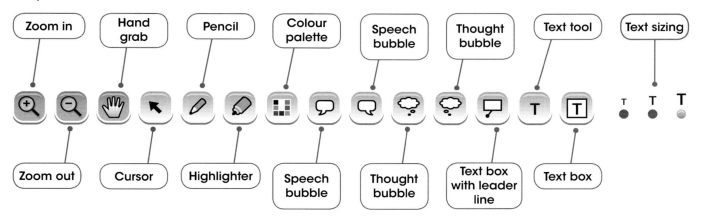

Film Tools (situated next to the annotation toolbar)

There are also a range of film tools available, including film markers, which let you add your own stop/start points to the film.

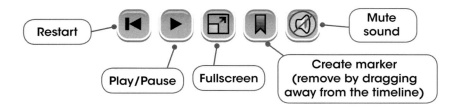

Printing

There is a print button located in the top right-hand corner of the player. Clicking this button will print the current page in view. You simply need to select the printer you wish to use from the list, as with your normal operating system.

Print

Loading

To load a previously saved screen, simply click the open button in the top right-hand corner of the player. This will then bring up a list of locations on your computer. Find the file that you wish to use and open as normal. This new file will then replace the screen currently open.

Open

Saving

To save your work on a current screen, click the save button located in the top right-hand corner of the player. You can then save the screen to a desired location on your computer.

Save

Exit

This button will close the program completely.

Assessment and I-Planner

Assessment for Learning practices are embedded through *Literacy Evolve*. Objectives are shared and reviewed at the beginning and end of every session. There are many opportunities for self- and peer-assessment, and success criteria are used for children to evaluate their work at each stage of its development.

All the lesson content is matched to Assessment Focuses. Assessment pointers are provided for every session which help you to identify what evidence has been identified for each Assessment Focus. This matches the approach of Assessing Pupil Progress and will help fulfil the requirements of this initiative.

I-Planner Online allows you to record evaluations of your children's learning, and from this will generate 'alerts' to remind you when your assessments are next relevant to your planning.

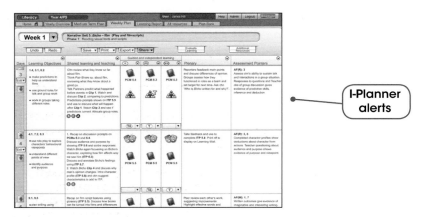

I-Planner alerts

In addition, I-Planner Online will create an ongoing Learning Report to summarise where the class are and which pupils you have identified as needing further support or extension.

Detailed information on how I-Planner works can be found on the Help tab of I-Planner.

The Learning Report is based on the Renewed Framework objectives. Underneath each of the Framework objectives are the *Literacy Evolve* 'We are learning to …' statements or learning objectives. These break down the broader Framework objectives into smaller chunks. You can use the Evaluate Learning feature in I-Planner Online to quickly assess these objectives and the Learning Report will then show at a glance how much progress your pupils are making towards the overall Framework objectives.

Teaching strategy glossary

Babble Gabble: The children work in pairs to retell a story they have just listened to. One child retells the story as fast as they can, whilst still including as much detail as possible, changing after a minute so their partner continues the tale.

Conscience Alley: One child takes on the role of the character whilst the other children create each side of the alley, putting forth their opposing views as the character walks down. The child in role listens to his 'conscience' before making a decision about the course of action to take.

Envoys: One member of each group moves between the other groups, sharing information and collecting ideas.

Expert Groups: Groups each focus on a specific subject, researching and discussing to become experts on it. (Leads to Jigsawing.)

Fortunately/Unfortunately: players take it in turns to tell a story which begins alternately with these words, e.g. unfortunately I lost my dinner money on the way to school. Fortunately I don't like school dinners!

Forum Theatre: A small group of children act out a scene, while the rest of the class work as directors.

Freeze Frame: A drama activity where the children use their bodies to form a still image to illustrate a specific incident or event.

Grammar Poetry: Groups try to make up nonsense sentences consisting of an adjective, noun and verb all beginning with the same letter or sound, e.g. angry aardvarks amble.

Hot-Seating: A drama technique where a child takes on the role of a character in the 'hot seat', while the other children ask the character either prepared or improvised questions.

Improvisation: A drama activity that is not planned in any way. The children take on roles and make up the dialogue, actions, etc. as they go along.

Jigsawing: Home groups are given a task to complete. Each member is then given a number and groups of children with the same number are formed (i.e. all the number 1s together) to undertake investigations, discuss their work and agree on the main points to report back to the home group.

Just a Minute: The children speak for one minute on a chosen subject, trying not to hesitate or repeat themselves.

Learning Wall: A place where key ideas, information and success criteria are stored in the classroom, so that children can easily refer to it throughout the sessions.

Mind Map: The children think of ideas about a particular topic, such as the personality traits of a character, the features of a story type, etc. Then they write down these ideas, usually in the form of a diagram.

Modelled Writing: The teacher models the writing process by orally rehearsing before writing, making and explaining out loud decisions and changes, while encouraging the children to share the writing process.

Rainbowing: Discussion is paused and each group is given a different colour. The class is reorganised into colour groups so that the children share ideas with children from other groups.

Role Play: The children take on the roles of different characters to act out a scene.

Role on the Wall: Key words and phrases are placed inside and outside an outline of a character, e.g. character's thoughts placed inside, other characters' opinions on the outside.

Signifier: A drama technique where a prop or item of clothing is used to signify a role being played.

Snowballing: Pairs discuss a subject then join with another pair to form a group and share ideas. Two groups then join together and so on until there is a whole-class discussion.

Statement Game: The children are given a set of cards on which statements are written. They then use the cards to discuss in groups or with a partner to decide how to categorise the statements.

Talk Partners: Pairs talk through and develop ideas together.

Teacher in Role: The teacher takes on the role of a character who is being focused on, in order to introduce, control or develop drama activities.

Think Alouds: Out loud, the teacher explains their thought processes during the writing process. This also includes aspects such as rereading the text to check for sense and making changes to the text, e.g. crossing out, improving words for effect.

Think-Pair-Share: The children are given think time, then talk though ideas with a partner, before sharing ideas with a larger group or the rest of the class.

Think Time: The children are given a brief amount of time to think about a question before answering.

Thought Tracking: The action in a novel or a film is frozen at a key moment and the thoughts of the character are spoken aloud, either by the child in role or by the rest of the group.

Two Stars and a Wish: When reviewing each other's work, the children identify two positive aspects and one negative aspect to feed back on.

Walking Bus: Music is played while the children walk around the classroom. When the music stops, the teacher asks a question which the children discuss with those nearest to them.

Word Tennis: In pairs, each child takes it in turn to say one word or phrase. This either makes up a continuous sentence or is used as a form of word association.

Curriculum Correlation – Proposed Primary Curriculum

Understanding English, communication and languages curriculum progression

MIDDLE	Narrative					Poetry		
	Unit 1 *Storm* (Settings)	Unit 2 *Dragon Slayer* (Myths and legends)	Unit 3 *Ottoline...* (Mystery)	Unit 4 *...Spud Murphy* (Author study)	Unit 5 *Dragon Slayer* (Play and film scripts)	Unit 1 McGough/ Douthwaite (Performance)	Unit 2 McGough/ Douthwaite (Shape)	Unit 3 McGough/ Douthwaite (Language play)
1. Speaking and listening								
Organise and shape what they say, selecting relevant ideas and using appropriate vocabulary to interest their listeners	✔	✔	✔	✔	✔	✔	✔	✔
Organise and adjust what they say according to listeners' needs, including the use of spoken standard English when appropriate	✔	✔	✔	✔	✔	✔	✔	✔
Identify the main points of what has been said and ask questions to clarify meaning	✔	✔	✔	✔	✔	✔		
Reflect on their own and others' speech and investigate how it varies								
Take different roles and make relevant contributions in group discussion and role-play	✔	✔	✔	✔	✔	✔		✔
Explain their opinions and ideas, modifying them in the light of what they have heard	✔	✔	✔	✔	✔	✔	✔	✔
Use dialogue and discussion to build up and refine ideas collaboratively in groups	✔	✔	✔	✔	✔	✔	✔	✔
Convey action, themes and emotions through role-play and drama.	✔	✔	✔	✔	✔	✔		✔
2. Reading								
Focus on the meaning of the text as a whole, identifying features of text and understanding their use	✔	✔	✔	✔	✔	✔	✔	✔
Use inference and deduction to find meaning beyond the literal	✔	✔	✔	✔	✔	✔	✔	
Make connections between different parts of a text and with other texts they have read	✔	✔	✔	✔	✔	✔	✔	✔
Skim, scan and use key word searches and other features of texts to locate and select information	✔	✔	✔	✔	✔			
Verify the accuracy and reliability of information, distinguishing between fact and opinion								
Recognise and describe how authors and poets select words and use a variety of language forms and structures to create effects	✔	✔	✔	✔	✔	✔	✔	✔
Recognise how authors of moving image and multimodal texts use different combinations of words, images and sounds to create effects and make meaning		✔			✔			
Identify different structural and organisational features and different presentational devices, layouts and combinations of formats and how they affect meaning		✔	✔	✔	✔	✔	✔	✔
Respond critically to arguments and recognise how they are constructed								
Explore and reflect on characters, ideas and themes in narratives	✔	✔	✔	✔	✔	✔	✔	✔

Understanding English, communication and languages curriculum progression

MIDDLE	Narrative					Poetry		
	Unit 1 *Storm* (Settings)	Unit 2 *Dragon Slayer* (Myths and legends)	Unit 3 *Ottoline...* (Mystery)	Unit 4 *...Spud Murphy* (Author study)	Unit 5 *Dragon Slayer* (Play and film scripts)	Unit 1 McGough/ Douthwaite (Perfor-mance)	Unit 2 McGough/ Douthwaite (Shape)	Unit 3 McGough/ Douthwaite (Language play)
3. Writing								
Create and shape their writing, using different techniques to interest the reader	✔	✔	✔	✔	✔	✔	✔	✔
Select form, content and vocabulary to suit particular purposes	✔	✔	✔	✔	✔	✔	✔	✔
Create effects by combining written text with illustration, moving image and sound		✔	✔				✔	
Share ideas and collaborate with others remotely using ICT								
Plan, develop and review their work in order to improve it, understanding how language varies in different formats	✔	✔	✔	✔	✔	✔	✔	✔
Use features of layout, presentation and organisation in print and on screen	✔	✔	✔	✔	✔		✔	✔
Understand how paragraphs, bullets, hyperlinks, screen layout and headings are used to organise and link ideas, and to use these in their own work	✔	✔	✔	✔				
Recognise and use different types of sentences, exploring how ideas are linked within and between sentences	✔	✔	✔	✔	✔			
Understand the function of punctuation within sentences and using it to clarify structure and represent emphasis	✔	✔	✔	✔	✔			
Recognise and apply common spelling patterns, conventions, and spell check techniques, using knowledge of word families and the roots and origins of words				✔				
Form and join letters fluently and correctly and type accurately		✔	✔	✔			✔	✔

Curriculum Correlation – Primary Framework

	Narrative					Poetry		
	Unit 1 *Storm* (Settings)	Unit 2 *Dragon Slayer* (Myths and legends)	Unit 3 *Ottoline...* (Mystery)	Unit 4 *...Spud Murphy* (Author study)	Unit 5 *Dragon Slayer* (Play and film scripts)	Unit 1 McGough/ Douthwaite (Performance)	Unit 2 McGough/ Douthwaite (Shape)	Unit 3 McGough/ Douthwaite (Language play)
1. Speaking								
Choose and prepare poems or stories for performance, identifying appropriate expression, tone, volume and use of voices and other sounds					✔	✔		✔
Explain process or present information, ensuring items are clearly sequenced, relevant details are included and accounts ended effectively		✔						
Sustain conversation, explain or give reasons for their views or choices	✔	✔	✔	✔	✔			
Develop and use specific vocabulary in different contexts		✔						
2. Listening and responding								
Follow up others' points and show whether they agree or disagree in whole-class discussion	✔				✔			
Identify the presentational features used to communicate the main points in a broadcast								
Identify key sections of an informative broadcast, noting how the language used signals changes or transitions in focus								
3. Group discussion and interaction								
Use discussion to organise roles and action		✔			✔	✔		
Actively include and respond to all members of the group		✔		✔				✔
Use the language of possibility to investigate and reflect on feelings, behaviour or relationships			✔	✔				
4. Drama								
Present events and characters through dialogue to engage the interest of an audience					✔			
Use some drama strategies to explore stories or issues	✔	✔	✔		✔			
Identify and discuss qualities of others' performances, including gesture, action and costume					✔	✔		✔
5. Word recognition (objectives covered by the end of Year 2)								
6. Word structure and spelling								
Spell high and medium frequency words								
Recognise a range of prefixes and suffixes, understanding how they modify meaning and spelling, and how they assist in decoding long, complex words								
Spell unfamiliar words using known conventions including phoneme/grapheme correspondences and morphological rules								
7. Understanding and interpreting texts								
Identify and make notes on the main points of section(s) of text		✔						
Infer characters' feelings in fiction and consequences in logical explanations	✔	✔	✔	✔	✔			

	Narrative					Poetry		
	Unit 1 Storm (Settings)	Unit 2 Dragon Slayer (Myths and legends)	Unit 3 Ottoline... (Mystery)	Unit 4 ...Spud Murphy (Author study)	Unit 5 Dragon Slayer (Play and film scripts)	Unit 1 McGough/ Douthwaite (Perfor-mance)	Unit 2 McGough/ Douthwaite (Shape)	Unit 3 McGough/ Douthwaite (Language play)
Identify how different texts are organised, including reference texts, magazines, leaflets, on paper and on screen		✔	✔	✔	✔			
Use syntax, context and word structure to build their store of vocabulary when reading for meaning								
Explore how different texts appeal to readers using varied sentence structures and descriptive language	✔	✔	✔	✔	✔	✔	✔	✔
8. Engaging with and responding to texts								
Share and compare reasons for reading preferences, extending range of books read		✔	✔	✔			✔	
Empathise with characters and debate moral dilemmas portrayed in texts	✔	✔	✔	✔	✔			
Identify features that authors use to provoke readers' reactions	✔	✔	✔	✔	✔	✔		✔
9. Creating and shaping texts								
Make decisions about form and purpose, identify success criteria and use them to evaluate their own writing	✔	✔	✔	✔	✔	✔	✔	✔
Use beginning, middle and end to write narratives in which events are sequenced logically and conflicts resolved		✔	✔		✔			
Write non-narrative texts using structures of different text types								
Select and use a range of technical and descriptive vocabulary	✔	✔	✔	✔	✔	✔	✔	✔
Use layout, format, graphics, illustrations for different purposes			✔	✔	✔		✔	
10. Text structure and organisation								
Signal sequence, place and time to give coherence		✔	✔					
Group related material into paragraphs			✔	✔				
11. Sentence structure and punctuation								
Show relationships of time, reason and cause, through subordination and connectives		✔	✔	✔				
Compose sentences using adjectives, verbs and nouns for precision, clarity and impact	✔	✔	✔					✔
Clarify meaning through the use of exclamation marks and speech marks			✔		✔			
12. Presentation								
Write with consistency in size and proportion of letters and spacing within and between words, using the correct formation of handwriting joins								✔
Develop accuracy and speed when using keyboard skills to type, edit and redraft				✔			✔	✔

Curriculum Correlation – Wales

The National Curriculum for Wales, English correlation chart

Wales Key Stage 2 Programme of Study	Narrative					Poetry		
	Unit 1 *Storm* (Settings)	Unit 2 *Dragon Slayer* (Myths and legends)	Unit 3 *Ottoline...* (Mystery)	Unit 4 *...Spud Murphy* (Author study)	Unit 5 *Dragon Slayer* (Play and film scripts)	Unit 1 McGough/ Douthwaite (Performance)	Unit 2 McGough/ Douthwaite (Shape)	Unit 3 McGough/ Douthwaite (Language play)
Skills Pupils should be given opportunities to:								
1. listen and view attentively, responding to a wide range of communication	✔	✔	✔	✔	✔	✔	✔	✔
2. identify key points and follow up ideas through question and comment, developing response to others in order to learn through talk	✔	✔	✔	✔	✔	✔	✔	✔
3. communicate clearly and confidently, expressing opinions, adapting talk to audience and purpose, using appropriate gesture, intonation and register in order to engage the listener	✔	✔	✔	✔	✔	✔	✔	✔
4. develop their awareness of the social conventions of conversation and discussion	✔	✔	✔	✔	✔	✔	✔	✔
5. develop their ability to use a range of sentence structures and vocabulary with precision, including terminology that allows them to discuss their work	✔	✔	✔	✔	✔	✔	✔	✔
6. develop their understanding of when it is necessary to use standard English, and use formal and informal language appropriately				✔		✔	✔	✔
7. evaluate their own and others' talk and drama activities and develop understanding of how to improve, considering how speakers adapt their vocabulary, tone, pace and style to suit a range of situations.	✔	✔	✔	✔	✔	✔	✔	✔
Range Pupils should be given opportunities to develop their oral skills through:								
1. seeing and hearing different people talking, including people with different dialects	✔			✔		✔	✔	✔
2. experiencing and responding to a variety of stimuli and ideas: visual, audio and written	✔	✔	✔	✔	✔	✔	✔	✔
3. communicating for a range of purposes, *e.g. presenting information, expressing opinions, explaining ideas, questioning, conveying feelings, persuading*	✔	✔	✔	✔	✔	✔	✔	✔
4. speaking and listening individually, in pairs, in groups and as members of a class	✔	✔	✔	✔	✔	✔	✔	✔
5. using a variety of methods to present ideas, including ICT, *e.g. drama approaches, discussion and debate*	✔	✔	✔	✔	✔	✔	✔	✔
6. presenting, talking and performing for a variety of audiences	✔	✔	✔	✔	✔	✔	✔	✔
7. increasing their confidence in language use by drawing on their knowledge of English, Welsh and other languages				✔	✔			
8. engaging in activities that focus on words, their derivation, meanings, choice and impact.		✔	✔	✔	✔	✔	✔	✔

Curriculum Correlation – Wales

The National Curriculum for Wales, English correlation chart

Wales Key Stage 2 Programme of Study	Narrative					Poetry		
	Unit 1 *Storm* (Settings)	Unit 2 *Dragon Slayer* (Myths and legends)	Unit 3 *Ottoline…* (Mystery)	Unit 4 *…Spud Murphy* (Author study)	Unit 5 *Dragon Slayer* (Play and film scripts)	Unit 1 McGough/ Douthwaite (Performance)	Unit 2 McGough/ Douthwaite (Shape)	Unit 3 McGough/ Douthwaite (Language play)
Reading Pupils should be given opportunities to:								
1. develop phonic, graphic and grammatical knowledge, word recognition and contextual understanding within a balanced and coherent programme	✔	✔	✔	✔		✔	✔	✔
2. develop their ability to read with fluency, accuracy, understanding and enjoyment	✔	✔	✔	✔		✔	✔	✔
3. read in different ways for different purposes, including:	✔	✔	✔	✔	✔	✔	✔	✔
• skimming, scanning and detailed reading	✔		✔	✔				
• using prediction, inference and deduction	✔	✔	✔	✔	✔			
• distinguishing between fact and opinion, bias and objectivity in what they read/view								
4. recognise and understand the characteristics of different genres in terms of language, structure and presentation	✔	✔	✔	✔	✔	✔	✔	✔
5. consider what they read / view, responding orally and in writing to the ideas, vocabulary, style, presentation and organisation of image and language, and be able to select evidence to support their views	✔	✔	✔	✔	✔	✔	✔	✔
6a. use a range of appropriate information retrieval strategies including ICT, *e.g. the alphabet, indexes and catalogues*	✔		✔	✔				
6b. retrieve and collate information and ideas from a range of sources including printed, visual, audio, media, ICT and drama in performance	✔		✔	✔				
7. use the knowledge gained from reading to develop their understanding of the structure, vocabulary, grammar and punctuation of English, and of how these clarify meaning	✔	✔	✔	✔				
8. consider how texts change when they are adapted for different media and audiences.		✔			✔	✔	✔	✔
Range Pupils should be given opportunities to develop their reading / viewing skills through:								
1. becoming enthusiastic and reflective readers	✔	✔	✔	✔	✔	✔	✔	✔
2. reading individually and collaboratively	✔	✔	✔	✔	✔	✔	✔	✔
3. experiencing and responding to a wide range of texts that include:	✔	✔	✔	✔	✔	✔	✔	✔
• information, reference and other non-literary texts, including print, media, moving image and computer-based materials	✔		✔	✔	✔			
• poetry, prose and drama, both traditional and contemporary	✔	✔	✔	✔		✔	✔	✔

Curriculum Correlation – Wales

The National Curriculum for Wales, English correlation chart

Wales Key Stage 2 Programme of Study	Narrative					Poetry		
	Unit 1 *Storm* (Settings)	Unit 2 *Dragon Slayer* (Myths and legends)	Unit 3 *Ottoline…* (Mystery)	Unit 4 *…Spud Murphy* (Author study)	Unit 5 *Dragon Slayer* (Play and film scripts)	Unit 1 McGough/ Douthwaite (Performance)	Unit 2 McGough/ Douthwaite (Shape)	Unit 3 McGough/ Douthwaite (Language play)
• texts with a Welsh dimension and texts from other cultures		✔	✔		✔			
4. reading / viewing extracts and complete texts:	✔	✔	✔	✔	✔	✔	✔	✔
• with challenging subject matter that broadens perspectives and extends thinking, *e.g. environmental issues, sustainability, animal rights, healthy eating*	✔		✔					
• with a variety of structural and organisational features	✔	✔	✔	✔	✔	✔	✔	✔
• that show quality and variety in language use	✔	✔	✔	✔	✔	✔	✔	✔
• that reflect the diversity of society in the twenty-first century			✔			✔		✔
• that reflect individual pupils' personal choice of reading matter.	✔			✔				
Writing Pupils should be given opportunities to communicate in writing and to:								
1. use the characteristic features of literary and non-literary texts in their own writing, adapting their style to suit the audience and purpose	✔	✔	✔	✔	✔	✔	✔	✔
2. use a range of sentence structures, linking them coherently and developing the ability to use paragraphs effectively	✔	✔	✔	✔	✔			
3. use punctuation to clarify meaning including full stop, exclamation and question marks, comma, apostrophe, bullet points, speech marks	✔	✔	✔	✔	✔			
4. choose and use appropriate vocabulary	✔	✔	✔	✔	✔	✔	✔	✔
5. use the standard forms of English: nouns, pronouns, adjectives, adverbs, prepositions, connectives and verb tenses	✔	✔		✔	✔			
6. develop and use a variety of strategies to enable them to spell correctly				✔	✔	✔		
7. use appropriate vocabulary and terminology to consider and evaluate their own work and that of others	✔	✔	✔	✔	✔	✔	✔	✔
8. draft and improve their work, using ICT as appropriate, to:	✔	✔	✔	✔	✔	✔	✔	✔
• plan	✔	✔	✔	✔	✔	✔	✔	✔
• draft	✔	✔	✔	✔	✔	✔	✔	✔
• revise	✔	✔	✔	✔	✔	✔	✔	✔
• proofread	✔		✔	✔	✔		✔	
• prepare a final copy		✔		✔	✔	✔	✔	✔
9. present writing appropriately:	✔	✔	✔	✔	✔	✔	✔	✔
• developing legible handwriting		✔		✔				

The National Curriculum for Wales, English correlation chart

Wales Key Stage 2 Programme of Study	Narrative					Poetry		
	Unit 1 *Storm* (Settings)	Unit 2 *Dragon Slayer* (Myths and legends)	Unit 3 *Ottoline...* (Mystery)	Unit 4 *...Spud Murphy* (Author study)	Unit 5 *Dragon Slayer* (Play and film scripts)	Unit 1 McGough/ Douthwaite (Performance)	Unit 2 McGough/ Douthwaite (Shape)	Unit 3 McGough/ Douthwaite (Language play)
• using appropriate features of layout and presentation, including ICT.		✔		✔	✔	✔	✔	✔
Range Pupils should be given opportunities to develop their writing skills through:								
1. writing for a range of purposes, *e.g. to entertain, report, inform, instruct, explain, persuade, recount, describe, imagine and to generate ideas*	✔	✔	✔	✔	✔	✔	✔	✔
2. writing for a range of real or imagined audiences	✔	✔	✔	✔	✔	✔	✔	✔
3. writing in a range of forms	✔	✔	✔	✔	✔	✔	✔	✔
4. writing in response to a wide range of stimuli: visual, audio and written.	✔	✔	✔	✔	✔	✔	✔	✔

Curriculum Correlation – NI

The Northern Ireland Curriculum, Language and Literacy correlation chart

Teachers should enable pupils to develop knowledge, understanding and skills in:	Narrative					Poetry		
	Unit 1 *Storm* (Settings)	Unit 2 *Dragon Slayer* (Myths and legends)	Unit 3 *Ottoline...* (Mystery)	Unit 4 *...Spud Murphy* (Author study)	Unit 5 *Dragon Slayer* (Play and film scripts)	Unit 1 McGough/ Douthwaite (Performance)	Unit 2 McGough/ Douthwaite (Shape)	Unit 3 McGough/ Douthwaite (Language play)
Pupils should be enabled to:								
listen and respond to a range of fiction, poetry, drama and media texts through the use of traditional and digital resources	✔	✔	✔	✔	✔	✔	✔	✔
tell, retell and interpret stories based on memories, personal experiences, literature, imagination and the content of the curriculum	✔	✔	✔	✔	✔			
participate in group and class discussions for a variety of curricular purposes	✔	✔	✔	✔	✔		✔	✔
know, understand and use the conventions of group discussion	✔	✔	✔	✔	✔		✔	✔
share, respond to and evaluate ideas, arguments and points of view and use evidence or reason to justify opinions, actions or proposals	✔	✔	✔	✔	✔	✔	✔	✔
formulate, give and respond to guidance, directions and instructions	✔	✔	✔	✔	✔	✔	✔	✔
participate in a range of drama activities across the curriculum	✔	✔	✔	✔	✔	✔		✔
improvise a scene based on experience, imagination, literature, media and/or curricular topics			✔		✔			
describe and talk about real experiences and imaginary situations and about people, places, events and artefacts	✔	✔	✔	✔	✔			
prepare and give a short oral presentation to a familiar group, showing an awareness of audience and including the use of multimedia presentations		✔			✔	✔	✔	✔
identify and ask appropriate questions to seek information, views and feelings	✔	✔	✔	✔	✔			
talk with people in a variety of formal and informal situations	✔	✔	✔	✔	✔	✔	✔	✔
use appropriate quality of speech and voice, speaking audibly and varying register, according to the purpose and audience	✔	✔		✔	✔	✔		✔
read aloud, inflecting appropriately, to express thoughts and feelings and emphasise the meaning of what they have read		✔		✔	✔	✔	✔	✔
recognise and discuss features of spoken language, including formal and informal language, dialect and colloquial speech.	✔			✔	✔			
Reading Pupils should be enabled to:								
participate in modelled, shared, paired and guided reading experiences	✔	✔	✔	✔	✔	✔	✔	✔
read, explore, understand and make use of a wide range of traditional and digital texts	✔	✔	✔	✔	✔	✔	✔	✔
engage in sustained, independent and silent reading for enjoyment and information								

Curriculum Correlation – NI

The Northern Ireland Curriculum, Language and Literacy correlation chart

Teachers should enable pupils to develop knowledge, understanding and skills in:	Narrative					Poetry		
	Unit 1 Storm (Settings)	Unit 2 Dragon Slayer (Myths and legends)	Unit 3 Ottoline… (Mystery)	Unit 4 …Spud Murphy (Author study)	Unit 5 Dragon Slayer (Play and film scripts)	Unit 1 McGough/ Douthwaite (Performance)	Unit 2 McGough/ Douthwaite (Shape)	Unit 3 McGough/ Douthwaite (Language play)
extend the range of their reading and develop their own preferences	✔	✔	✔	✔	✔	✔	✔	✔
use traditional and digital sources to locate, select, evaluate and communicate information relevant for a particular task								
represent their understanding of texts in a range of ways, including visual, oral, dramatic and digital	✔	✔	✔	✔	✔	✔	✔	✔
consider, interpret and discuss texts, exploring the ways in which language can be manipulated in order to affect the reader or engage attention	✔	✔	✔	✔	✔	✔	✔	✔
begin to be aware of how different media present information, ideas and events in different ways	✔	✔	✔	✔	✔	✔	✔	✔
justify their responses logically, by inference, deduction and/or reference to evidence within the text	✔	✔	✔	✔	✔	✔	✔	
reconsider their initial response to texts in the light of insight and information which emerge subsequently from their reading	✔	✔	✔	✔	✔			
read aloud to the class or teacher from prepared texts, including those composed by themselves, using inflection to assist meaning		✔	✔	✔	✔	✔	✔	✔
use a range of cross-checking strategies to read unfamiliar words in texts								
use a variety of reading skills for different reading purposes.	✔	✔	✔	✔	✔	✔	✔	✔
Writing Pupils should be enabled to:								
participate in modelled, shared, guided and independent writing, including composing onscreen	✔	✔	✔	✔	✔	✔	✔	✔
discuss various features of layout in texts and apply these, as appropriate, within their own writing	✔	✔	✔	✔	✔	✔	✔	✔
experiment with rhymes, rhythms, verse structure and all kinds of word play and dialect						✔	✔	✔
write for a variety of purposes and audiences, selecting, planning and using appropriate style and form	✔	✔	✔	✔	✔	✔	✔	✔
use the skills of planning, revising and redrafting to improve their writing, including that which they have composed digitally	✔	✔	✔	✔	✔	✔	✔	✔
express thoughts, feelings and opinions in imaginative and factual writing	✔	✔	✔	✔	✔	✔	✔	✔
use a variety of stylistic features to create mood and effect	✔	✔	✔	✔	✔	✔	✔	✔
begin to formulate their own personal style	✔	✔	✔	✔	✔	✔	✔	✔
create, organise, refine and present ideas using traditional and digital means, combining text, sound or graphics	✔	✔	✔	✔	✔		✔	✔

Curriculum Correlation – NI

The Northern Ireland Curriculum, Language and Literacy correlation chart

Teachers should enable pupils to develop knowledge, understanding and skills in:	Narrative					Poetry		
	Unit 1 *Storm* (Settings)	Unit 2 *Dragon Slayer* (Myths and legends)	Unit 3 *Ottoline...* (Mystery)	Unit 4 *...Spud Murphy* (Author study)	Unit 5 *Dragon Slayer* (Play and film scripts)	Unit 1 McGough/ Douthwaite (Perfor-mance)	Unit 2 McGough/ Douthwaite (Shape)	Unit 3 McGough/ Douthwaite (Language play)
understand the differences between spoken and written language			✔	✔	✔			
use a variety of skills to spell words correctly	✔			✔				
develop increasing competence in the use of grammar and punctuation to create clarity of meaning	✔	✔	✔	✔	✔			✔
develop a swift and legible style of handwriting.		✔						

Curriculum Correlation – Scotland

The Curriculum for Excellence, Literacy and English correlation chart

FIRST	Narrative					Poetry		
	Unit 1 *Storm* (Settings)	Unit 2 *Dragon Slayer* (Myths and legends)	Unit 3 *Ottoline…* (Mystery)	Unit 4 *…Spud Murphy* (Author study)	Unit 5 *Dragon Slayer* (Play and film scripts)	Unit 1 McGough/ Douthwaite (Performance)	Unit 2 McGough/ Douthwaite (Shape)	Unit 3 McGough/ Douthwaite (Language play)
Experiences and Outcomes The development of literacy skills plays an important role in all learning.								
I develop and extend my literacy skills when I have opportunities to:								
– communicate, collaborate and build relationships	✔	✔	✔	✔	✔	✔	✔	✔
– reflect on and explain my literacy and thinking skills, using feedback to help me improve and sensitively provide useful feedback for others	✔	✔	✔	✔	✔	✔	✔	✔
– engage with and create a wide range of texts in different media, taking advantage of the opportunities offered by ICT	✔	✔	✔	✔	✔	✔	✔	✔
– develop my understanding of what is special, vibrant and valuable about my own and other cultures and their languages		✔	✔			✔	✔	✔
– explore the richness and diversity of language, how it can affect me, and the wide range of ways in which I and others can be creative	✔	✔	✔	✔	✔	✔	✔	✔
– extend and enrich my vocabulary through listening, talking, watching and reading.	✔	✔	✔	✔	✔	✔	✔	✔
In developing my English language skills:								
– I engage with a wide range of texts and am developing an appreciation of the richness and breadth of Scotland's literary and linguistic heritage	✔	✔	✔	✔	✔	✔	✔	✔
– I enjoy exploring and discussing word patterns and text structures.	✔	✔	✔	✔	✔	✔	✔	✔
Listening and talking **Enjoyment and choice** – within a motivating and challenging environment, developing an awareness of the relevance of texts in my life								
I regularly select and listen to or watch texts which I enjoy and find interesting, and I can explain why I prefer certain sources.	✔	✔	✔	✔	✔	✔	✔	✔
I regularly select subject, purpose, format and resources to create texts of my choice. **LIT 1-01a / LIT 2-01a**	✔	✔		✔		✔	✔	✔
Tools for listening and talking – to help me when interacting or presenting within and beyond my place of learning								
When I engage with others, I know when and how to listen, when to talk, how much to say, when to ask questions and how to respond with respect. **LIT 1-02a**	✔	✔	✔	✔	✔	✔	✔	✔
I am exploring how pace, gesture, expression, emphasis and choice of words are used to engage others, and I can use what I learn. **ENG 1-03a**	✔	✔	✔	✔	✔	✔	✔	✔

Curriculum Correlation – Scotland

The Curriculum for Excellence, Literacy and English correlation chart

FIRST	Narrative					Poetry		
	Unit 1 *Storm* (Settings)	Unit 2 *Dragon Slayer* (Myths and legends)	Unit 3 *Ottoline…* (Mystery)	Unit 4 *…Spud Murphy* (Author study)	Unit 5 *Dragon Slayer* (Play and film scripts)	Unit 1 McGough/ Douthwaite (Performance)	Unit 2 McGough/ Douthwaite (Shape)	Unit 3 McGough/ Douthwaite (Language play)
Finding and using information – when listening to, watching and talking about texts with increasingly complex ideas, structures and specialist vocabulary								
As I listen or watch, I can identify and discuss the purpose, key words and main ideas of the text, and use this information for a specific purpose. LIT 1-04a	✔	✔	✔	✔	✔	✔	✔	✔
As I listen or watch, I am learning to make notes under given headings and use these to understand what I have listened to or watched and create new texts. LIT 1-05a	✔	✔	✔	✔	✔	✔	✔	✔
I can select ideas and relevant information, organise these in a logical sequence and use words which will be interesting and/or useful for others. LIT 1-06a	✔	✔	✔	✔	✔	✔	✔	✔
Understanding, analysing and evaluating – investigating and/or appreciating texts with increasingly complex ideas, structures and specialist vocabulary for different purposes								
I can show my understanding of what I listen to or watch by responding to and asking different kinds of questions. LIT 1-07a	✔	✔	✔	✔	✔			
To help me develop an informed view, I am learning to recognise the difference between fact and opinion. LIT 1-08a								
Creating texts – applying the elements others use to create different types of short and extended texts with increasingly complex ideas, structures and vocabulary								
I can communicate clearly when engaging with others within and beyond my place of learning, using selected resources as required. LIT 1-10a	✔	✔	✔	✔	✔	✔	✔	✔
Reading **Enjoyment and choice** – within a motivating and challenging environment, developing an awareness of the relevance of texts in my life								
I regularly select and read, listen to or watch texts which I enjoy and find interesting, and I can explain why I prefer certain texts and authors. LIT 1-11a / LIT 2-11a	✔	✔	✔	✔	✔	✔	✔	✔
Tools for reading – to help me use texts with increasingly complex or unfamiliar ideas, structures and vocabulary within and beyond my place of learning								

Curriculum Correlation – Scotland

The Curriculum for Excellence, Literacy and English correlation chart

FIRST	Narrative					Poetry		
	Unit 1 *Storm* (Settings)	Unit 2 *Dragon Slayer* (Myths and legends)	Unit 3 *Ottoline...* (Mystery)	Unit 4 *...Spud Murphy* (Author study)	Unit 5 *Dragon Slayer* (Play and film scripts)	Unit 1 McGough/ Douthwaite (Performance)	Unit 2 McGough/ Douthwaite (Shape)	Unit 3 McGough/ Douthwaite (Language play)
I can use my knowledge of sight vocabulary, phonics, context clues, punctuation and grammar to read with understanding and expression. **ENG 1-12a**	✔	✔	✔	✔	✔			✔
I am learning to select and use strategies and resources before I read, and as I read, to help make the meaning of texts clear. **LIT 1-13a**								
Finding and using information – when reading and using fiction and non-fiction texts with increasingly complex ideas, structures and specialist vocabulary								
Using what I know about the features of different types of texts, I can find, select, sort and use information for a specific purpose. **LIT 1-14a**								
I am learning to make notes under given headings and use them to understand information, explore ideas and problems and create new texts. **LIT 1-15a**	✔	✔	✔	✔	✔	✔	✔	✔
Understanding, analysing and evaluating – investigating and/or appreciating fiction and non-fiction texts with increasingly complex ideas, structures and specialist vocabulary for different purposes								
To show my understanding across different areas of learning, I can identify and consider the purpose and main ideas of a text. **LIT 1-16a**	✔	✔	✔	✔	✔	✔	✔	✔
To show my understanding, I can respond to different kinds of questions and other close reading tasks and I am learning to create some questions of my own. **ENG 1-17a**	✔	✔	✔	✔	✔	✔	✔	✔
To help me develop an informed view, I can recognise the difference between fact and opinion. **LIT 1-18a**								
I can share my thoughts about structure, characters and/or setting, recognise the writer's message and relate it to my own experiences, and comment on the effective choice of words and other features. **ENG 1-19a**	✔	✔	✔	✔	✔	✔	✔	✔
Writing **Enjoyment and choice** – within a motivating and challenging environment, developing an awareness of the relevance of texts in my life								
I enjoy creating texts of my choice and I regularly select subject, purpose, format and resources to suit the needs of my audience. **LIT 1-20a / LIT 2-20a**	✔	✔	✔	✔	✔	✔	✔	✔

Curriculum Correlation – Scotland

The Curriculum for Excellence, Literacy and English correlation chart

FIRST	Narrative					Poetry		
	Unit 1 *Storm* (Settings)	Unit 2 *Dragon Slayer* (Myths and legends)	Unit 3 *Ottoline...* (Mystery)	Unit 4 *...Spud Murphy* (Author study)	Unit 5 *Dragon Slayer* (Play and film scripts)	Unit 1 McGough/ Douthwaite (Perfor-mance)	Unit 2 McGough/ Douthwaite (Shape)	Unit 3 McGough/ Douthwaite (Language play)
Tools for writing – using knowledge of technical aspects to help my writing communicate effectively within and beyond my place of learning								
I can spell the most commonly-used words, using my knowledge of letter patterns and spelling rules and use resources to help me spell tricky or unfamiliar words. *LIT 1-21a*	✔	✔		✔				
I can write independently, use appropriate punctuation and order and link my sentences in a way that makes sense. *LIT 1-22a*	✔	✔	✔	✔	✔			
Throughout the writing process, I can check that my writing makes sense. *LIT 1-23a*	✔	✔	✔	✔	✔	✔	✔	✔
I can present my writing in a way that will make it legible and attractive for my reader, combining words, images and other features. *LIT 1-24a*		✔	✔	✔	✔		✔	✔
Organising and using information – considering texts to help create short and extended texts for different purposes								
I am learning to use my notes and other types of writing to help me understand information and ideas, explore problems, generate and develop ideas or create new text. *LIT 1-25a*	✔	✔	✔	✔	✔	✔	✔	✔
By considering the type of text I am creating, I can select ideas and relevant information, organise these in a logical sequence and use words which will be interesting and/or useful for others. *LIT 1-26a*	✔	✔	✔	✔	✔	✔	✔	✔
Creating texts – applying the elements which authors use to create different types of short and extended texts with increasingly complex ideas, structures and vocabulary								
I can convey information, describe events or processes, share my opinions or persuade my reader in different ways. *LIT 1-28a / LIT 1-29a*	✔	✔	✔	✔	✔			
I can describe and share my experiences and how they made me feel. *ENG 1-30a*	✔	✔	✔	✔	✔			
Having explored the elements which authors use in different genres, I can use what I learn to create my own stories, poems and plays with interesting structures, characters and/or settings. *ENG 1-31a*	✔	✔	✔	✔	✔	✔	✔	✔

Narrative Unit 1

STORM – novel (Settings)

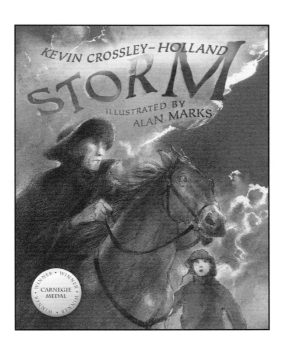

Medium term plan (3 weeks)	
Phase	**Learning Outcomes**
Phase 1: Engaging with the text (7 days)	• Children can identify and respond to the mood of a text. • Children can identify and discuss how characters are feeling. • Children can find evidence in the text to support their views.
Phase 2: Analysing setting descriptions (3 days)	• Children can identify how the author's use of language creates a mood. • Children can select appropriate vocabulary to describe a setting.
Phase 3: Writing setting descriptions (5 days)	• Children can draw on modelled writing as a basis for their own writing. • Children can write a setting description that creates a particular mood. • Children can manipulate their language choices to create contrasting moods.

Narrative Unit 1

STORM

Big picture

The children read *Storm*. They explore the setting, characters and their thoughts and feelings, using visualisation, artwork responses, discussion and drama. The children read an extract from *The Thing in the Basement* and identify language that creates mood. They try out creating similar effects using modelled writing. In pairs, the children identify a setting and write their own descriptions of it, focusing on sensory language to create mood, and using powerful words to add a character's thoughts and feelings. Finally they extend their understanding of the effects of language choices by rewriting their description to create a different mood.

Prior learning

This unit assumes that the children can already:
• read and respond to stories and discuss how characters are feeling
• use drama strategies to explore characters
• work collaboratively to explore their views and discuss creative ideas.

Key aspects of learning

Communication: Express ideas through speaking, listening and writing.
Creative thinking: Identify an interesting setting as a stimulus for writing; use imaginative writing with evocative language to create a mood.

Empathy: Explore characters' feelings through role play and drama.
Enquiry: Understand how reference books such as thesauruses can be used to extend language choices.
Social skills: Work collaboratively in pairs to create ideas for a setting description; offer constructive feedback during peer evaluation.

Progression in narrative

In this unit the children will:
• infer characters' feelings and empathise with characters
• identify features that writers use to create settings and characters
• write descriptions using powerful adjectives, verbs and nouns.

Cross-curricular links

Art and Design: The children could create artwork to illustrate the settings described, conveying the differences in mood of the alternative descriptions.
ICT: The children could combine the stimulus photographs they have taken with their written descriptions

Reading time

25 minutes

PHASE 1: ENGAGING WITH THE TEXT (7 DAYS)

Session 1

We are learning to ...	Resources
• discuss the text giving reasons for our views • use hot-seating to explore characters' views and feelings • understand how authors use settings to create different feelings or moods (PNS Strands 1.3, 4.2, 8.3) **Assessment Focuses** AF (R):3	*Storm* ITP: 1.1

Shared teaching

• Discuss the 'Big Picture' for this unit and share the learning objectives.
• Read Chapter 1 with the children following in their books. Encourage the children to picture the scene being described. *What have you learned about where Annie lives? Does this remind you of any place you know? How does Annie feel about her home?*
• Continue reading to the end of Chapter 3. Talk Partners discuss predictions for what might happen next in the story.
• Take feedback. Encourage the children to refer back to the book to support their responses. *Is there anything that puzzles you about the story so far? Can anyone else answer that? Are there any strange characters?* (the ghost)
• Talk Partners discuss the story of the ghost. *How do you feel about the ghost? Do you believe he is real? What would you do if you met him on the marsh?*
• Take feedback. *Does the ghost change the way Annie feels about the marsh? Does it make it seem scarier?*
• Explain that they are going to look in more detail at the setting for the

story. Show Screen 1 of 'The marsh' (ITP 1.1) *What does the marsh look like in summer time? What is the weather like?*
• Now show Screen 2 on ITP 1.1. *It is still summer time. How do we know Annie is enjoying the marsh?*
• Finally, show Screen 3 on ITP 1.1. *What season is it now? How do we know? How does Annie feel about the marsh now?*

Independent and Guided

• The children work in mixed ability groups to perform a Hot-Seating activity. Each group chooses one person to be Annie in the hot-seat. The rest of the group ask Annie questions, e.g. *What do you like about living near the marsh? What do you like playing? What is it like in the winter? Do you miss your sister? How do you feel about the ghost?* Encourage the children playing Annie to give reasons for their answers. Support the children with an identified need. (T/TA)

Plenary

• Recap the learning objectives. Take feedback and encourage the children to describe Annie in detail.
• Ask the children to close their eyes and imagine the marsh in summer time. *What can you hear/see/touch/smell/taste?*
• Discuss what the children have learned about the story setting. *Would you like to live on the marsh?*

Assessment pointers

• S&L: hot-seating will show how far the children can sustain roles and recount ideas.
• AF3 (R): observation of classroom discussion and drama groups shows how far the children are able to make simple inferences from the text, understand how a character is feeling and how the setting changes.

Session 2

We are learning to ...	Resources
• understand how authors use settings to create different feelings or moods (PNS Strands 8.3) **Assessment Focuses** AF (R): 3	*Storm* ITP: 1.2

Shared teaching

• Share the learning objective and remind the children of what they learnt in Session 1 about where the book is set (the marsh).

• Explain that they are now going to think about all the places Annie mentions in her description. Reread pages 8–11. Ask the children to listen carefully and try to remember the places mentioned.

• *What different places does Annie mention?* (the cottage, the marsh, the track along the edge of the marsh, the ford, the river, the crossroads, Waterslain village)

• Show 'Map' (ITP 1.2) to help the children remember where each of the places are located. Explain that the children are going to draw a picture of the marsh including some of the other places mentioned in the text.

• Remind the children that the marsh looks different in summer time and winter time. Ask the children to close their eyes. *Imagine the marsh in summer. What colour is the sky? What colour is the water? What is the weather like? What can you see/hear/smell? How do you feel?*

• Now ask the children to imagine the marsh in winter. *What is the weather like now? What has happened to the trees and grass? What colour is the sky? What other details might make the marsh feel gloomy and unfriendly? How do you feel now?*

Independent and Guided

• The children work independently and choose either to draw the setting in winter or in summer. They draw and colour the setting including as many of the places on ITP 1.2 as they can. Support the children with an identified need. (T/TA)

Plenary

• Ask the children who drew the setting in summer to show their pictures. *What words and phrases describe these pictures?* Encourage the children to think of synonyms. Show ITP 1.2. Click on the places and add descriptions.

• Now ask the children who drew the setting in winter to show their pictures and repeat the process.

• Recap the learning objective and discuss how different settings create different moods. *How does Annie feel about the different places? Does this change in summer and winter? Why do you think that is?* Explain that they will look again at the different moods and the words the author uses to describe them in later sessions.

Assessment pointers

• AF3 (R): contributions to the list of places and to the descriptive words and phrases during the plenary shows how far the children are able to engage with the details of the setting given in the text.

Session 3

We are learning to ...	Resources
• listen to others, saying whether we agree/disagree and giving reasons to support our ideas • explore characters using evidence from the text (PNS Strands 2.1, 7.2) **Assessment Focuses** AF (R): 2, 3	*Storm* ITP: 1.3 PCM: 1.1

Shared teaching

• Play Babble Gabble to recap Chapters 1, 2 and 3.

• Share the learning objectives. Explain that the children are now going to focus on the characters in *Storm*.

• Focus on Annie's sister. *What do you know about Willa? What does she look like? How old is she? Does she live with Annie?* Model referring back to *Storm* to find details about Willa, e.g. *Yes, it says on page 6 that* ... ,etc.

• *What do you remember about Annie?* Allow the children Think Time to look back through the text and collect details about Annie.

• Take feedback. Encourage the children to refer to the text to support their answers.

• Show 'Character statements' (ITP 1.3). *What do you know about each of the characters from what we have read? Where does it say that in the story?*

• Click on the picture of Annie to get a character statement relating to her. *Do you agree or disagree with this statement?* Explain that there may not be a right answer, but the children must use what they are told in the story to support their decision.

• Talk Partners discuss the statement and use their copies of *Storm* to find evidence.

• Share responses and prompt discussion, e.g. *Who has a different view, more to add or evidence from a different part of the text?*

• If there is time, repeat the process with the other statements on ITP 1.3, asking the children to Think-Pair-Share their responses, referring to the text.

Independent and Guided

• In pairs, the children discuss 'Character statements' (PCM 1.1). They listen and respond to what each other says, giving reasons for their ideas. Support the children with an identified need. (T+/TA+)

Plenary

• Recap the learning objectives. *What did you think about the statements? How did you come to your decisions? How did you support your answers? Have you got a better idea about the characters now?*

Assessment pointers

• S&L: pair work will show how far the children can listen and respond to others.

• AF2, 3 (R): observation of paired/group discussion and oral responses shows how far the children are able to make inferences, deductions and reference to the text.

Session 4

<table>
<tr><td>We are learning to ...
• use drama to explore characters' thoughts and feelings
• put ourselves in the role of a character to help us understand their feelings, thoughts and actions (PNS Strands 4.2, 8.2)
Assessment Focuses
AF (R): 2, 3</td><td>Resources
Storm
ITP: 1.4
PCM: 1.2, 1.3</td></tr>
</table>

Shared teaching

• Recap the story so far and the children's predictions about what might happen next. Read Chapter 4, emphasising the changing moods. *What is the weather on the marsh like now?*
• Model a personal response to the events, e.g. *I don't think I'd want to go out in that storm. Would you have volunteered? Is it a good idea? How would you feel if it were you in that situation?*
• Share the learning objectives and explain that the children will be using drama to see events from Annie's point of view and to understand why she volunteered to help.
• Read pages 26–27 of 'Storm' (ITP 1.4), emphasising the mood of optimism at this point. Select a group of children to Freeze Frame the scene, thinking about posture and facial expression. Allow Think Time, then invite other children to stand behind the characters and speak their thoughts. Encourage thoughtful responses. *Why do you think that? Can you say more?*
• Read pages 28–29 on ITP 1.4, emphasising the growing sense of panic. Ask a group of children to Freeze Frame this scene. Invite the children to speak the characters' thoughts at this point. *How have the characters' thoughts and feelings changed?*

• Bring the focus onto Annie. The children perform a Hot-Seating activity to explore what Annie is thinking and feeling just before she volunteers to go out in the storm. One child takes on the role of Annie whilst the other children ask her questions about this point in the story, e.g. *Are you excited about the baby coming? Do you want to help your sister? How do you feel about going out in the storm?*
• Explain that the children are now going to explore the characters' thoughts and feelings just after Annie has decided to go out in the storm.

Independent and Guided

• The children use Thought Tracking to explore the moment after Annie decides to go out in the storm (page 30) and then record their ideas.
  - Complete 'Thought bubbles' (PCM 1.2) about any character. (T+)
  - Complete PCM 1.2 about Annie.
  - Use 'Annie's thought bubbles' (PCM 1.3). (TA+)

Plenary

• Choose a group to present their Thought Tracking. Prompt others to comment. *Do you think that's what Annie is thinking? What makes you say that?*
• Recap the learning objectives. Discuss how the freeze frame and thought tracking activities helped to understand the actions of the characters.

Assessment pointers

• S&L: drama activities will show how far the children can sustain roles and understand the characters.
• AF2, 3 (R): observation of drama activities will show how how far the children can use ideas and make inferences from the text.

Session 5

<table>
<tr><td>We are learning to ...
• understand how authors use settings to create different feelings or mood
• say what makes a story effective, looking at powerful words
(PNS Strands 8.3)
Assessment Focuses
AF(R): 2, 5, 6</td><td>Resources
Storm
ITP: 1.5
PCM: 1.4</td></tr>
</table>

Shared teaching

• Recap the events of Chapter 4 then read Chapter 5 using appropriate expression.
• Encourage the children to respond and make predictions. *I wonder what might happen next? Do you think something bad will happen? What makes you think that? How do you think Annie feels about the stranger? I wonder who he is?*
• Focus attention on the mysterious stranger. *What is the stranger like?* Identify examples of words used to describe the mysterious stranger, e.g. 'tall and unsmiling', 'a dark voice'. *What does this suggest about him?*
• Share the learning objectives. Explain that an author's choice of words affect the way we feel about characters and settings. Use Think Alouds to focus on the use of language, e.g. *I really liked where it said they were 'swallowed in the stormy darkness.' That sounded very frightening. Was there any phrase or sentence that you particularly liked?*
• Reread the opening of Chapter 5 (pages 34–35). *How does the description of the setting make you feel? What is the mood?*
• Show 'Storm' (ITP 1.5). *Which words and phrases helped to create this mood?* Highlight words and phrases identified, commenting on

choices and discussing the effect, e.g. *Yes, 'snatched' sounds very unfriendly. I wonder why the author has used the word 'ashen' three times in that sentence? How do these words make you feel about Annie's journey into the storm?*

Independent and Guided

• The children continue to focus on words and phrases used for impact in Chapter 5. They complete activities in pairs then discuss them in groups, focusing on the effect created.
  - Complete 'Powerful words' (PCM 1.4).
  - As above. (T+)
  - Choose four star phrases, e.g. the most effective phrases, and then record these on sticky notes. (TA+)

Plenary

• Recap the learning objectives. Use the above activity to focus on how the choice of words can change the impact of a sentence. *Why is the book version better? How does it make you feel?*
• Add the author's choice of words and star phrases to the Learning Wall.

Assessment pointers

• S&L: pair and group work will show how well the children can adopt group rules and express and respond to opinions.
• AF2 (R): observation of responses to questions and evidence from independent activities show how far the children can refer to the text.
• AF5, 6 (R): evidence from independent activities shows how far the children can identify effective language.

We are learning to ...	Resources
• put ourselves in the role of a character to help us understand their feelings, thoughts and actions • understand how authors use settings to create different feelings or moods (PNS Strancs 8.2, 8.3) **Assessment Focuses** AF (R): 2, 3, 5	*Storm* ITP: 1.6 PCM: 1.5

Shared teaching (1)

• Recap Chapter 5 and some of the children's predictions that followed.
• Read Chapter 6. Allow the children Think Time to discuss whether their predictions have now changed. *What do you think now? Does this change your view of the horseman? What if he is a ghost?*
• Read Chapter 7 with pace and dramatic expression. Encourage further response. *What do you think now? Does anything puzzle you? How would you feel if you were Annie?*
• Share the lecrning objectives. *Imagine you were Annie. What would you remember about this journey? How would you feel?*
• Show 'Memories map' (ITP 1.6). Click on the first marker (Home) and read the quote that appears. Demonstrate using the page reference, then scanning to find this part of the text. Read the complete paragraph. *Imagine you are Annie. What would she remember about this moment?* The children Think-Pair-Share ideas.
• Take feedback, encouraging reference to the text. *Why do you say that?* Use the children's suggestions to model noting what Annie would remember in the pop-up box on ITP 1.6.
• Repeat this activity for the second marker on ITP 1.6 (Ford). *What would Annie remember about this moment? How might the*

horseman's words affect Annie's thoughts and feelings? What made her feel less scared? Again add notes to ITP 1.6.

Independent and Guided

• In pairs, the children annotate 'Memories map' (PCM 1.5) with notes about what Annie might remember from her journey with the horseman.

   Annotate all points on the map using details from the text. (TA)

   Annotate the map using the phrase 'I remember ...'

   As above. (T+)

Shared teaching (2)

• Take feedback and add notes to ITP 1.6.
• Introduce the idea of using the memory maps and annotations to imagine being Annie telling someone what they remember about that night.
• Model how this might start, incorporating ideas from ITP 1.6, e.g. *I remember being swallowed up into the stormy darkness. My heart was beating so fast … .* Ask the children to continue in pairs.

Plenary

• Recap the learning objectives. *What did it feel like to be Annie? What words, phrases or sentences from the text did you use to help you?*

Assessment pointers

• S&L: oral retellings will show how well the children can recount ideas.
• AF2, 3 (R): story maps and talking in role will show how far the children can refer to the text and infer characters' thoughts and feelings.
• AF5 (R): further questioning will show how far the children understand the effect of words and phrases.

We are learning to ...	Resources
• share our opinions about a story (or poem) and give reasons for our views • listen and respond to others • say what mckes a story effective, looking at powerful words (PNS Strands 1.3, 2.1, 8.3) **Assessment Focuses** AF (R): 6	*Storm* ITP: 1.7 PCM: 1.6

Shared teaching

• Remind the children that there are still some questions to be answered, e.g. we are still not sure who the horseman is. *What would you like to find out?*
• Read Chapter 8 using appropriate dramatic expression. Pause at the end of the stcry for the children to reflect on the ending. *Was that what you expected? Did anything surprise you? Does anything still puzzle you? Can we answer these puzzles or are some things left open? What do you think happened next?*
• Share the lea·ning objectives. Show 'Discussion starters' (ITP 1.7). Click on 'Setting' and read the statement. *Would it be the same if the events happened on a bright sunny summer day or in a town? How does the setting make us feel?* Talk Partners consider whether they agree or disagree with the statement.
• Take feedback, encouraging the children to explain their opinions by referring to the story, e.g. how weather and darkness influenced mood; how stories about the ford built up expectations.
• Click on 'Language' and read the statement. Explain that powerful words are ones that have a big impact on the reader. They make the

reader feel a certain way as well as helping to create a picture of events. Talk Partners consider whether they agree or disagree with the statement using *Storm* or the Learning Wall to locate examples.
• Take feedback, encouraging the children to support their comments with examples of powerful words. *Why is that word really effective? Does anyone have another example? What mood does that word or phrase create?*
• If there is time, discuss the other statements ('plots and characters') on ITP 1.7.

Independent and Guided

• In mixed ability groups the children use 'Discussion starters' (PCM 1.6) to help them discuss their opinions of the story. Explain that everyone should express their own personal opinion, giving reasons for what they say whilst respecting each other's opinions. Support the children with an identified need. (T+/TA)

Plenary

• Recap the learning objectives and ask a member from each group to comment on whether their group achieved the first two objectives. *Did everyone get a chance to give their opinion? Did you agree or disagree? Did you give reasons for your views? What do you think your group needs to work on when discussing stories in future? What did you think about the book?*

Assessment pointers

• S&L: group work and debate will show how far the children can express ideas and listen to others.
• AF6 (R): observation of groups, peer assessment and responses to questioning will show how far the children are able to express personal responses, describe overall effects and comment on author's purpose.

Session 8

We are learning to …	Resources
• discuss the text, giving reasons for our views • explore how authors use descriptive language to appeal to readers • understand how authors use settings to create different feelings or moods (PNS Strands 1.3, 7.5, 8.3) **Assessment Focuses** AF (R): 2, 3, 5	*Storm* ITP: 1.8, 1.9, 1.10 PCM: 1.7, 1.8

Shared teaching

• Refer to the 'Big Picture' and explain the purpose of the next three sessions (to look more closely at the details the author uses). Share the learning objectives.
• Reread *Storm* pages 8–9. Remind the children that this describes the marsh in summer time. *What mood is being created? Which words and phrases help to create this mood?*
• Show 'Target board' (ITP 1.8). Explain that the centre zone is for words that best describe the setting; the middle zone is for words which are less relevant and that you are unsure about; and the outer zone is for words which least describe the settings. Talk Partners find the three most appropriate words to describe the setting, giving reasons for their choices.
• Take feedback, encouraging extended answers. *Why do you think that? What do you mean by … ? Do you have a particular word or phrase?*
• Show '*Storm*' (ITP 1.9). *What mood is being created now?* (fear) *What words and phrases give us this mood?* (E.g. 'salty lips', 'gnashed its sharp teeth', etc.) Highlight them on screen. *How does it make Annie feel?* (scared) *Where does she imagine she is?* (on a boat on the sea)
• Show '*Storm*' (ITP 1.10). Ask the children to imagine that they are Annie riding through the storm. *What can you see, hear, touch? What words are used to describe the rain? How does this make you feel?*
• Explain that children are now going to create their own mood boards based on the marsh during the storm.

Independent and Guided

• The children work with a partner to create a 'Target board' (PCM 1.7) for the setting during the storm. They can use words from the bottom of PCM 1.7, their own words or words from the text.

∞ Use 'Clues bookmark' (PCM 1.8) to record evidence as they complete PCM 1.7. (T+)

∞ Complete PCM 1.7.

◉ Complete PCM 1.7. (TA+)

Plenary

• Display the children's completed PCMs. *Which three words best describe the marsh during the storm?* Write a list of the best words and phrases to add to the Learning Wall.
• Recap the learning objectives and discuss how the mood changes between summer and winter. *Would you use the same three words to describe the marsh in winter? How does the change to the setting affect the story?*

Assessment pointers

• S&L: pair work will show how far the children can express and explain relevant ideas.
• AF2, 3, 5 (R): observation of pair discussions and evidence from word targets shows how far the children can find information in the text and understand an author's use of language to create moods.

Session 9

We are learning to …	Resources
• say what powerful verbs and adjectives are and why they are used • write sentences using powerful verbs and adjectives (PNS Strands 9.4, 11.2) **Assessment Focuses** AF (W): 6, 7	ITP: (1.5), 1.11, 1.12, 1.13 PCM: 1.9

Shared teaching

• Recap Session 8. *How do authors use small details and the senses to create pictures and moods?* Share the learning objectives.
• Recall '*Storm*' (ITP 1.5). Explain to the children that a verb describes actions. Perform some simple actions, e.g. walking across the classroom, writing on the whiteboard, brushing your hair, etc. *What am I doing?* Prompt the children to identify the action words (the verbs).
• Talk Partners think of two verbs which they can demonstrate with actions. Choose pairs to demonstrate actions while the class guess the verb they are acting.
• Recall ITP 1.5. *Which words describe the actions of the wind and the family?* Highlight them. Ask a group to perform the powerful verbs of the wind ('snatched', 'slammed') and family ('huddled' and 'staring'). *Why did the author choose these words? What do they tell us about the wind and the family?*
• Show 'Powerful verbs' (ITP 1.11). Click on the 'Powerful verbs' button. *Why did the author choose these verbs rather than verbs like 'sending', 'stopping', 'came'? What effect do they have?*
• Show '*Storm* storyboard' (ITP 1.12). Ask the children to imagine the sequence of pictures, thinking about the features of the landscape, e.g. rivers, trees, wildlife. *What do you see, hear, smell?*
• Allow Think Time then invite responses and add notes to ITP 1.12.
• Explain that the children are going to write a sentence for each picture on the storyboard as if Annie were describing her ride through the storm.
• Use Think Alouds to construct a sentence orally using one of the annotations (e.g. wind) and the construction 'I felt … ', e.g. *I felt the wind snatch my scarf, I felt the wind whip the air … , I saw the wind bend the trees.*
• *How can we improve these sentences? How can we make the wind sound more fierce?* Model how to choose powerful verbs to improve the sentences, e.g. 'snatch', 'whip'.
• Show 'Descriptive sentences' (ITP 1.13) to introduce the success criteria. Encourage the children to add to the list.

Independent and Guided

• The children write sentences to describe Annie's journey through the storm, using as many powerful verbs as they can.

∞ Use 'Annie's journey' (PCM 1.9). (TA+)

∞ As above. (T+)

◉ As above.

Plenary

• Recap the learning objectives.
• Share the children's sentences. Invite the rest of the class to check against the success criteria on ITP 1.13. *Have they used powerful verbs? Have they described what Annie could hear/see/touch?*

Assessment pointers

• AF 6, 7 (W): written sentences show how far the children can construct descriptive, accurate sentences, choosing words for effect.

We are learning to ...
- understand how authors use settings to create different feelings or moods
- write sentences choosing details to create a mood
- edit details in a sentence to change the mood
(PNS Strands 8.3, 11.2)

Assessment Focuses
AF (R): 2, 5; AF (W): 6, 7

Resources
ITP: (1.13), 1.14
PCM: 1.10

Shared teaching (1)
- Share the learning objectives. Explain that the children are going to read an extract from another story with a different setting.
- Read 'The Thing in the Basement' (ITP 1.14) with the children listening for details that help them picture the setting. *What mood is created? What words and phrases help to create this mood?*

Independent and Guided
- In pairs, the children identify details about the setting and discuss their feelings about the place.
- **OOO** The children label 'School setting' (PCM 1.10) with words to describe the mood.
- **OO** As above. (TA)
- **O** As above. (T)

Shared teaching (2)
- Focus on what Scott's old school was like. *Imagine that Scott first approached his old school, the one that was very friendly. What details might he use to describe that school? How is the mood different from his new school?*
- Model using sentences from ITP 1.14 and changing details to create a different setting, e.g. *All around the school there was grass and tall trees. It looked like the trees were protecting the little school.*
- Recap how to write sentences with the correct punctuation. *What should all sentences have?* (a capital letter and a full stop)
- Recall 'Descriptive sentences' (ITP 1.13). *Do your sentences meet this criteria? How could you improve them?*
- In pairs, the children orally rehearse and write two more sentences to describe the 'friendly' school using the sentence starters: *Scott could see ... He could hear ... .*

Plenary
- Recap the learning objectives and share some of the children's sentences. The rest of the class check against the success criteria on ITP 1.13.
- Discuss what the children have learnt about how authors use details to create different moods. *How is Scott's old school described? How does this compare to his new school? Why are details important when describing settings?*

Assessment pointers
- AF5 (R): observation of oral responses indicate how far the children can respond to the author's use of language and its effect.
- AF6 (W): written sentences marked against the success criteria will show how far the children can construct/punctuate sentences and choose vocabulary for effect.
- AF7 (W): annotations on PCM 1.10 show how far the children are able to select appropriate and effective vocabulary.

PHASE 3: WRITING SETTING DESCRIPTIONS (5 DAYS)

We are learning to ...
- collect suitable words and phrases before we write
- use photographs (and real experience) to help us describe settings
(PNS Strands 9.4)

Assessment Focuses
AF (W): 7

Resources
ITP: 1.15
PCM: 1.11, 1.12

Shared teaching
- Remind the children of the 'Big Picture'. Recap what they learnt in Phase 2 and how this will be useful in writing their own setting descriptions.
- Share the learning objectives and explain that authors often use familiar settings so they have a real place in mind when writing. Explain that the children will write about a place familiar to them. Decide on a specific purpose and audience for the writing, e.g. exchanging descriptions with a school in a contrasting location.
- There are two alternative approaches to this task: one is to visit the location that children will write about (e.g. the school playground, a park, etc.). The other is to use 'Setting photographs' (ITP 1.15).
- If visiting the setting, take clipboards and 'Using your senses' (PCM 1.11) and 'Looking close-up' (PCM 1.12) to record the things the children see, touch, hear, smell and feel. Encourage the children to look for details by taking digital photographs, sketching items, etc.
- If using the photographs, show ITP 1.15 and discuss the images. *What can you tell about the setting?* (time/place/weather) *What words would you use to describe the mood?* The children Think-Pair-Share ideas.
- Choose a photo from ITP 1.15. Talk Partners describe the setting in as much detail as they can. Encourage them to list as many words as possible based on the picture.
- Invite responses, selecting and refining ideas. Click and add words and phrases to ITP 1.15.
- Remind the children what they learned from Phase 2 (using the senses and focusing on details). Ask the children to imagine themselves in the scene. *Step into the picture. What would it be like to be there? What would you hear, touch, smell? What details might you focus on?*
- Take feedback and add additional words and phrases to ITP 1.15.

Independent and Guided
- The children describe their chosen setting in more detail using PCM 1.11 and PCM 1.12. They either use the setting they visited or the photographs on ITP 1.15 as a stimulus. Support the children with an identified need. (T+/TA+)

Plenary
- The children create a 'sense of place' target board to display on the Learning Wall. Include words and phrases from the PCMs, sketches and photos. Praise, question and comment on their suggestions.
- Recap the learning objectives.

Assessment pointers
- AF7 (W): PCMs, target boards, contributions to the learning wall and annotations will show how far the children are able to select adventurous words and words for effect.

We are learning to ...	Resources
• develop success criteria • write an effective description using interesting vocabulary • write sentences using powerful verbs and adjectives (PNS Strands 9.1, 9.4, 11.2) **Assessment Focuses** AF(W): 1, 2, 6, 7	ITP: 1.16, 1.17 PCM: (1.11, 1.12)

Shared teaching

• Share the learning objectives. Recap what the children have learnt about good setting descriptions, e.g. use of details, using powerful verbs, creating mood.
• Show 'Describing settings' (ITP 1.16), encouraging the children to add to the list.
• Explain that the children will write a setting description based on the location they explored in Session 11.
• Use Modelled Writing and 'Model description' (ITP 1.17) to create a description of a park scene. *Imagine your character is walking through the park, a place that they know well, like Annie on her way to school in* Storm. Compose the opening of this story, using Think Alouds to rehearse the sentences.
• Use Think Alouds to model improving word choice, e.g. *'walked' is a rather ordinary verb. I want something to suggest that they are happy and comfortable in the setting. Do you have any suggestions?* Click 'Powerful words' on ITP 1.17 and discuss alternatives, trying out the effect by saying the sentence aloud and giving reasons for the final choice.
• Use Modelled Writing to create the next few sentences using 'Powerful words' from ITP 1.17 and turning them into complete sentences. Explain how you are choosing verbs for accuracy and impact, e.g. 'The sunlight peeped through the leaves' ... *I like peeped, it sounds shy.*
• Use Think Alouds to improve the writing. Click on the 'Openers' button and discuss how to vary the sentences by using a where/when starter, e.g. Overhead, the sunlight ...
• Begin the next sentence and ask the children to contribute ideas for how it might continue, focusing on the choice of verb, e.g. *Somewhere in the distance ... .*
• Save changes to ITP 1.17 for use in Session 13.

Independent and Guided

• The children write their own setting descriptions using the model for support but drawing on the notes they made in Session 11, 'Using your senses' (PCM 1.11) and 'Looking close-up' (PCM 1.12). Encourage them to think about the purpose of the writing and the success criteria on ITP 1.16. Support the children with an identified need. (T+/TA)

Plenary

• Recap the learning objectives and encourage the children to assess progress against the success criteria on ITP 1.16. *What have you done well? What do you need to work on in the next session?*
• Select sentences to be revised in Session 13 and identify focus groups for guided work.

Assessment pointers

• AF1, 2, 7 (W): setting descriptions will show how far the children can use powerful verbs and an awareness of the effect created.
• AF6 (W): drafted writing will show how far the children are able to construct and punctuate sentences accurately.

We are learning to ...	Resources
• edit writing to make it more effective • edit writing to choose more adventerous words • change simple verbs in sentences and explain how this affects the meaning (PNS Strands 9.1, 9.4, 11.2) **Assessment Focuses** AF (W): 1, 2, 5, 7	ITP: (1.16, 1.17)

Shared teaching

• Share the learning objectives.
• Recall annotated 'Model description' (ITP 1.17) and explain that together you will check the writing against the success criteria on 'Describing settings' (ITP 1.16), suggesting improvements. Explain that later, the children will work in pairs to check their own writing in the same way.
• Read annotated ITP 1.17 aloud. *Can you picture the setting? What mood is created? Does the mood come across strongly? Which words and phrases are most effective?*
• Invite feedback, encouraging the children to explain their comments by referring to the text. Highlight words and phrases that the children agree are effective. Add these to the Learning Wall.
• Look at ITP 1.16. *Which success criteria have been achieved by the model description? What needs to be worked on?*
• Focus on the need to use more powerful verbs. Read each sentence and identify the verb used. *Is this the best word? Can you think of a more accurate verb or a more powerful verb to help the mood?*
• Click on the 'Powerful words' button on ITP 1.17. Explain that not all of the words will fit the mood. Encourage the children to Think-Pair-Share possibilities, trying out the effect by rehearsing the new sentences.
• Model changing the verbs in the sentences, explaining your choice and demonstrating altering the tense of the verbs (past). Reread the whole passage to explore the impact of these changes. *How has this improved the effect of the writing?*
• Ask the children to select and note verbs from the 'Powerful words' box on ITP 1.17 to use in their own writing.

Independent and Guided

• The children work in pairs to check the effectiveness of their own writing, focusing particularly on their choice of verbs.
  - ●●● Use a thesaurus to find more adventurous verbs.
  - ●● Work on the sentences highlighted by the teacher. (T+)
  - ● Discuss suggestions to improve their choice of verbs. (TA+)

Plenary

• Recap the learning objectives. Ask the children to share sentences they have improved by changing the verb. *Why did you choose that verb? How does it improve the effect of your writing?*
• Use the Learning Wall to summarise what the children have learnt from writing their first setting description. Explain that they are going to write a second description of their setting. *What should we remember to work on when we start writing our second setting description?*

Assessment pointers

• S&L: pair work will show how sensitively the children can express and respond to opinions.
• AF1, 2, 5, 7 (W): draft sentences and the final version will show how far the children can create imaginative texts that use appropriate vocabulary and understand the effect of using powerful verbs.

Session 14

We are learning to ...	Resources
• collect suitable words and phrases before we write • write an effective description using interesting vocabulary • write sentences choosing details to create a mood (PNS Strands 9.4, 11.2) **Assessment Focuses** AF (W): 7	ITP: (1.15, 1.17) PCM: (1.11, 1.12)

Shared teaching

• Remind the children of the writing task and summarise their learning from Sessions 11–13.
• Share the learning objectives. Explain that now they will write a second setting description, describing the same setting but with a different mood.
• Show the other photo from 'Setting photographs' (ITP 1.15). *How is this different to the first picture? What mood will we need to convey in our writing?* The children Think-Pair-Share ideas for suitable words and phrases.
• Show the annotated version of 'Model description' (ITP 1.17). Remind the children that this described a bright, sunny day. *Now you are going to make it night in the middle of winter and the mood is going to be cold, dark and frightening as in* Storm. *What do you need to change?*
• Use Modelled Writing to compose the opening for the new description, using Think Alouds and rehearsing each sentence, e.g. *It was almost midnight when Josh reached the park. The chilly winter air bit at his fingers and toes.*
• Compose another sentence, using an idea from the original description but changing the mood. Model using words from the

Learning Wall explaining your choices, especially when using verbs, e.g. *The spiky trees moaned as the wind whipped their branches.*
• Model rereading the writing from the beginning, making alterations to improve the flow of the sentences, e.g. joining together the first two sentences with 'and', inserting a 'where' or 'when' starter to vary sentence openings.

Independent and Guided

• The children write a second description of their setting creating a different mood, using notes from 'Using your senses' (PCM 1.11) and 'Looking close-up' (1.12) to help them.

ꝏ Write a description using a thesaurus to select powerful words and phrases.

ꝏ As above. (TA)

◉ As above. (T+)

Plenary

• Recap the learning objectives. Ask the children to choose a sentence in their writing that uses a powerful verb and creates a mood. Listen to some, with the rest of the class commenting on the mood created and the choice of verb. *What mood did you create? Which phrases were effective? Are there any you would change?*
• Use success criteria to mark the descriptions before Session 15.

Assessment pointers

• AF (W) 7: the children's descriptions show how far they can select and use appropriate vocabulary to enhance their writing.

Session 15

We are learning to ...	Resources
• work with an editing partner to improve our writing (PNS Strands 9.1) **Assessment Focuses** AF (W): 1, 2, 5, 6, 7	ITP: (1.16), 1.18

Shared teaching

• Share the learning objective and discuss how the children's descriptions will be published, e.g. on a school website, sent to another school, displayed in a public place, etc. Explain that before publishing it is important to check their writing is the best it can possibly be. Refer to 'Describing settings' (ITP 1.16).
• Explain that in this session, the children will take on an editor's role by reading a partner's writing and giving advice on what can be improved. Show 'Editor's questions' (ITP 1.18) and read the questions.
• Read a description written by one of the children. Allow Think Time and ask the children to comment using ITP 1.18 to help them. *Which parts of the description were the most effective?*
• Expand on the children's comments referring to ITP 1.18, e.g. *Yes, that powerful verb does make the setting sound really unfriendly.* Explain that the editor should highlight those effective parts.
• Allow Think Time and ask the children to comment on what could be improved. Again expand on the children's comments referring to ITP 1.18, e.g. *Perhaps they should have joined those two ideas together to make a longer sentence.* Explain that the editor marks words, phrases or sentences to be improved.
• Model how to summarise the advice for the writer, focusing on how changes at word and sentence level improve the overall effect of the writing.

Independent and Guided

• The children work in editing pairs using ITP 1.18 and the success criteria on ITP 1.16 to evaluate the effectiveness of each other's descriptions. They highlight what is effective and mark the parts to be improved. The children then use this feedback to improve their writing. Hold editing meetings with small groups with similar strengths and areas for development. Support the children with an identified need. (T+/TA+)

Plenary

• Share examples of those sentences highlighted as effective. *Which words and phrases were effective?* Add these to the Learning Wall.
• Recap the learning objective and discuss the changes that were made to the writing in response to feedback. *Which parts did you change? How did this help to improve your description?*
• Recap the unit as a whole. *What did you enjoy most? What do you think you did well? What do you think you still need to work on? Would you like to read more books by this author?*

Assessment pointers

• S&L: pair work will show how sensitively the children can express and respond to opinions.
• AF1, 2 (W): the children's finalised descriptions show how far they are able to write imaginative and interesting texts that are appropriate to task.
• AF5, 6, 7 (W): the children's writing will show how far they are able to vary sentences for effect, write with technical accuracy and use effective vocabulary.

Character statements

Discuss the statements with your partner.

Annie's mother is very happy living in the cottage.

Willa likes living in town.

Annie believes in ghosts.

Annie likes everything about living near the marsh.

Annie and Willa are very different.

Annie and Willa find it hard to get along.

Literacy Evolve Year 3 © Pearson Education 2009

Thought bubbles

Choose a character and draw their picture. Write their thoughts and feelings.

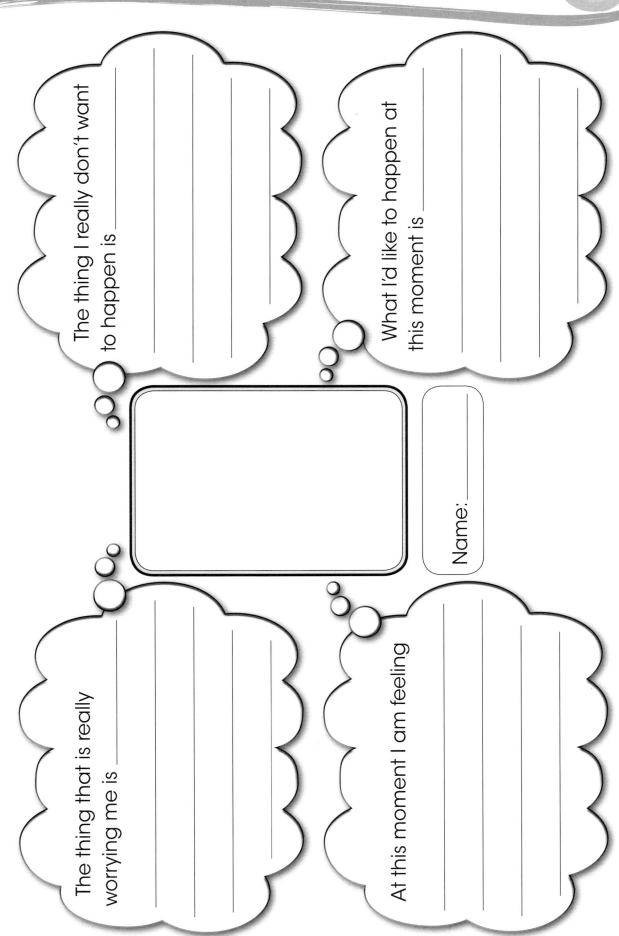

The thing I really don't want to happen is _____

What I'd like to happen at this moment is _____

Name: _____

The thing that is really worrying me is _____

At this moment I am feeling _____

Annie's thought bubbles

Annie is getting ready to go out into the storm. Write her thoughts in the bubbles below.

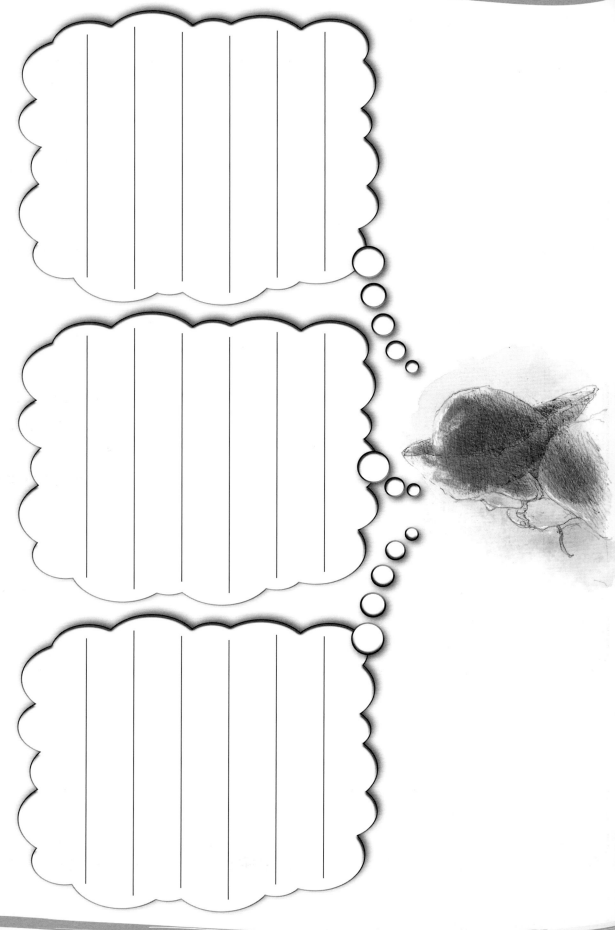

Powerful words

The words in bold are different in _Storm_. Write the words the author chose.

[ ] → [ ]

It seemed to be **going** behind grey lumpy clouds, **going** away from something that was **going after** it. (Page 35)

↑ [ ]

[ ] [ ]

The hooves **got** louder and louder, **quite close to** them, and round the corner of the cottage **came** a horseman on a fine chestnut mare. (Page 36)

↑ [ ]

[ ]

The wind **blew** and Annie was unable to catch his reply.
… "I can walk," **said** Annie. (Page 39)

↑ [ ]

[ ]

Annie's heart was beating **fast**.
… she and the horseman **went off** in the stormy darkness. (Page 41)

[ ]

Literacy Evolve Year 3 © Pearson Education 2009

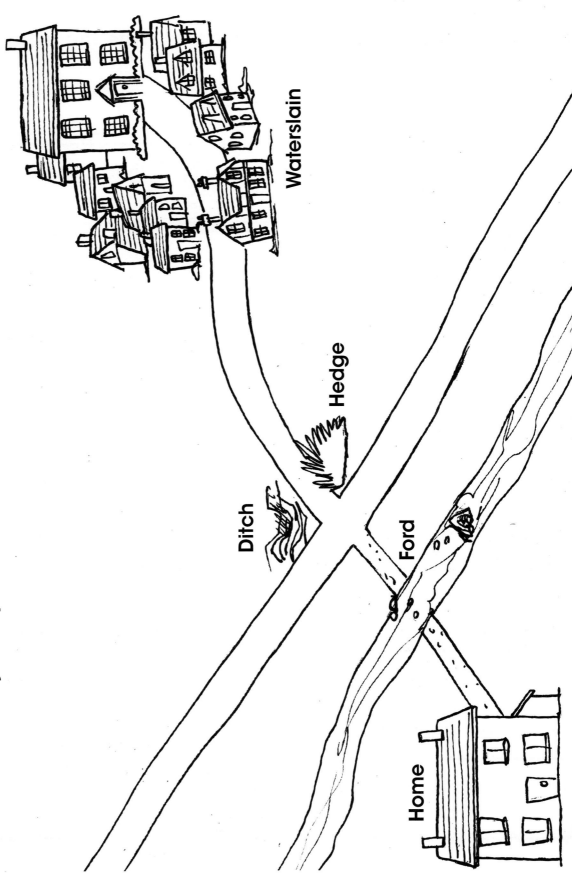

Memories map

Add words to the picture to describe how Annie was feeling and what she might remember from her journey.

Name: _____ Date: _____ 1.5

Waterslain

Hedge

Ditch

Ford

Home

Discussion starters

Discuss the questions with a partner.

What did you like about this story?

Was there anything you didn't like?

Was there anything that surprised you?

If the author were here what would you ask him?

Would you recommend this story to other children?

How would you describe the story to a friend?

Would you like to read another book about Annie? Why/Why not?

Who was your favourite character? Why?

Target board

Write the words on the board to describe the setting. Add your own words.

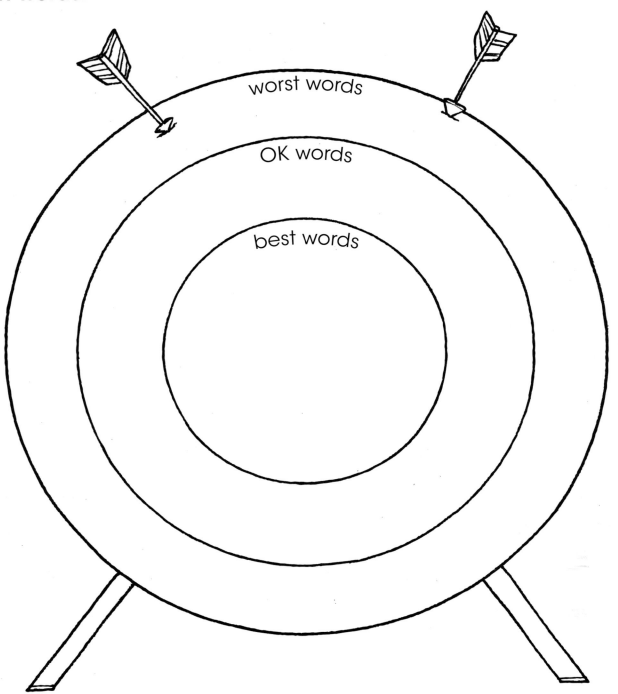

worst words

OK words

best words

peaceful	friendly	safe	threatening	cold
frightening	exciting	unfriendly	wild	bleak

Clues bookmark

Write the 'clues' from the text that helped you to complete your target board.

Clues bookmark

Name: _____

Title: _Storm_ _____

Sights

Page   *Clue*

_____ : _____

_____ : _____

_____ : _____

Sounds

Page   *Clue*

_____ : _____

_____ : _____

_____ : _____

Imaginings

Page   *Clue*

_____ : _____

_____ : _____

_____ : _____

_____ : _____

Feelings

Page   *Clue*

_____ : _____

_____ : _____

_____ : _____

_____ : _____

Fold

Name: _____ Date: _____

1.9

Annie's journey

Imagine you are Annie. Describe her journey through the storm.

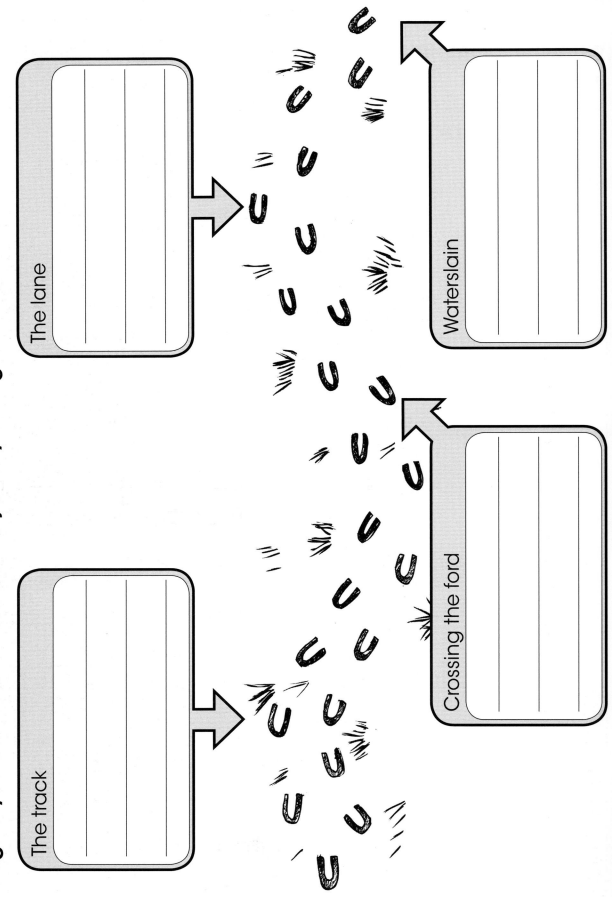

The lane

The track

Waterslain

Crossing the ford

School setting

Label the picture with descriptive words and phrases.

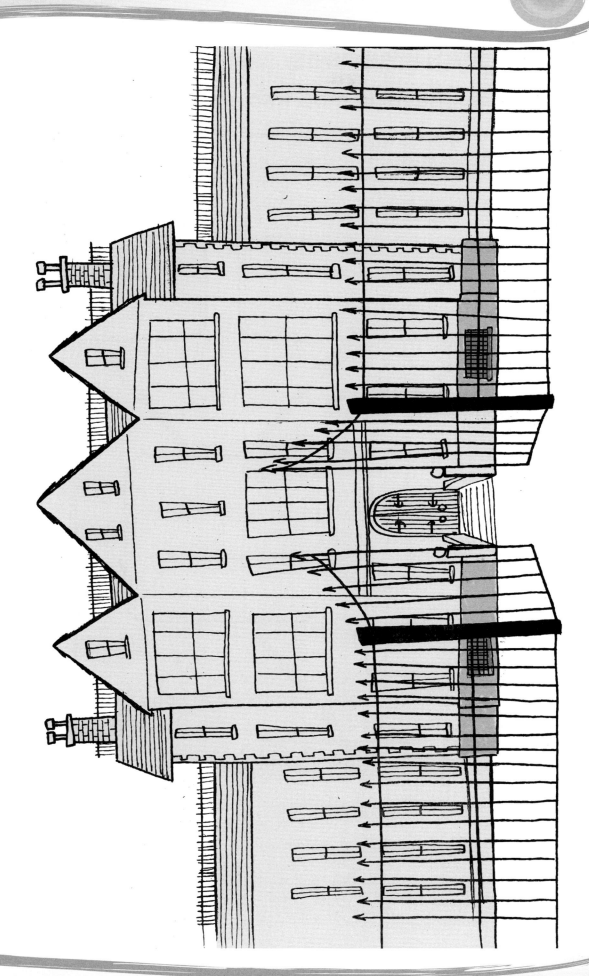

Literacy Evolve Year 3 © Pearson Education 2009

Using your senses

Complete the mind map with notes about your setting.

I can see …

I can hear …

I can smell …

My setting

I can taste …

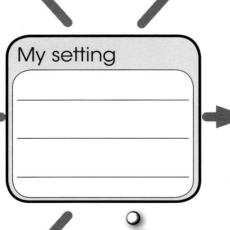

I can touch …

I feel … _____

Looking close-up

Draw close-up pictures of your setting inside the magnifying glasses. Then label and describe your pictures.

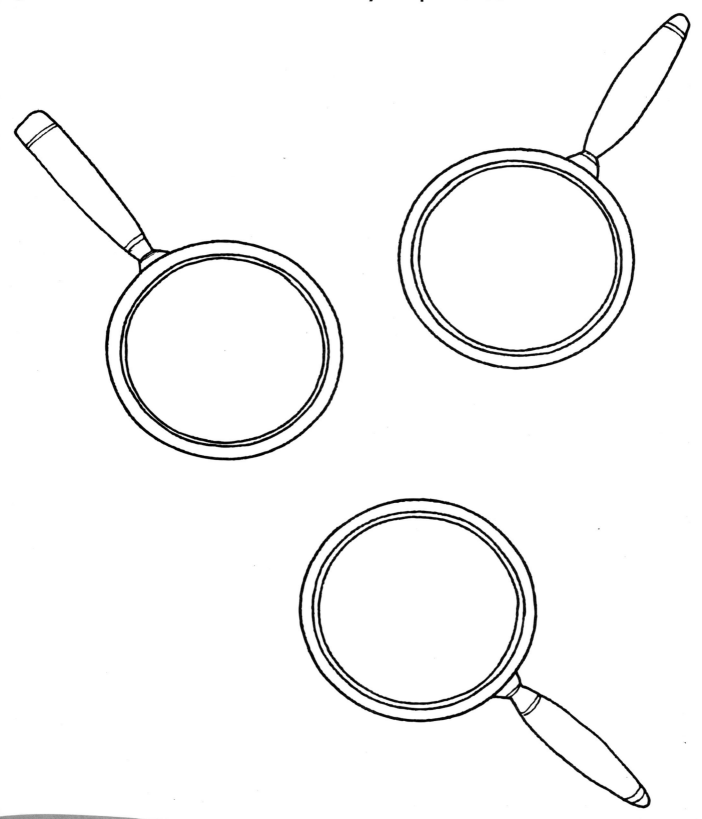

Narrative Unit 2

DRAGON SLAYER – film (Myths and legends)

Medium term plan (4 weeks)	
Phase	**Learning Outcomes**
Phase 1: Familiarisation with genre (5 days)	• Children can identify the key features of legends. • Children can work in groups to compare stories in the legend genre. • Children can understand the effect of the language used in legends.
Phase 2: Looking closely at film and narrative (7 days)	• Children can identify film techniques, including types of shot, pace, music and use of colour. • Children can understand and respond to the impact of film techniques. • Children can use drama to explore a dilemma. • Children can identify the story structure of a legend.
Phase 3: Writing and editing (8 days)	• Children can draw on modelled writing as a basis for their own writing. • Children can create an original written story based on the structure of a film story. • Children can use powerful words to create settings, characters, mood and emotions.

DRAGON SLAYER

Big picture

The children compare two legend texts: *Saint George and the Dragon* and *The Beast with a Thousand Teeth*. They use drama strategies to explore the characters' feelings, and identify key features of the language of the genre. The children then watch the film *Dragon Slayer*. They identify film techniques and explore how character, mood and emotions are conveyed visually. They retell the story in descriptive narrative, then go on to write their own legend based on the structure of the film, adding their own characters and settings.

Prior learning

This unit assumes that the children can already:
- read and respond to stories and discuss settings and characters giving reasons for their views
- infer and describe how a character is feeling
- select language that will convey setting, mood and character
- understand the structure of a story.

Key aspects of learning

Communication: Convey a character's feelings through expressive language; express own ideas through speaking, listening and writing; retell a story in a different medium.

Creative thinking: Invent imaginative variations on a given story, creating new settings, characters and dilemmas.
Empathy: Respond to a character's feelings; understand a character's dilemma.
Social skills: Engage in group discussion; offer constructive feedback during peer evaluation.

Progression in narrative

In this unit the children will:
- identify key features of the legend genre
- identify techniques of film and written storytelling
- discuss the effect of film techniques on the viewer
- transform a film story into a written text
- use the structure of a film story as the basis of an original written story.

Cross-curricular links

Art and Design/Design and Technology: Create finished books of the completed legends, with illustrations.
Citizenship: Explore themes of caring for others; resolving dilemmas; taking responsibility for our actions; making choices.
History: Explore the place of legends in history, across different cultures.

Viewing time

8 minutes 10 seconds approx.

PHASE 1: FAMILIARISATION WITH GENRE (5 DAYS)

Session 1

We are learning to …	Resources
• retell a story in sequence • use the language of legends when telling the story • explore how the features of legends appeal to readers (PNS Strands 1.2, 1.4, 7.5) **Assessment Focuses** AF (R): 4	ITP: 2.1, 2.2 PCM: 2.1

Shared teaching

- Explain that in this unit, the children are going to be exploring legends. *Do you know what a legend is?* (A legend is a traditional story about a heroic character, which may be based on truth but has been exaggerated over the years.) *Can you give any examples?* (E.g. King Arthur, Saint George, Robin Hood, etc.)
- Share the learning objectives.
- Explain that legends often tell the tale of a hero/heroine who has to go on a dangerous journey, or quest, to overcome a problem.
- Read 'Saint George and the Dragon' (ITP 2.1) until the end of paragraph 4, Screen 2. Highlight and discuss the meaning of any new vocabulary, e.g. 'rolling hills', 'lush', 'harvest', 'sacrifice', etc.
- Talk Partners discuss what they have learnt about the legend so far. *When is the legend set? What kind of place is it? Are the people happy? What is the beast like? What does the beast want?*
- Explain that in most legends one character (the hero/heroine) represents good and another character (often the beast or monster) represents evil. Read ITP 2.1 to the end of paragraph 7, Screen 3. *What words and phrases tell you that Saint George is a hero?*
- Show 'Legend ingredients' (ITP 2.2). Click on 'Hero', and 'Problem'. *Is*

Saint George a typical hero? What problem does Saint George have to solve?
- Ask the children if they can identify similar features in any other legend they know, e.g. *What problem does Robin Hood have to solve?* Ask the children if they can identify similar features in any films, cartoons or television programmes they know.

Independent and Guided

- In pairs the children take turns to retell specific parts of the story, using as much language from the text as possible, while their partner asks questions to help prompt descriptions. The children support each other using cut-up 'Story prompts' (PCM 2.1). They should be prepared to retell their part of the story to the class during the plenary.

  ⬤⬤⬤ Use C and D from PCM 2.1 to retell part of the story.

  ⬤⬤ Use A and B from PCM 2.1 to retell part of the story. (TA+)

  ⬤ Use B from PCM 2.1 to retell part of the story. (T+)

Plenary

- Retell the story as a class. Invite pairs to volunteer retelling their parts of the story in the correct order (A, B, C, D). Encourage the children to add as much information as they can. *How well do you think you retold the story? What language did you use from the text?*
- Recap the learning objectives. *What have you learnt about legends so far?*

Assessment pointers

- S&L: oral retellings will show how well the children can recount ideas.
- AF4 (R): discussion in the shared teaching shows how far the children respond to the language and features in texts.

<table>
<tr><td>

We are learning to ...
- retell a story in sequence
- use talk to organise roles and action
- work together effectively in groups, including all group members
(PNS Strands 1.2, 3.1, 3.2)

Assessment Focuses
AF (R): 2, 4

</td><td>

Resources
ITP: (2.1, 2.2), 2.3
PCM: 2.2, 2.3

</td></tr>
</table>

Shared teaching

- Share the learning objectives. Recap Session 1. *What has happened so far in* Saint George and the Dragon?
- Read '*Saint George and the Dragon*' (ITP 2.1) until the end. *Did anything surprise you?*
- Recall 'Legend ingredients' (ITP 2.2). Click on 'Plot'. Explain that plot is the word we use to describe the sequence of events or 'what happens' in a story.
- Ask the children to recap what happens in *Saint George and the Dragon. Is this a typical plot for a legend?*
- Click on the 'Language' button on ITP 2.2. Read the pop-up text with the children, then look back at ITP 2.1. *Can you identify powerful words in the descriptions in* Saint George and the Dragon?
- Explain that the children are going to work in groups to put the events of the story in order. Everyone in the group will need to agree on the order of events.
- Show 'Group work' (ITP 2.3). Discuss the success criteria with the children. *Are there any you would like to add or change?* Remind them to remember these while they work in their groups.

Independent and Guided

- The children work in groups to order and/or retell part of the story, paying attention to the rules for group work on ITP 2.3. They share out the retelling so that everyone in the group has a part of the story to focus on.
- **⊙⊙⊙** Use 'Jumbled up' (PCM 2.2) to order and retell the story, adding more detail.
- **⊙⊙** As above. (TA+)
- **⊙** Use 'Story starters' (PCM 2.3) to retell the story. (T+)

Plenary

- Each group presents its sequence and retells part of the story. Encourage the children to offer feedback. *What did you like about their retelling? What did they do well? What could be improved?*
- Recap the learning objectives.
- Ask the children to reflect on how well they worked in their groups. *Did everyone have a chance to contribute? Did you all agree on the order? Could you improve on how you worked together?*

Assessment pointers

- S&L: group work will show how well the children can adopt group roles, drawing ideas together and promoting effective discussion.
- AF2, 4 (R): group work and retellings will show how far the children are able to identify powerful words and understand the structure of a legend.

Session 3

<table>
<tr><td>

We are learning to ...
- make notes about the text using headings
- explore how the features of legends appeal to readers
(PNS Strands 7.1, 7.5)

Assessment Focuses
AF (R): 4

</td><td>

Resources
ITP: 2.4, 2.5
PCM: 2.4

</td></tr>
</table>

Shared teaching

- Share the learning objectives. *Can you remember the main features of a legend?* (hero/heroine, beast, language, etc.)
- Explain that the children are going to read another fantastic tale which shares many features of legends. Explain that later in the session, the children are going to be 'legend detectives' so they should think about the main ingredients of legends as they listen to the story.
- Read '*The Beast with a Thousand Teeth*' (ITP 2.4) up to line 122 ('"Great" said the beast and ate the lot.') *What ingredients of legends does this story have? Did anything about this story surprise you? What problem did Sam solve? What do you think is going to happen next?*
- Read the rest of *The Beast with a Thousand Teeth. Is this story typical of a legend? What was different? What surprised you?*
- Explain that to help keep track of our thoughts and responses to a story, we can make notes to help us remember things later. It is also useful to make notes under headings.
- Show 'Detective's notebook' (ITP 2.5). Use Modelled Writing to show how to write notes under headings, encouraging the children to suggest ideas for the notes. *What clues tell us about the setting? Who is the hero? What do we learn about the beast?* Model how to refer to the text to support your answers.
- Explain that when making notes we don't need to write in full

sentences, but we can underline and circle things to help us remember them later.

Independent and Guided

- The children use 'Detective's notebook' (PCM 2.4) to continue making notes on the text.
- **⊙⊙⊙** Complete PCM 2.4. Encourage the children to refer directly to the text to support their ideas.
- **⊙⊙** As above. (T+)
- **⊙** Make notes under the first three headings on PCM 2.4. (TA+)

Plenary

- Recap the learning objectives.
- Ask the children to share their notes. *Have you noted similar things? Is there anything you can add to your notes?*
- Discuss how far *The Beast with a Thousand Teeth* shares the features of a typical legend. *How is it different? What extra features are there?*

Assessment pointers

- AF4 (R): shared discussion and completed PCMs show how far the children can identify the main features of a legend in another story.

We are learning to ...	Resources
• use talk to organise roles and action • work together effectively in groups, including all group members • compare different stories, looking for similarities and differences (PNS Strands 3.1, 3.2, 8.1) **Assessment Focuses** AF (R): 2	ITP: (2.3), 2.6 PCM: 2.5

Shared teaching

• Share the learning objectives. Explain that the children are going to compare *Saint George and the Dragon* and *The Beast with a Thousand Teeth*. *Which story did you like best?*

• Use Babble Gabble to recap the stories of *Saint George and the Dragon* and *The Beast with a Thousand Teeth*.

• Talk Partners discuss the heroes from both legends. *What are the heroes like? What do they do? How are they similar or different? Is Sam a typical hero?* (No, because he is not a knight; he doesn't want to fight; he wants money.)

• Take feedback and add suggestions about the heroes to 'Comparison chart' (ITP 2.6).

• Use Hot-Seating to explore the heroes in each story. Choose one child to be George and another to be Sam. The class ask them questions and they answer in role, e.g. *Where do you come from, George? Where did you learn to cook, Sam? Were you scared of the beast? What did you think was going to happen?*

• Discuss the battles in each story and add notes about how the stories are resolved to ITP 2.6. *How are they different? How are they similar?*

• Explain that the children are going to compare the stories in their groups. Remind the children of the success criteria on 'Group work' (ITP 2.3).

Independent and Guided

• The children work in groups, using 'Question time' (PCM 2.5) to compare the features of each legend. They should appoint one group member to chair, one to take notes and another to share the group's answers with the class.

 Use the questions in part A on PCM 2.5.

 Use the questions in part B on PCM 2.5. (TA+)

 Use the questions in part C on PCM 2.5. (T+)

Plenary

• Take feedback from each of the groups and use this to complete ITP 2.6. Encourage the children to point out specific differences between the two legends, e.g. Sam has two problems to solve: saving himself and relieving the beast's toothache.

• Recap the learning objectives. *How well did you work in your groups? What could you do better next time?*

Assessment pointers

• S&L: hot-seating will show how far the children can sustain roles to explore ideas. Group work will show how far they can adopt group roles, drawing ideas together and promoting effective discussion.

• AF2 (R): shared and independent discussions show how far the children are able to make reference to ideas, information and events in the text when drawing comparisons.

We are learning to ...	Resources
• say what makes a story effective, looking at powerful words (PNS Strands 8.3) **Assessment Focuses** AF (R): 5	ITP: (2.1)

Shared teaching

• Share the learning objective. Explain that so far the children have looked at the legend features of character and plot. There is another special feature of legends. *Does anyone know what this is?* (powerful words and phrases)

• Explain that today, the children will be collecting powerful words and phrases to use when they are writing their own legend.

• Reread the first paragraph of 'Saint George and the Dragon' (ITP 2.1). Highlight a couple of descriptive phrases, e.g. 'shining, heavy armour', 'loud as thunder', etc.

• Talk Partners identify their favourite descriptive phrases in ITP 2.1, Screen 1 and give reasons for their choices. (If whiteboards are available children could write the words or phrases on this.)

• Take feedback and add the children's suggestions to the Learning Wall. *Why have you chosen these words and phrases? How do they make you feel?*

• Discuss why the words or phrases are effective, e.g. they paint a better picture for the reader, they make the story seem scarier and more exciting, etc.

• Remind the children of the work they did on verbs and adjectives in Unit 1. *Can you identify any verbs or adjectives in your selected words and phrases?*

Independent and Guided

• The children highlight key words and phrases in a specific part of the text (printed from ITP 2.1).

 Highlight powerful words and phrases on Screens 4 to 6.

 Highlight powerful words and phrases on Screens 2 and 3. (TA+)

 Point out powerful words and key phrases on pages 3 and 4 while the teacher reads. (T+)

Plenary

• Recap the learning objective and invite the children to share some of the descriptive words and phrases they located in the text they examined. Encourage the children to discuss the words and phrases. *Why did you choose that word/phrase? What picture does it paint? How does it make you feel?* Add words and phrases to the Learning Wall.

Assessment pointers

• AF5 (R): talk partner activity and contributions to ITP 2.1 will show how far the children can identify and comment on the use of powerful language.

Session 6

We are learning to ...	Resources
• understand a character's thoughts and feelings • explore how film directors use film techniques to tell us about characters • choose powerful verbs and adjectives (PNS Strands 7.2, 8.3, 9.4) **Assessment Focuses** AF (R): 3, 5	*Dragon Slayer* (film) ITP: 2.7, 2.8 PCM: 2.6

Shared teaching (1)

• Share the learning objectives. Explain that today, the children are going to explore how the features of legends are used in film. They are also going to find out how the person who made the film (the director), helps the audience to understand the characters and story.
• Introduce the film *Dragon Slayer* and play from the beginning until Marker 1. *What characters are introduced? What is the purpose of the 'orange' scene at the beginning?* (gives background information, sets the scene) *What do you think the dragon slayer is going to do?*
• Talk Partners discuss the dragon slayer in more detail. *What does he look like? How does he move? How do you think he feels at the beginning of the film?* (weary, tired) *What happens when he sees the villagers?*
• Explain that the children are going to explore adjectives to describe the dragon slayer.
• Show 'Target board' (ITP 2.7). and remind the children about the significance of the different zones.
• Model placing adjectives into the most relevant zones to describe the dragon slayer. Invite the children to debate where each adjective should be positioned.

Independent and Guided

• The children work in groups to choose adjectives to describe the dragon slayer. Groups use 'Target board' (PCM 2.6) to write the adjectives on the target according to how well they think they describe the dragon slayer. Support the children with an identified need. (T/TA)

Shared teaching (2)

• Take feedback and change the position of adjectives on ITP 2.7 accordingly. Encourage the children to support their answers with reference to the film. Print off ITP 2.7 and add to the Learning Wall.
• Explain that the director uses different camera shots to tell us about the character.
• Show 'Film shots' (ITP 2.8) and talk through the main shots: long shot (often scene-setting), mid shot (often action) and close-up (often of characters' faces to show feelings or of objects to show importance).
• Rewatch *Dragon Slayer* from the beginning to Marker 1. Ask the children to identify the different shots.
• Take feedback. *What do the different shots tell us? Do they give us any clues about the characters or the story?*

Plenary

• Recap the learning objectives. Discuss what the children have learnt about the dragon slayer. *What is his behaviour like at the beginning of the film clip? Did he appear to change? What do the old man and the boy think about him?*

Assessment pointers

• AF3 (R): choice of adjectives shows how far the children are able to make inferences about the dragon slayer.
• AF5 (R): the discussion of film shots shows how far the children are able to engage with the choices directors make.

Session 7

We are learning to ...	Resources
• explore how film directors use film techniques to make us think and feel • explore how directors use settings to create different feelings and moods (PNS Strands 8.3, 11.2) **Assessment Focuses** AF (W): 1, 6, 7	ITP: (2.7), 2.9, 2.10 PCM: (2.6), 2.7

Shared teaching

• Recap Session 6. Ask the children to play Word Tennis to describe the setting they saw in *Dragon Slayer* in Session 6. *How did the setting make you feel?*
• Share the learning objectives. Remind the children of the work they did previously on adjectives and explain that they will be using this information to write 'super sentences' to describe the dragon slayer.
• Show '*Dragon Slayer*' (ITP 2.9). Ask the children to choose adjectives to annotate one or both of the stills. Click the still image to add suggested words to ITP 2.9. Demonstrate how to develop some of these words into phrases and add these to ITP 2.9, e.g. *dark, cloudy sky*.
• Now write a very simple sentence, e.g. *The dragon slayer rode into the village*. Discuss how to improve this sentence by using some of the adjectives from annotated 'Target board' (ITP 2.7).
• Improve the sentence further by adding information about how the dragon slayer rode into the village, e.g. *Slowly, the weary dragon slayer rode into the half-deserted village*.
• Use Modelled Writing to create a sentence that gives more detail about the dragon slayer's appearance, e.g. *He wore an old helmet with sharp, shiny horns*.

• Talk Partners orally rehearse a sentence describing the dragon slayer's powerful arms.
• Take feedback and add examples of super sentences to ITP 2.9, expanding on the words and phrases already noted and explaining why particular ideas have been chosen.
• Explain that the children will now write their own 'super sentences'. Show 'Super sentences' (ITP 2.10). Invite the children to make further suggestions to add to the list. Save annotations for future sessions.

Independent and Guided

• The children write 'super sentences' to describe the dragon slayer using their 'best words' from annotated 'Target board' (PCM 2.6) to help them.
  ◉◉◉ Use PCM 2.6 to write a series of 'super sentences'.
  ◉◉ As above. (T+)
  ◉ Use PCM 2.6 and 'The dragon slayer' (PCM 2.7) to write 'super sentences'. (TA+)

Plenary

• Recap the learning objectives. Encourage the children to share their 'super sentences' while the rest of the class check against ITP 2.10 to ensure that all points are covered. *What did you like about the sentences? How could the sentences be improved?*
• Add some of the descriptive words and 'super sentences' to the Learning Wall.

Assessment pointers

• AF1, 6, 7 (W): sentences show how far the children can write with technical accuracy and how far they can select appropriate vocabulary.

Session 8

We are learning to ...	Resources
• retell a story in sequence • explore how authors use powerful verbs and adjectives • explore how film directors use film techniques to make us think and feel (PNS Strands 1.2, 8.3, 10.1) **Assessment Focuses** AF (R): 6	*Dragon Slayer* (film) ITP: 2.11 PCM: 2.8

Shared teaching

• Share the learning objectives. Recap the story so far. *What do you think is going to happen next?*
• Watch *Dragon Slayer* from Marker 1 to Marker 3. Ask the children to look for how the film director uses different shots (long, mid and close-up) for effect and to listen to how music is used. *Did you find the battle scene exciting? What was the effect of the different camera shots? What did you notice on the close-up of the shield? How did the music make you feel?*
• Explain that the children are now going to compare how an author describes a similar scene in words. Talk Partners discuss what happened in the battle scene of *Saint George and the Dragon*.
• Take feedback and show 'Verbs and connectives' (ITP 2.11). Read the passage.
• Remind the children that verbs are words that describe actions. Ask the children to identify powerful verbs on ITP 2.11. Click 'Powerful verbs' to highlight them. *How do these powerful verbs make you feel?*
• Talk Partners write down powerful verbs to describe the dragon slayer's actions and the dragon's actions in the battle scene (two verbs for each character).

• Take feedback and add powerful verbs to the Learning Wall.
• Show ITP 2.11 again. Click 'Time connectives' to highlight the time connectives. *What do you notice about the highlighted words?* E.g. they introduce the next action or event or tell us how much time has passed.
• Explain that time connectives help to tell the reader when a new event or action is taking place or how much time has passed. *Can you think of any other time connectives?* (E.g. soon, suddenly, the next minute, in a split second, next, at once, after that, etc.).

Independent and Guided

• The children work in groups to prepare an oral retelling of the battle scene using the prompts on 'Battle starters' (PCM 2.8). The children should use time connectives and powerful verbs. They should take it in turns to tell parts of the story. Support the children with an identified need. (T/TA)

Plenary

• Recap the learning objectives.
• Each group shares their oral retelling of the battle scene with the class. *Which time connectives have they used? Which powerful words have they used?* Scribe a list of time connectives to add to the Learning Wall.

Assessment pointers

• S&L: group work and oral retellings will show how far the children structure and vary talk to maintain listener's attention.
• AF6 (R): oral responses show how far the children are able to engage with the director's choices and viewpoint.

Session 9

We are learning to ...	Resources
• use drama to explore dilemmas • understand a character's thoughts and feelings • debate moral dilemmas • explore how film directors use film techniques to make us think and feel (PNS Strands 4.2, 7.2, 8.2, 8.3) **Assessment Focuses** AF (R): 3, 5	*Dragon Slayer* (film)

Shared teaching (1)

• Remind the children that at the end of Session 8, the dragon lay dead on the ground. *How did the dragon slayer feel at that point? What do you think is going to happen next?*
• Watch *Dragon Slayer* from Marker 3 to Marker 4. *How do you think the dragon slayer feels about the death of the dragon? Is he sorry or not? What might he be thinking as he adds a notch to his shield? What could have made the noise he heard?* (Notice how a close-up shot is used to show his surprise.)
• Watch *Dragon Slayer* from Marker 4 to Marker 5. *How did this scene make you feel?* Explore how the film director makes us feel this way (close-ups of characters' faces, sad music, use of colour).
• Discuss how the dragon slayer feels about the baby dragon. *Why does he seem angry at first? What does he want to do? How do you feel about the baby dragon?* Discuss how the film director makes us feel this way, e.g. the baby dragon waves its tail like a little puppy dog.
• Explore this part of *Dragon Slayer* further. *Why does the baby dragon roar after the dragon slayer does?* (For a moment it sees the image of its mother in the shape of the dragon slayer.) *Why do you think the horse nudged the dragon slayer closer to the dragon? Why do you*

think it is taking so long for the dragon slayer to make up his mind about what to do with the baby dragon?
• Explain that the children are going to work in pairs to explore what the dragon slayer should do next.

Independent and Guided

• In pairs, the children explore reasons why the dragon slayer should save the baby dragon (for) and reasons why he should just walk away (against). Each partner then selects one favourite reason from each category. Support the children with an identified need. (T/TA)

Shared teaching (2)

• Perform a Conscience Alley to explore the dragon slayer's dilemma. Choose one child to be the dragon slayer. One side of the alley represents 'reasons for' and the other represents 'reasons against' saving the baby dragon.
• After performing this once, discuss how it could be made more dramatic, e.g. by adding actions, body language and facial expressions.
• Ask what the child in role as the dragon slayer has decided to do.

Plenary

• Recap the learning objectives and take the children's predictions as to what the dragon slayer will do next.

Assessment pointers

• S&L: group work and drama will show how well the children can adopt group roles and explore issues.
• AF3 (R): discussion and drama show how far the children can infer characters' feelings and engage in their dilemmas.
• AF5 (R): responses during shared teaching show how far the children can comment on the use of film techniques.

We are learning to ...	Resources
• understand a character's thoughts and feelings • write sentences in the first person using powerful words (PNS Strands 7.2, 11.2) **Assessment Focuses** AF (R): 3; AF (W) 6, 7	*Dragon Slayer* (film) ITP: (2.10), 2.12 PCM: 2.9, 2.10

Shared teaching

• Share the learning objectives.
• Recap Session 9 and the children's predictions of what will happen next.
• Watch *Dragon Slayer* from Marker 5 to Marker 6. *What do you think the noise was? Were your predictions right?*
• Continue watching until Marker 7. *What surprised you about the ending? How do you think the dragon slayer feels at the end?*
• Explain that the children are going to explore how the dragon slayer's thoughts and feelings change throughout the film.
• Show 'Feelings web' (ITP 2.12). Talk Partners discuss what the dragon slayer heard, saw, thought and felt. Take feedback and add notes to ITP 2.12.
• Use Modelled Writing to show how to transform the notes into super sentences in the first person, e.g. *I could hear the heavy rain lashing down around me. After a while, I could see a village ahead of me. I was very tired. Another day, another dragon hunt! I wanted to rest.*
• Explain that when we use 'I' as in the above sentences we are writing in the first person – that is, we are writing as if we are the dragon slayer. (If we were writing in the third person we would write 'He could see a village ahead of him', or 'He wanted to rest'.)

• Go to Screen 2 on ITP 2.12. Talk Partners makes notes about the dragon slayer. Then construct sentences orally in the first person based on their notes.
• Take feedback and add suggestions to ITP 2.12.

Independent and Guided

• The children annotate pictures with words to describe what the dragon slayer thinks and feels. They then use these to write 'super sentences' in the first person.

○○○ Use 'Thoughts and feelings 1' (PCM 2.9).

○○ As above. (T+)

◉ Use 'Thoughts and feelings 2' (PCM 2.10). (TA+)

Plenary

• Recap the learning objectives.
• Encourage the children to share their 'super sentences'. The rest of the class check them against the success criteria on annotated 'Super sentences' (ITP 2.10) to ensure that all points are covered. *What do you like about these sentences? How could we make these sentences even better?*

Assessment pointers

• AF3 (R): the children's annotations show how far they can infer a character's feelings.
• AF6, 7 (W): the children's sentences show how far they can write with technical accuracy and select effective vocabulary.

We are learning to ...	Resources
• use conjunctions to join sentences (PNS Strands 11.1) **Assessment Focuses** AF (W): 5, 6	ITP: 2.13 PCM: (2.9, 2.10), 2.11

Shared teaching

• Share the learning objective and explain that the children are now going to improve their 'super sentences' by using conjunctions. *Does anyone know what conjunctions are?*
• Explain that conjunctions are words which join sentences together. *'And', 'but' and 'so' are conjunctions that we often use. Can you think of any others?*
• Ask the children to volunteer their favourite 'super sentences' from Session 10. *How could we improve these sentences?* Use Modelled Writing to show how to improve some of these sentences using conjunctions.
• Ask the children to volunteer examples of simple sentences for the other children to join together using conjunctions.
• Show 'Where's the conjunction?' (ITP 2.13). Read the extract and ask the children to identify conjunctions. Click on the 'Conjunctions' button to highlight them.
• Look again at the third sentence on ITP 2.13. *How would this read if it was written in only simple sentences?* Explain that 'when' is also a conjunction and write the simple sentence: 'George heard this story'. Ask the children to say the next simple sentences orally and scribe. ('George heard this story. He was determined to try to save the princess. He rested that night in the hermit's hut. At daybreak he set out to the hillside where the dragon lived.') *What is the effect of using*

conjunctions? (they make the sentences flow better) *Do they make the writing more interesting?*
• Discuss success criteria for using conjunctions and add this to the Learning Wall.

Independent and Guided

• Using sentences with conjunctions, the children write a description of the dragon slayer approaching the village.

○○○ The children write a description of the dragon slayer approaching the village using sentences with a variety of conjunctions. (T+)

○○ The children use 'Conjunctions' (PCM 2.11) to join sentences with conjunctions. They then write a few sentences to describe the dragon slayer's approach to the village, using conjunctions.

◉ As above. (TA+)

Plenary

• Recap the learning objective and select some of the children to read their sentences.
• Encourage the children to evaluate the sentences and discuss any improvements that can be made. *Have you used a variety of conjunctions? Have you used the first person?*

Assessment pointers

• AF5, 6 (W): sentences will show how far the children can write using a range of conjunctions and how far they can vary the length of sentences for effect.

We are learning to ...	Resources
• identify the story structure (PNS Strands 7.3) **Assessment Focuses** AF (R): 4	*Dragon Slayer* (film) ITP: (2.1, 2.2), 2.14 PCM: 2.12

Shared teaching

- Share the learning objective.
- Explain that today, the children are going to explore the overall structure of *Dragon Slayer* in preparation for writing their own legends.
- Recap what the children learnt about legends at the beginning of this unit, showing 'Legend ingredients' (ITP 2.2).
- Show 'Story plan' (ITP 2.14). *What do you know about how stories are structured?* (Stories have a beginning, middle and end.) Explain that stories often have more stages in between the beginning, middle and end. They often have a problem to be solved, and a build-up to the resolution. Explain that this plan (ITP 2.14) shows the structure of a typical legend.
- Reread '*Saint George and the Dragon*' (ITP 2.1). Explain that the children are going to map the structure of *Saint George and the Dragon* onto ITP 2.14.
- Use Modelled Writing to show how to map details of the legend onto ITP 2.14.
- Explain that many stories have a similar structure with some variations.
- Explain that during independent work, the children will map the structure of the *Dragon Slayer* film.
- Watch *Dragon Slayer* again. Pause at Marker 7. *Do you think this is the end of the film? What do you think happens in the future?* Continue watching the film to the end.

Independent and Guided

- The children use 'Story plan' (PCM 2.12) to map the structure of *Dragon Slayer*.

  ⊙⊙⊙ Use PCM 2.12 to map the structure of *Dragon Slayer*. If the children finish early they can map the structure of *The Beast with a Thousand Teeth* on a second copy of PCM 2.12.

  ⊙⊙ Use PCM 2.12 to map the structure of *Dragon Slayer*. (T)

  ⊙ As above. (TA+)

Plenary

- Recap the learning objective. Remind the children that stories have different structures but will often follow a similar basic pattern: opening, problem, solution, ending. Ask the children to help you summarise the key points in *Dragon Slayer*.
- Ask for volunteers to discuss a story they have read recently (one that they remember well). Ask the child to summarise the story for the rest of the class. *Does the story have a clear beginning and ending? Is there a problem to be solved? Does the story build up to this?*

Assessment pointers

- AF4 (R): completed PCMs will show how far the children can identify the structure of a story.

PHASE 3: WRITING AND EDITING (8 DAYS)

We are learning to ...	Resources
• discuss our choices with our talk partners • develop ideas for writing (PNS Strands 1.3, 9.1) **Assessment Focuses** AF (W): 3	ITP: (2.14), 2.15, 2.16 PCM: 2.13, 2.14, 2.15

Shared teaching (1)

- Share the learning objectives.
- Explain that the children will be writing their legends following the structure of *Dragon Slayer* step-by-step. However, the children are free to substitute their own heroes/heroines, monsters and settings.
- Explain that today, the children are going to plan their legends. They will have an opportunity to draw and describe their own hero/heroine, monster and setting.
- Remind the children of the work they did earlier in this unit on adjectives and powerful verbs. Refer to the Learning Wall for examples.
- Show 'Ideas' (ITP 2.15). Use Modelled Writing to show how to generate ideas for a new setting. *Where does the story take place? What kind of place is it? What does it look like?* Take feedback and add a few ideas to ITP 2.15.
- Talk Partners discuss ideas for the monster in their legends. *Where is my monster? Is it a traditional dragon or something different? What does it do to scare people? What does it look like? Smell like?*

Independent and Guided (1)

- The children use 'Story ideas' (PCM 2.13) to generate ideas for their own setting, monster and hero/heroine. Encourage the children to write down descriptive words and phrases. In pairs, the children discuss their ideas and ask each other questions. Support the children with an identified need. (T/TA)

Shared teaching (2)

- Take feedback. *What did you like about your partner's ideas? What were your favourite descriptive words and phrases?* Add suggestions to ITP 2.15.
- Quickly recap the different stages of a legend. Refer back to 'Story plan' (ITP 2.14) if necessary.
- Show 'Legend planner' (ITP 2.16). Use Modelled Writing to show how to complete the 'Opening' section, using one of the children's ideas from PCM 2.13.

Independent and Guided (2)

- The children complete 'Legend planner' (PCM 2.14), using completed PCM 2.13 and 'Prompts for writing' (PCM 2.15) to help them. Support the children with an identified need. (T/TA)

Plenary

- Talk Partners share their legend planners and offer feedback.
- Take feedback. *Did your partner's plan include all the legend ingredients? What did you like about your partner's plan? Is there anything they could add?*
- Recap the learning objectives.

Assessment pointers

- S&L: pair work will show how sensitively the children can express and respond to opinions.
- AF3 (W): completed legend planners will show how far the children understand the organisation of legends and how far they can plan their own stories using this structure.

We are learning to ...	Resources
• think about who we are writing for and why (our audience and purpose) • develop success criteria • write an opening that catches the reader's attention • choose powerful verbs and adjectives (PNS Strands 9.1, 9.2, 9.4) **Assessment Focuses** AF (W): 1, 6, 7	ITP: (2.10), 2.17 PCM: (2.14, 2.15)

Shared teaching (1)

• Share the learning objectives. Explain that the children are going to write their opening of their legends based on the plans they made.
• Explain who they are writing for and remind the children why they are writing their legends (to entertain the reader). *How can you make the legends entertaining?*
• Show 'Writing legends' (ITP 2.17). Read the success criteria and encourage the children to add to the list.

Independent and Guided (1)

• In pairs, the children discuss the plans they made on 'Legend planner' (PCM 2.14). Each child gives their partner Two Stars and a Wish. Give the children time to complete plans if they haven't finished and to revise plans based on feedback from their partner's comments. Support the children with an identified need. (T/TA)

Shared teaching (2)

• Explain that the openings to the children's legends should describe the setting and characters. Explain that while writing the opening, they should focus particularly on using interesting adjectives and ensuring

they write well-constructed and powerful sentences. Briefly remind the children of the success criteria on annotated 'Super sentences' (ITP 2.10).
• Use Modelled Writing to compose the first few sentences of the opening to *Dragon Slayer*, focusing on selecting the most effective vocabulary to describe the setting. Use of Think Alouds to model the process, e.g. *Long ago in a faraway land there was a beautiful village surrounded by green fields ... .*
• Continue the narrative, encouraging the children to suggest ideas. Select the most effective words suggested, introducing new words if necessary and always giving reasons for the choices made.

Independent and Guided (2)

• The children work independently to write the openings to their legends using their completed 'Legend planner' (PCM 2.14) and 'Prompts for writing' (PCM 2.15) to help them. Encourage them to think about how to make their writing entertaining for the reader. Support the children with an identified need. (T+/TA+)

Plenary

• Recap the learning objectives.
• Share some of the children's openings. Encourage the rest of the class to comment, referring back to the success criteria. *Do you think you have written an effective story opening? How could you improve it?*

Assessment pointers

• S&L: pair work will show how sensitively the children can express and respond to opinions.
• AF1, 6, 7 (W): story openings will show how far the children can write imaginatively, using interesting sentences with powerful words and also technical accuracy.

We are learning to ...	Resources
• introduce and describe the hero or heroine • write sentences using powerful verbs and adjectives • write in the third person (PNS Strands 9.2, 11.2) **Assessment Focuses** AF (W): 1, 7	PCM: (2.14, 2.15)

Shared teaching

• Share the learning objectives. Explain that the children are going to be writing the next part of their legend: the problem and introducing the hero/heroine.
• Remind the children that in previous sessions they wrote sentences about the dragon slayer's thoughts in the first person. Explain that when they write their legends, they are going to use the third person (he/she or him/her). They must be sure to write in the third person consistently.
• Use Modelled Writing to compose the first few sentences of this part of the narrative. Begin by using a time connective to signal that time has passed before the hero's arrival, e.g. *Several weeks later, the dragon slayer and his faithful horse ... .*
• Set up a whole-class Hot-Seating activity. Invite one child to take the role of the dragon slayer and the other children to ask questions, e.g. *Where have you come from? How do you feel? What is the problem you have to solve?*
• Use ideas from the hot-seating to compose the next part of the narrative, adding in more description to show what the dragon slayer looks like and what he is feeling. Encourage the children to contribute to the composition.

Independent and Guided

• In pairs, the children take it in turns to hot-seat their hero/heroine at this point in their story. The children then use these ideas to continue writing this part of their own legends using completed 'Legend planner' (PCM 2.14) and 'Prompts for writing' (PCM 2.15). Support the children with an identified need. (T+/TA+)

Plenary

• Recap the learning objectives. Recap the key things that the children are looking for in this part of the legend (the use of descriptive words and 'super sentences').
• Take in the children's work for marking and evaluate them against the objectives and the prompts on PCM 2.15.
• Give the children feedback and identify areas for praise, and note where improvements could be made.

Assessment pointers

• S&L: hot-seating will show how far the children can sustain roles to explore ideas.
• AF1, 7 (W): stories show how far the children can write imaginatively using descriptive language.

We are learning to ...	Resources
• write our stories including the build-up, climax and resolution • use time connectives to show time passing • write super sentences to make our writing more effective (PNS Strands 9.2, 11.1, 11.2) **Assessment Focuses** AF (W): 3, 5, 6, 7	*Dragon Slayer* (film) PCM: (2.14, 2.15)

Shared teaching

• Share the learning objectives. *What features have we included in our legends so far? What do we need to write about next?* Explain that the children will be writing the part of the legend: how the problem is resolved.
• Rewatch *Dragon Slayer* from the beginning to Marker 3. Encourage the children to note what the dragon slayer sees, hears and feels as they watch the clip again.
• Freeze Frame the key events in this section of the film and ask the children to Thought Track the dragon slayer.
• Use Modelled Writing ideas from the drama to compose the next part of the story, explaining the need to use the senses to describe what the dragon slayer can see, hear and feel as he gets closer to the dragon's lair.
• Remind the children of the work they did on 'super sentences' in previous sessions. Talk Partners write a super sentence to describe the setting of this part of the dragon slayer's story.
• Take feedback. *How can we improve our sentences?*
• Remind the children of the work they did on time connectives in

previous sessions. Ask the children to suggest time connectives to show how time passes as the dragon slayer approaches the lair.
• Use Modelled Writing to compose 'super sentences' to describe the battle.

Independent and Guided

• The children write this part of their own legend (the journey and resolution), using 'Legend planner' (PCM 2.14) and 'Prompts for writing' (PCM 2.15) to help them. Support the children with an identified need. (T+/TA+)

Plenary

• Recap the learning objectives. *What did this part of the legend need to describe?* (the journey and the battle)
• As a class, evaluate samples of the children's writing against the prompts on PCM 2.15. Identify areas for praise and note where improvements could be made.

Assessment pointers

• S&L: freeze frames will show how far the children can create roles and empathise with characters.
• AF3, 5 (W): independent writing shows how far the children can sequence paragraphs using time connectives and vary sentences for effect.
• AF6, 7 (W): independent writing shows how far the children can select interesting vocabulary and write with technical accuracy.

We are learning to ...	Resources
• write our stories including a second problem • use time connectives to show time passing • use conjunctions to compose some longer sentences • write sentences using powerful verbs and adjectives (PNS Strands 9.2, 11.1, 11.2) **Assessment Focuses** AF (W): 1, 7	*Dragon Slayer* (film) PCM: (2.14, 2.15)

Shared teaching

• Recap Session 16 and refer to annotated 'Legend planner' (PCM 2.14) to identify the point that the children have reached in their writing.
• Share the learning objectives, explaining that the children will be writing the part of the legend in which a new problem is introduced.
• Remind the children of the drama activity, Conscience Alley, from Session 9, where they explored the dragon slayer's dilemma when he saw the baby dragon and thought about what he might be thinking or feeling. *It will be important to include some of these thoughts in our writing today.*
• Rewatch *Dragon Slayer* from Marker 3 to Marker 5. Pause the film at key moments and Thought Track the dragon slayer. *What is the dragon slayer thinking at the beginning of the clip? Do his thoughts change? How does the dragon slayer feel about the baby dragon? How do you know?*
• Use Modelled Writing to introduce the second problem facing the dragon slayer (what to do about the baby dragons). As you do so, explain why you have chosen certain words above others, e.g. 'stumbled' instead of 'walked'; 'budge' instead of 'move'. Encourage

the children to suggest words and phrases to describe the dragon slayer's thoughts and feelings.

Independent and Guided

• The children take it in turns to Role Play their stories and ideas for a second problem. The children then use these ideas to write this section of their stories, using 'Legend planner' (PCM 2.14) and 'Prompts for writing' (PCM 2.15) to help them. Support the children with an identified need. (T+/TA+)

Plenary

• Ask for volunteers to share the second problem part of their legends. The rest of the class comment on how well the hero or heroine's thoughts and feelings have been described. *Which words and phrases have they used to describe the hero or heroine's feelings? Can you suggest any improvements? How do you think the hero or heroine will solve the problem?*
• Recap the learning objectives.
• You may wish to mark the children's compositions in order to identify key areas that they need to work on in the following sessions.

Assessment pointers

• S&L: role plays will show how well the children can explore and develop ideas through drama.
• AF1, 7 (W): independent writing shows how far the children are able to write imaginatively, using powerful vocabulary.

Session 18

<table>
<tr><td>We are learning to …
• write our stories including the resolution
• choose powerful verbs and adjectives
(PNS Strands 9.2, 9.4)
Assessment Focuses
AF (W): 1, 3, 4, 7</td><td>Resources
Dragon Slayer (film)
PCM: (2.14, 2.15)</td></tr>
</table>

Shared teaching

- Recap the dilemma from Session 17. *How did the dragon slayer's feelings change? How did he decide to solve the problem?* Share the learning objectives.
- Talk Partners play Just A Minute taking it in turns to tell each other their legends so far.
- Explain that the children will now be writing the resolution to their legends. Remind the children that the reader needs to know how the second problem (the dilemma) is resolved.
- Talk Partners discuss how their second problem will be resolved. *How will your hero or heroine solve the second problem?*
- Take feedback and discuss any questions or concerns the children might have. *Does anyone need help to solve their second problem? Is there anything puzzling you?*
- Use Modelled Writing to compose the solution to the second problem in *Dragon Slayer* (what to do with the baby dragons). Encourage the children to offer suggestions. Discuss the choice of vocabulary, e.g. more powerful words that could be used. *How could you improve the sentences?* (add time connectives, conjunctions)
- If you have checked over the children's compositions, hand these back and allow time for the children to read through your comments. Talk Partners discuss how these comments could be addressed.

Independent and Guided

- The children work independently to complete this section of their legends (the resolution). They use their 'Legend planner' (PCM 2.14) and 'Prompts for writing ' (PCM 2.15) to help them. Support the children with an identified need. (T/TA)

Plenary

- Ask for volunteers to tell the class how their legend ended. Encourage the children to offer feedback. *Do we know how the problem was resolved?*
- Recap the learning objectives.

Assessment pointers

- AF1, 7 (W): legends will show how far the children can write imaginative stories using powerful vocabulary.
- AF3, 4 (W): legends will also show how far the children can construct stories sequentially with a clear structure and how far they can use paragraphs and time connectives effectively.

Session 19

<table>
<tr><td>We are learning to …
• write convincing endings where all the puzzles and problems are solved
• edit writing to choose more adventurous words
(PNS Strands 9.2, 9.4)
Assessment Focuses
AF (W): 1, 3, 4, 7</td><td>Resources
PCM: (2.14, 2.15)</td></tr>
</table>

Shared teaching

- Share the learning objectives and explain that in this session, the children will be writing the ending to their legends.
- Talk Partners discuss traditional legend endings. *How do legends normally end?* (E.g. they lived happily ever after.) *How did Saint George and Dragon end?* ('So Camellia and Saint George … were married and lived happily ever after.')
- Take feedback. *Do you think* Dragon Slayer *is a traditional legend? How did* Dragon Slayer *end?* (There are two endings: the first shows them riding off into the sunset and the second shows what happens in the future in more detail.) Explain that the children are going to write an ending similar to *Dragon Slayer* which tells the reader what happens in the future.
- Use Modelled Writing to compose the ending to *Dragon Slayer*. Encourage the children to offer suggestions. Use Think Alouds to demonstrate the process of orally rehearsing sentences, e.g. *I think I'll begin by describing the setting as they leave and the golden colour at the end of the film which makes you think everything will be fine in the end.*
- Review the ending and encourage the children to draw on their knowledge from previous sessions to add more powerful verbs to

create 'super sentences'. *What words could we change to make the story more interesting? Are there any time connectives we could add to make the story flow better?*

Independent and Guided

- The children work in groups to take it in turns to Role Play their stories and develop ideas for how the story ends. Encourage the children to think about how the character, especially the hero/heroine, feels at the end. The children then use these ideas and 'Legend planner' (PCM 2.14) and 'Prompts for writing' (PCM 2.15) to write the ending to their stories. Support the children with an identified need. (T/TA)

Plenary

- Recap the learning objectives and encourage the children to share their legend endings. *Why did you choose to end the story in that way? How did the role play help you develop your ideas? Is there anything you would like to change?*
- Explain that in Session 20, the children will have time to make final changes to their legends.

Assessment pointers

- S&L: role plays will show how well the children can explore and develop ideas through drama.
- AF1, 7 (W): legends will show how far the children can write imaginative stories using powerful vocabulary.
- AF3, 4 (W): legends will also show how far the children can construct stories sequentially with a clear structure and how far they can use paragraphs and time connectives effectively.

We are learning to ...	Resources
• evaluate writing using a marking ladder • edit writing to make it more effective (PNS Strands 9.1) **Assessment Focuses** AF (W): 1, 2, 3, 6	ITP: (2.17) PCM: 2.16

Shared teaching (1)

• Share the learning objectives. Explain that today, the children are going to evaluate their legends. 'Evaluate' means they will review the legends to see what they like, what they think is good and what they think they might do better.

• Explain that once they have evaluated their legends, the children will have an opportunity to edit their legends, present them in different ways and add illustrations.

• Show 'Writing legends' (ITP 2.17). Remind the children that they looked at these success criteria before they started writing. *How well do you think you have done? Did you include all the points on the list?* Explain that the points on the marking ladder are based on the success criteria.

Independent and Guided (1)

• The children evaluate their work using 'Marking ladder' (PCM 2.16). Support the children with an identified need. (T+/TA+)

Shared teaching (2)

• Ask for volunteers to feedback on their evaluations. *Can you name one thing you have done really well? Can you suggest one thing you would like to improve? How will you do this?*

• Ask the children if they are clear about any points they would like to improve before making a final copy.

• Remind the children that the audience they are writing for is children of a similar age. Discuss how the children might like to present their stories, e.g. in an illustrated class book with a cover and blurb, either handwritten or typed, or perhaps several smaller 'group' books.

Independent and Guided (2)

• The children prepare final versions of their legends, ready for publication. Support the children with an identified need. (T+/TA+)

Plenary

• Recap the learning objectives. *What changes did you make to your legend? What are you really pleased about? What do you think you could do better next time?*

• Remind the children that the focus for this whole unit has been on legends. *What did you enjoy most about this unit? What have you learnt about legends? What are the 'ingredients' of legends? Would you like to read or watch more legends in the future?*

Assessment pointers

• AF1, 2 (W): final compositions will show how far the children are able to produce texts which are imaginative and appropriate to task and purpose.

• AF3, 6 (W): final compositions will show how far the children can sequence texts effectively and write with technical accuracy.

Story prompts

Use the pictures and prompts to retell the story.

A

- Where is the town?
- Is it a happy place?
- Why not?
- Who lives in the cave?

B

- What did the dragon look like?
- Can you describe him in more detail?
- What did he do to scare people?

C

- What did the dragon threaten to do?
- How did the townspeople keep the dragon happy?
- How did the townspeople feel?

D

- What did the King decide?
- How were the maidens chosen?
- Which maiden was picked first?

Jumbled up

Order the sentences and retell part of the story in more detail.

George met Princess Camellia on his way to find the dragon.

The king offered a prize for killing the dragon.

George threw his spear at the dragon.

George decided to try and save Princess Camellia.

George pierced the dragon under its wing.

The spear broke into a thousand pieces.

George rode to the dragon's cave.

The dragon knocked George into the enchanted water.

Princess Camellia's name was drawn from the casket.

Story starters

Use the sentence starters to retell part of the story.

George rode into town.
He was dressed in

George met an old man.
The old man told him

Princess Camellia's name was drawn from the
casket. She was going to be

The king offered a prize for killing the
dragon. The prize was

George wanted to save Princess Camellia.
The next morning he

George saw Princess Camellia on
his way to find the dragon. He told her to

George arrived at the dragon's cave.
The dragon roared and

George was not afraid. He held his
shield and

Detective's notebook

Write clues about the features of *The Beast with a Thousand Teeth*.

Other characters:

Problems:

Journey:

Battle:

Ending:

Question time

Discuss the questions.

What are the problems in each legend?

How are they the same or different?

How are the problems solved?

How is the journey described in each legend?

What are the problems in each legend?

What happens when George meets the dragon?

What happens when Sam meets the beast?

What is similar or different about the ending of each story?

What things are the same about the two beasts?

What things are different about the two beasts?

Which beast do you think is scariest? Why?

What things are the same about Sam and George?

What things are different about Sam and George?

Target board

Write the words on the target to describe the dragon slayer.

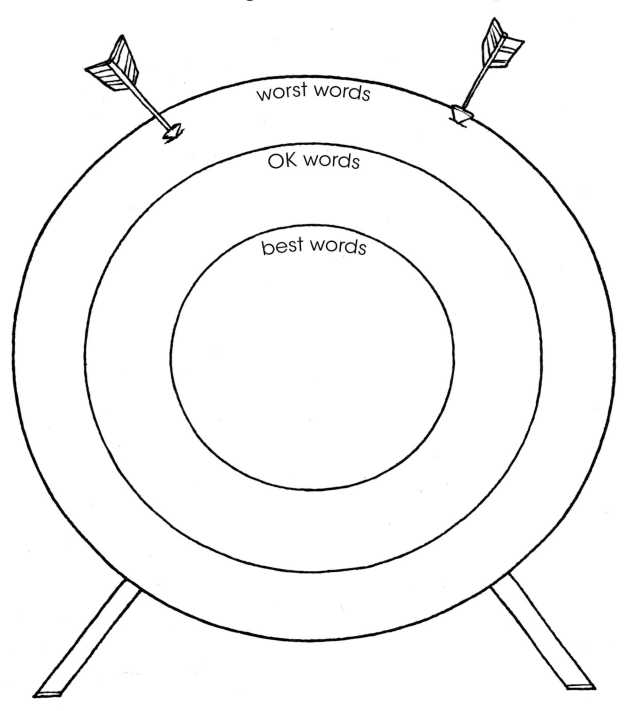

worst words

OK words

best words

| brave | evil | strong | proud | kind |
| cheerful | shy | tired | grumpy | weak |

The dragon slayer

Complete the advert to describe the dragon slayer.

The Dragon Slayer

If you have a problem,
a great, big dragon to slay
give us the money
and we'll send him your way!

Our most famous and _____ dragon slayer
has killed _____ dragons. He is _____ and
_____ . He has _____
_____ . His _____ are _____
and he _____ .

Name: _____ Date: _____

Battle starters

Use the sentence starters to retell the battle scene. Use as many powerful verbs and time connectives as you can.

Meanwhile

During

Next

Then

Suddenly

After

the dragon slayer grasps

the horse chomps

the dragon slayer changes

the dragon roars

the horse watches

the dragon flaps

Thoughts and feelings 1

Write the dragon slayer's thoughts and feelings. Then write super sentences.

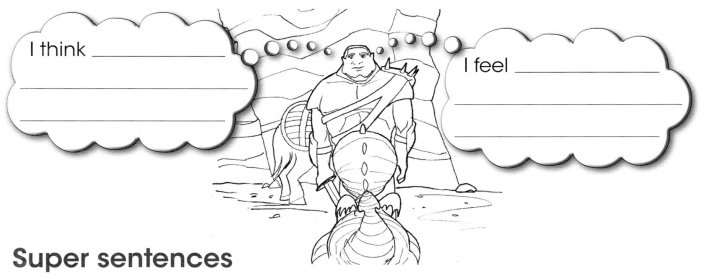

I think _____

_____

_____

I feel _____

_____

Super sentences

_____

_____

_____

I think _____

_____

_____

I feel _____

_____

_____

Super sentences

_____

_____

_____

Thoughts and feelings 2

1. Write the dragon slayer's thoughts and feelings.

I think _____

_____

_____

_____

I feel _____

_____

_____

_____

2. Write his thoughts and feelings as sentences in the first person.

_____

_____

_____

3. Turn your sentences into super sentences.

_____

_____

_____

Literacy Evolve Year 3 © Pearson Education 2009

Conjunctions

1. Re-write the sentences using conjunctions to join them together.

and but so or while because if when as

a. The thunder rumbled. The rain poured from the sky. I rode into the tiny village.

_____

_____

_____

b. I was very tired. I had killed so many dragons over the years.

_____

_____

c. I saw people. I got closer to the village.

_____

_____

2. Write sentences to describe the dragon slayer's journey. Use conjunctions to join your sentences.

_____

_____

_____

_____

_____

Literacy Evolve Year 3 © Pearson Education 2009

Story plan

Add notes about the structure of the *Dragon Slayer*.

Opening	Problem 1	Resolution 1	Problem 2	Resolution 2	Ending

Story ideas

Write your ideas for a new setting, monster and hero or heroine.

Hero/heroine

Monster

Setting

Legend planner

Complete the planner with details of your own legend.

Opening

_____
_____
_____
_____

Problem 1

_____
_____
_____
_____

Resolution 1

_____
_____
_____
_____

Problem 2

_____
_____
_____
_____

Resolution 2

_____
_____
_____
_____

Ending

_____
_____
_____
_____

Prompts for writing

Use the prompts to help you write your legend.

Use powerful verbs and adjectives.

Write in the third person.

Use time connectives.

Opening
- Describe the setting
- Describe the hero or heroine

Problem 1
- Describe the problem
- How do the people feel?
- What can be done?

Resolution 1
- Describe the journey
- Describe the monster
- What happens?

Problem 2
- What is the second problem?
- What does the hero/heroine do?
- How do they feel?

Resolution 2
- How was the second problem solved?
- What happens?

Ending
- What happens in the end?
- How do the characters feel?

Use super sentences.

Use conjunctions.

Describe thoughts and feelings.

Name: _____ Date: _____

Marking ladder

Use the marking ladder to check your work.

My teacher's comments

My comments

| My story has a hero or a heroine and a monster. |
| It has a clear beginning, middle and end. |
| My sentences have capital letters and full stops. |
| My story uses interesting adjectives to describe characters. |
| It uses conjunctions. |
| It uses time connectives to link sentences. |

Narrative Unit 3

OTTOLINE AND THE YELLOW CAT – novel (Mystery)

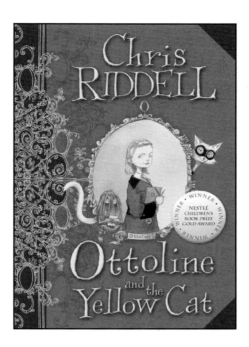

Medium term plan (4 weeks)	
Phase	**Learning Outcomes**
Phase 1: Reading; engaging with the text (7 days)	• Children can make inferences from pictures as well as text. • Children can make predictions based on clues in the text. • Children can recognise and use the language of possibility.
Phase 2: Analysing and comparing mystery story features (4 days)	• Children can identify key features of a mystery story. • Children can identify the techniques used to make a mystery story intriguing. • Children can use language to build suspense and excitement.
Phase 3: Planning and writing a sequel (9 days)	• Children can develop ideas for their own mystery story. • Children can organise a story to create suspense, build to a peak and resolve the puzzle. • Children can combine words and illustrations to create an interesting text.

OTTOLINE AND THE YELLOW CAT

Big picture

The children read the mystery story *Ottoline and the Yellow Cat*. They keep a reading diary to note their ideas as the mystery unfolds, spotting clues and making inferences from both the text and pictures. They use drama strategies to explore character and feelings, identify the structure of the story and analyse mystery story features. The children write another mystery story using the characters from the book and following modelled writing sessions. They work independently and in pairs to write effective, varied sentences, and give and respond to peer feedback.

Prior learning

This unit assumes that the children can already:
- make inferences about characters and their feelings
- identify a story structure
- identify features that authors use to provoke readers' reactions
- plan and organise a story.

Key aspects of learning

Communication: Use speaking, listening and writing to explore story ideas; use drama to explore character and plot.
Creative thinking: Write a story in the style of a given text, using imagination and improvisation to plan appropriate details of plot, character and dialogue.

Empathy: Respond to a character's feelings; understand a character's dilemma.
Enquiry: Ask questions about a mystery as it unfolds; make inferences from visual and textual clues; note and revise ideas.
Social skills: Work in small groups; offer constructive feedback during peer evaluation.

Progression in narrative

In this unit the children will:
- identify key features of the mystery genre
- identify the structure of a mystery story
- write a story in which events are sequenced logically in paragraphs
- use time connectives to signal time passing
- write dialogue for a character using appropriate punctuation.

Cross-curricular links

Art and Design: Explore visual humour; create artwork in the style of the book.
Citizenship: Explore themes of people who help us.
ICT: Create an illustrated book of the children's stories.

Reading time

35 minutes

PHASE 1: READING; ENGAGING WITH THE TEXT (7 DAYS)

Session 1

We are learning to ...	Resources
• share our opinions about a story (or poem) and give reasons for our views • find information about the characters and ask questions • explore how the features of mystery stories appeal to readers (PNS Strands 1.3, 7.2, 7.5) **Assessment Focuses** AF (R): 2, 7	*Ottoline and the Yellow Cat* ITP: 3.1 PCM: 3.1

Shared teaching

- Share the learning objectives and let the children look at the book cover.
- Read Chapter 1 with the children following in their own books. Model how to read a book that combines illustration with text, e.g. *There's the Pepperpot Building. Apartment 243 – that must be where Ottoline lives. Look at the names of the other buildings.* Pause occasionally to allow Talk Partners to explore the illustrations and the captions, labels and speech bubbles within them.
- Encourage the children to respond to Chapter 1. *What did you like about it? Does it remind you of any other stories?*
- Show 'What type of story?' (ITP 3.1).
- Talk Partners discuss what type of story they think *Ottoline and the Yellow Cat* will be, based on the book cover and Chapter 1.
- Take feedback and move the words into position on the screen.
- *Have you read or seen any mystery stories?* (E.g. Scooby Doo.) *What makes you think* Ottoline and the Yellow Cat *might be a mystery?*
- Encourage the children to find elements of mystery in Chapter 1, e.g.

the posters found by Mr Munroe, Ottoline working out clever plans, etc. *What might the story be about?*

Independent and Guided

- The children work in pairs as 'reading detectives', retrieving and recording information about Mr Munroe or Ottoline. Encourage the children to ask questions about the characters and record these on sticky notes. Remind the children to look at the pictures and the text.

  ∞∞ Do Role on the Wall for Ottoline and/or Mr Munroe.

  ∞ Create a 'Character profile' (PCM 3.1). (TA+)

  ○ As above. (T+)

Plenary

- Recap the learning objectives. *How did you find out about the characters? Which reading detective skills did you use? What aspects of the story caught your interest or made you want to read on?*
- Display the Role on the Wall character profiles, the children's questions on sticky notes and a copy of ITP 3.1 on the Learning Wall.
- Introduce the 'The Big Picture' for the unit.

Assessment pointers

- S&L: pair work will show how well the children can express and explain relevant ideas.
- AF2 (R): observation of response to questions, role on the wall and PCM 3.1 show how far the children can find information and ideas in the text.
- AF7 (R): responses to ITP 3.1 will show how far the children are aware of genre.

We are learning to ...	Resources
• use the language of possibility • explore how the features of mystery stories appeal to readers (PNS Strands 3.3, 7.5) **Assessment Focuses** AF (R): 2, 3,	*Ottoline* ITP: 3.2, 3.3, 3.4 PCM: 3.2

Shared teaching

• Share the first two learning objectives. Show 'Reading detectives' (ITP 3.2) and explain that in a mystery story the author creates a puzzle that, as reading detectives, we have to try and solve. Discuss the pointers on ITP 3.2.

• *What puzzles did you notice in Chapter 1?* (E.g. the lost dogs – the hook) *What details did you notice 'hidden' in the illustrations? What does this make you do as you read the book?*

• Show 'Reading detective's notebook 1' (ITP 3.3). Explain that like Ottoline the children are going to keep a notebook of the ideas they have and the things they notice when reading the book. Provide the children with notebooks or paper to record their ideas whilst reading *Ottoline and the Yellow Cat* in this and the following phases.

• Read the notes already included in ITP 3.3. Discuss the term 'lapdog'.

• Read pages 22–35. Remind the children to be reading detectives, listening and looking for new information. Discuss difficult vocabulary, e.g. 'extensive enquiries', 'prolonged investigations', 'audacious', etc.

• Talk Partners discuss clues or new information in the newspaper articles. Add suggestions to ITP 3.3. *Are there any connections?* Draw arrows to show the link between page 13 (the missing dogs) and the

victims of the burglaries. *Could the burglaries be connected to the missing dogs? I wonder how?*

• Share the last objective. Show 'Language of possibility' (ITP 3.4). Explain that we use these words when suggesting ideas that we are not sure about. For example sentences click on the words.

• Invite predictions of what Ottoline might do next, using the language of possibility.

• Look at the pictures on pages 36–37. Use the language of possibility, e.g. *Why have they come here? What might be going on here?*

• Read to the end of Chapter 2. *What do you think the Yellow Cat is up to? What have the poker players been doing?*

Independent and Guided

• The children work in groups to record details and ideas about the burglaries in *Ottoline and the Yellow Cat*.

ⓒⓒⓒ Complete 'Crime scenes' (PCM 3.2).

ⓒⓒ As above. (T+)

ⓞ As above. (TA+)

Plenary

• Ask a group to share their ideas about the burglaries in Chapter 2. Encourage them to use the language of possibility, e.g. *The dogs are ...* (definitely known) or *They could be ...* (a possibility).

• Recap the learning objectives. *What reading detective skills did you use? How has the author encouraged you to keep reading? What questions has the author left you with?*

Assessment pointers

• S&L: group work will show how far the children can adopt group roles and express opinions.

• AF2, 3 (R): responses to questioning, observation of reading and independent work show how far the children can find and interpret information in the text and make inferences about character and plot.

Session 3

We are learning to ...	Resources
• use drama to explore characters' thoughts and feelings • work out characters' feelings and relationships from their actions (PNS Strands 4.2, 7.2) **Assessment Focuses** AF (R): 3	*Ottoline* PCM: 3.3

Shared teaching

• Read Chapter 3. *How does Ottoline feel when her parents are far away? Is there anything puzzling about the postcard? What do you think is going to happen next? Are there any connections between the recent burglary and the other ones? What might the special disguise be?*

• Share the learning objectives. Explain that today, the children will focus on the thoughts and feelings of Mr Munroe.

• Reread pages 50–51. *How is Ottoline feeling? Do you think Mr Munroe is a good friend?*

• Now read Chapter 4. Ask the children to think about how Mr Munroe is feeling as you read.

• Explain that as Mr Munroe can't speak, the children will have to look for clues about his feelings in his actions, behaviour and his body language, using the text and the pictures.

• Organise a Forum Theatre activity based on Chapter 4. Start at the end of Chapter 3: *"I think it's time you practised your Special Disguises."*. Read the text as two children re-enact the events, if possible using available props. The other children check against the book.

• Encourage the other children to advise 'Mr Munroe' on how he should stand, walk, sit and act to show his feelings, referring to the pictures

and the text. Invite the children to speak Mr Munroe's (and Ottoline's) thoughts at various points. *Why does he feel this way? Have you ever felt like this?*

Independent and Guided

• The children work in groups to write down Mr Munroe's thoughts at key moments throughout Chapter 4.

ⓒⓒⓒ Track and note Mr Munroe's thoughts and feelings in their 'reading detective notebooks'. Write some on sticky notes for the Learning Wall.

ⓒⓒ As above. (T+)

ⓞ Complete 'Mr Munroe's feelings' (PCM 3.3). (TA+)

Plenary

• Recap the learning objectives. *What have you learnt about working out a character's feelings? How did the drama help you understand the characters?*

• Update the character profiles on the Learning Wall with additional information. *Can any of the questions be answered now?*

Assessment pointers

• S&L: drama activites will show how far the children can sustain roles and understand the characters.

• AF3 (R): PCM 3.3, independent activites and sticky notes show how far the children can infer characters' feelings.

<table>
<tr><td>

We are learning to ...
- explore how the features of mystery stories appeal to readers
- identify the ways the author keeps us guessing and asking questions
  (PNS Strands 7.5, 8.3)

Assessment Focuses
AF (R): 3, 6

</td><td>

Resources
Ottoline
ITP: (3.2), 3.5, 3.6
PCM: 3.4

</td></tr>
</table>

Shared teaching

- Share the learning objectives.
- Recall annotated 'Reading detectives' (ITP 3.2) to recap prior learning and remind the children of the skills reading detectives need.
- Recap how Mr Munroe felt at the end of Chapter 4. Read Chapter 5. Pause on page 91. *How did Mr Munroe feel at first? How did his mood change?*
- Continue reading and at the end of the chapter close the book dramatically. *Why does the author end the chapter like this? What is the effect on the reader?*
- Explain that ending the chapter with a hook that leaves the reader wanting to know more, is a technique used to keep the reader guessing or reading on. Show 'Writers' clever tricks' (ITP 3.5). Explain that mystery writers use a lot of clever tricks to get you hooked on the story and to keep you guessing. *Can you think of any more tricks an author could use?* Add ideas to ITP 3.5.
- Encourage predictions about what the clever plan might be, thinking about the purpose of the plan. *I wonder who or what it might involve?*
- Show 'Ottoline and the Yellow Cat' (ITP 3.6). Read the extract and

use Think Alouds to model looking for clues, e.g. *It doesn't say what Ottoline's plan was. Let's read on; we might find out soon.*

- Encourage the children to work out who the new lapdog is. *What makes you say that?* Highlight clues in the text, e.g. 'small hairy dog', and circle clues in the pictures, e.g. Ottoline's bow; clues on the card.
- Read to the end of Chapter 6 with the children following in their books. *Is this part of Ottoline's plan? Who might be at the door?*
- Turn the page and read the opening of Chapter 7. *I wonder who this lady is? What clues can you see in the picture?*

Independent and Guided

- The children record clues about what Ottoline's plan might be and what the Yellow Cat is up to.
- ⊂⊃⊃ Use reading dectective notebooks to record ideas. (T)
- ⊂⊃ Use 'Mystery clues bookmark' (PCM 3.4).
- ◉ As above. (TA+)

Plenary

- Recap the learning objectives. *When and how did you guess who Mrs Jansen-Smith was?* Discuss the clues on pages 104–105. *What reading detective skills did you use? How did the author keep us guessing and wanting to read on?* (E.g. disguising/hiding information; giving a few clues at a time; showing rather than telling us; using page breaks to hide things.)

Assessment pointers

- AF3 (R): class and group discussion of clues show how far the children can make deductions.
- AF6 (R): responses to questioning will show how far the children understand the author's purpose in deliberately hiding information and the effect this has on the reader.

<table>
<tr><td>

We are learning to ...
- use the language of possibility to make predictions about events
- identify the ways the author keeps us guessing and asking questions
  (PNS Strands 3.3, 8.3)

Assessment Focuses
AF (R): 3

</td><td>

Resources
Ottoline
ITP: (3.4), 3.7
PCM: 3.5, 3.6

</td></tr>
</table>

Shared teaching

- Share the learning objectives. Recall 'Language of possibility' (ITP 3.4).
- Recap predictions about what the Yellow Cat is up to and then read up to the end of Chapter 7. *What do you know about Ottoline's clever plan?* Show 'Reading detective's notebook 2' (ITP 3.7) and read the entries. *Is there anything that puzzles you? What questions would you like to ask Ottoline or the other characters at this point?* Add puzzles and questions to ITP 3.7.
- The children Think-Pair-Share their predictions of what might happen next, drawing on what is already known and using the language of possibility. *What might Ottoline / the Yellow Cat / Mr Munroe do next?* Record suggestions on Screen 2 of ITP 3.7, highlighting the language of possibility.
- Encourage class discussion of the suggestions. *Do you think that is likely or unlikely? What might happen if the character did this? Would that be what you want to happen?*
- Explain that as we continue reading we will be checking what happens against our predictions and seeing if any puzzles are answered.
- Read pages 118–129 modelling questioning to encourage predictions, e.g. *I wonder what Mr Munroe is doing? Where could he be going?*
- Pause after page 129 to update ITP 3.7, basing the predictions and

puzzles on the actions of Ottoline and Mr Munroe in the chapter. *Should we change, cross out or add to our predictions? Is anything now definite?* (If so, change the language.) *Have any puzzles or questions been answered? Do you have any new questions or puzzles?* (E.g. *I wonder why Ottoline put up the poster?*)

- Read to the end of Chapter 8. *What is Mr Munroe up to?*

Independent and Guided

- In groups, the children make predictions about what the characters might do next and how the story could end. Recall ITP 3.4 for the children to refer to.
- ⊂⊃⊃ Use 'Plot detective cards' (PCM 3.5).
- ⊂⊃ As above. (T+)
- ◉ Use 'Character cue cards' (PCM 3.6). (TA+)

Plenary

- Recap the learning objectives. *How does the author keep you guessing?*
- Recall the language of possibility. Ask a spokesperson from each group to feedback on their discussion. *What have you learnt about making predictions? Can you agree on a preferred ending?* (E.g. *We all agree that the Yellow Cat should be caught.*)

Assessment pointers

- S&L: group work will show how well the children can organise and sustain collaboration and discussion.
- AF3 (R): group discussion of PCMs and responses during shared teaching will show how far the children are able to make predictions about future events and endings.

We are learning to ...
- identify ways the author builds the story to the most exciting part
(PNS Strands 8.3)

Assessment Focuses
AF (R): 2, 4, 6

Resources
Ottoline
ITP: 3.8
PCM: 3.7

Shared teaching

- Read Chapters 9 and 10 with the children before the start of this session with few interruptions so that the children can enjoy the build-up and ending. *What did you like about the ending? Did you predict this? What surprises were there?*
- Explain that although we expect a mystery story to end with everything resolved, the fun part is how the author achieves this. *Did this ending leave you surprised or satisfied? Did the author do a good job?*
- Share the learning objective and show 'Story plan' (ITP 3.8). Explain that this shows the build up of excitement as we near the end of a story.
- Talk Partners look through Chapters 9 and 10 and decide what was the most exciting part of the resolution. Discuss suggestions, encouraging the children to give reasons for their choices, e.g. use of language, visual techniques, exciting action, etc.
- Add a page reference and notes to ITP 3.8.
- In the 'Ending' section, make a brief note of the less exciting but important events that happen after this as shown by the dip in the excitement level, e.g. the Yellow Cat and Clive are taken away.

- Talk Partners refer to their copies of the story and summarise what happened before the resolution. Take feedback and make short notes of events from Chapter 9 on ITP 3.8.
- Look through Chapter 9 again. *What do you notice? What is the author doing? Why does the author keep cutting to show the Yellow Cat climbing across the big city skyline? What changes each time?*

Independent and Guided

- In groups, the children explore the story ending in more detail. Groups then Jigsaw to share information from the three activities.
- ⬤⬤⬤ Explore problems at the end of Chapter 8 and how they are resolved. (T+)
- ⬤⬤ Use 'What's the link?' (PCM 3.7).
- ⬤ List each character and decide how he/she feels at the end. Give reasons. (TA+)

Plenary

- Recap the learning objective. *Why was Chapter 9 important in this story?* (E.g. because it builds up the excitement.) *What would you say makes a good resolution and ending for a mystery story?* (E.g. problems solved, questions answered, loose ends tied up, a surprise, etc.)

Assessment pointers

- S&L: group work will show how far the children can express and respond to opinions.
- AF2 (R): group activities will show how well the children can make reference to the text.
- AF4, 6 (R): responses to questioning show how far the children can comment on the effect of the text on a reader.

We are learning to ...
- use hot-seating to explore characters' views and feelings
- write in the role of a character
- develop success criteria
(PNS Strands 4.2, 8.2, 9.1)

Assessment Focuses
AF (R): 3; AF (W): 1, 2

Resources
Ottoline
ITP: 3.9

Shared teaching (1)

- Share the learning objectives and explain that the children will be focusing on the different characters, their actions and feelings.
- Ask the children to imagine they work for a local paper and they are going to interview Ottoline and Mr Munroe about their role in catching the Yellow Cat.
- Think-Pair-Share questions for each character. *Why did you ... ? How did you feel? What was the most worrying moment?* Etc.
- Set up a whole-class Hot-Seating activity with two children playing Ottoline and Mr Munroe. Or take on one of the roles yourself if you feel you need to model how to answer the questions drawing on the story. (For this activity, explain that Mr Munroe can talk.)

Independent and Guided (1)

- Continue Hot-Seating in small, mixed ability groups so more of the children have the opportunity to take on the roles and ask questions. Encourage the children to use details from the book to help develop the characters and ask questions. Support the children with an identified need. (T/TA)

Shared teaching (2)

- Share good examples of hot-seating where the children used the text and their imagination to get inside the character.
- Explain that they are now going to write a postcard to Ottoline's parents, either writing in role as Ottoline or as Mr Munroe.
- Show 'Writing in role' (ITP 3.9) and discuss the success criteria. *What do you need to remember when you are writing in the role of a character?* Encourage the children to offer suggestions and add these to ITP 3.9.

Independent and Guided (2)

- The children work independently to write their postcards, using ITP 3.9 to help develop their work. Support the children with an identified need. (T+/TA)

Plenary

- Recap the learning objectives. *How did you use the success criteria to help you when writing? What makes your writing sound like the character? Does anything still puzzle you about your character?*

Assessment pointers

- S&L: hot-seating will show how far the children can sustain roles to explore characters.
- AF1, 2 (W): individual writing using success criteria shows how far the children can write imaginatively in a chosen form.
- AF3 (R): responses to questioning, drama and written work show how far the children can infer how characters are feeling.

Session 8

We are learning to ...	Resources
• explore how the features of mystery stories appeal to readers • choose other stories to read and explain our choices • compare different stories, looking for similarities and differences (PNS Strands 7..5, 8.1) **Assessment Focuses** AF (R): 6, 7	*Ottoline* ITP: 3.10 PCM: 3.8, 3.9, 3.10

Shared teaching

• Remind the children of 'The Big Picture' and share the learning objectives. *Why might* Ottoline and the Yellow Cat *be called a mystery story?*

• Display a collection of words from the text, e.g. 'enquiries', 'disguise', 'cat burglar', 'clue', 'victim', 'detective', 'subterfuge', 'criminal', 'evidence', 'burglary', 'suspect' and 'investigate'. Explain that these are some words we often find in mystery stories and clarify any unknown vocabulary. Play a game of charades: one child chooses a word and acts it out, while the others guess the word.

• Show 'Mystery story ingredients' (ITP 3.10). *Does* Ottoline and the Yellow Cat *have all these ingredients?* Allocate each group one element to discuss in relation to the story. If the children are sat in ability groups, assign the elements accordingly, e.g. lower ability (characters and events) and higher ability (themes, puzzles and settings). Ask one member to act as scribe to note the group's ideas.

• Take feedback from the different groups and fill in ITP 3.10.

• *Have you read or seen any other mystery stories? Does* (a TV detective programme the children are familiar with) *have these features?* Ask the children to Think-Pair-Share before taking responses. Identify common features, e.g. the detective or solver of the mystery often has a helper; the theme is putting things right, catching the criminal, etc. *Do you usually enjoy this type of story?*

Independent and Guided

• The children read the blurbs or opening pages of other mystery stories to see if they interest them. Alternatively, use 'Book tasters' (PCM 3.8). Groups discuss the books comparing mystery story ingredients and personal preferences. They should come to a decision about which book they would like to read.

◦◦◦ Use 'Mystery story ingredients' (PCM 3.9).

◦◦ As above. (T+)

◦ Use 'Comparing stories' (PCM 3.10). (TA+)

Plenary

• Recap the learning objectives and ask a spokesperson from each group to explain mystery story features and their book preferences. *What examples have been noted? What features seem to be common in all mystery stories? Why do these features appeal to readers? What features are similar or different to* Ottoline and the Yellow Cat*?* Add notes to ITP 3.10.

• Encourage the children to start thinking about ideas and ingredients to use in the story they will write later.

Assessment pointers

• S&L: group work will show how far the children can engage with others, draw ideas together and promote discussion.

• AF6 (R): response to questioning and group discussion show how far the children can express personal response; likes and dislikes.

• AF7 (R): PCMs will show how far the children can identify and compare the common features of mystery stories.

Session 9

We are learning to ...	Resources
• identify the main sequence of events in a story • identify the story structure (PNS Strands 7.3) **Assessment Focuses** AF (R): 4	*Ottoline* ITP: (3.8), 3.11 PCM: 3.11, 3.12, 3.13

Shared teaching

• Share the learning objectives. *How did the story open? What was the key event (the trigger) that started the story off?*

• Show 'Sequence of events' (ITP 3.11). Explain that these are from the problem and build-up parts of the story. Talk Partners discuss which event they think came first. Encourage the children to refer to *Ottoline* for ideas.

• Take feedback and drag the first event to the beginning. *How do you know this is the first event? Where did you get your information from?*

Independent and Guided

• The children work in groups to order the cut out strips from 'Sequence of events' (PCM 3.11). Encourage them to refer to the book. Support the children with an identified need. (T/TA)

Shared teaching

• Take feedback from the groups. Encourage the children to justify their choices by referring to the book.

• Look at the connectives on ITP 3.11. Explain that these are time/place connectives that help to move the story on. Demonstrate moving the time/place connectives into the right place to make a timeline. *How can we check in the book?* Encourage the children to go back to the book, scanning for the phrases used at the opening of paragraphs to clearly signal time/place.

• Show annotated 'Story plan' (ITP 3.8). Remind the children that this shows the build up of the story from when the mystery is first introduced, through the gradual build up of the investigation and the plan, to the excitement of the resolution and then the quieter ending. The children will need these sections when they come to planning and writing their own story.

Independent and Guided

• The children organise the key events from *Ottoline* onto story plans to show the main stages in the story structure. If there is time, the children use the plans to retell the story around the group.

◦◦◦ Use PCM 3.11 and 'Story plan flow chart' (PCM 3.12).

◦◦ Use PCM 3.11 and 'Story plan' (PCM 3.13). (T+)

◦ Use PCM 3.11. Make a flowchart to show the beginning, middle and end of the story. (TA+)

Plenary

• Recap the learning objectives.

• Display examples of PCM 3.12 and PCM 3.13 on the Learning Wall and ask the children to explain why they have placed events in the different stages. *What have you learnt about the opening, build-up and ending of a mystery story?*

Assessment pointers

• S&L: group work will show how far the children can adopt group roles, drawing ideas together and promoting effective discussion.

• AF4 (R): sequencing of the story and group work show how far the children can identify and understand key features of the story structure.

We are learning to ...	Resources
• explore the language and sentence structure used to build up suspense • understand how authors use settings to create different feelings or moods • identify how pictures can create an effect on the reader (PNS Strands 7.5, 8.3) **Assessment Focuses** AF (R): 5, 6	*Ottoline* ITP: 3.12 PCM: 3.14

Shared teaching (1)

• Share the learning objectives and explain that in this session, the children will be looking at how mystery authors use settings.
• Remind the children that settings do not just create a picture for the reader; they can also affect how the reader feels.
• Ask the children to find pages 130–131 in their books. *Where does this come in the story? How does the picture make you feel? What does it make you think?* Allow Think Time before taking responses.
• Ask different groups to now focus on one aspect of the picture. *Who is in the picture? What is in the picture? How is colour used?*
• Take feedback of the group's responses.

Independent and Guided

• In groups, the children use 'Discussion prompts' (PCM 3.14) to discuss the sequence of pictures between pages 28–33, using sticky notes to annotate features on the pages. The children work in pairs, focusing on one set of questions. They then share their ideas with the group. Support the children with an identified need. (T/TA)

Shared teaching (2)

• Take feedback on how the different elements contribute to a feeling of mystery, growing unease, a build up of uncertainty and danger.
• Explain that the children are now going to look at the use of setting in another mystery story – one that uses descriptive language rather than pictures.
• Read 'The Postbox Mystery' (ITP 3.12) and ask the children to visualise the events and think about how it makes them feel.
• Discuss the mood created: one of fear, mystery, expecting something to happen. *How has the author achieved this?*
• Reread the first paragraph. *What details create the sense of mystery and fear?* Highlight on ITP 3.12 sights in one colour and sounds in another.
• Read the second paragraph. *What powerful words and phrases help create the effect of mystery and suspense?* Highlight these on ITP 3.12, e.g. 'the snap of a twig'; 'someone ... '; 'this dim, green place'; 'footfalls came closer', etc.

Plenary

• Recap the learning objectives. *What have you learnt about how mystery authors use settings?* (E.g. to create a sense of mystery, suspense, tension, danger, expectation, etc.) *How can this be done in words? What about pictures?* Add suggestions of powerful words and phrases to the Learning Wall.

Assessment pointers

• S&L: group work will show how far the children can adopt group roles, drawing ideas together and promoting effective discussion.
• AF5, 6 (R): responses to questioning and PCM 3.14 show how far the children can identify and begin to comment on an author's choice of language and the overall effect on the reader.

We are learning to ...	Resources
• explore the language and sentence structures used to build up suspense (PNS Strands 7.5) **Assessment Focuses** AF (R): 5; AF (W): 7	*Ottoline* ITP: 3.13

Shared teaching

• Share the learning objective.
• Show 'The simple version' (ITP 3.13) and read the extract. Remind the children that this is the most exciting point in the story.
• Dramatically read, taking particular note of punctuation. *What makes this effective? What builds up the suspense and excitement?*
• Highlight on ITP 3.13 particular words or phrases that the children choose, e.g. 'carefully', 'crept on tiptoe', 'slipped inside', 'sneaked', 'slowly', etc.
• Discuss the use of ellipsis, e.g. 'slowly opened it ... '. *Why has the author used this?* (To suggest something will happen.)
• Click 'Simpler version' and ask the children to compare it to the original. Think-Pair-Share ideas. *Is the original more exciting?*
• Focus on the original version again. Highlight and discuss sentence features: longer sentences (compound and complex) make the story flow, e.g 'The Yellow Cat climbed in through the window ... and looked around'; and one short sentence ('She didn't make a sound.') adds to the suspense.
• Discuss the sentence openings that add detail and slow the pace. Highlight 'With one gloved paw ... ' and explain that this is a 'how' sentence starter as it tells us how something was done.

• Highlight 'Opening the door a crack ...' and explain that this is an -*ing* sentence starter. Authors often use these for effect.
• Ask the children to look at pages 160–161. *Can you find examples of 'how' sentence starters?*
• Explain how the children might use these sentence starters in their own writing. Use an example sentence, e.g. 'With a startled miaow the Yellow Cat sprang to her feet and dashed for the door.' Use Modelled Writing to compose a new sentence using this as a model, e.g. 'With silent footsteps the burglar crept into the apartment'. Ask the children for more examples.

Independent and Guided

• The children orally compose sentences using models from the text, recording examples in their notebooks for use when writing their own stories.

 Focus on 'how' and '-*ing*' starters.

 Focus on 'how' starters. (TA+)

 Focus on compound sentences. (T+)

Plenary

• Ask the children to feedback examples of their sentences. Add these to the Learning Wall.
• Recap the learning objective. *How can the type of sentence used help build up suspense and add excitement and pace?*

Assessment pointers

• AF5 (R): responses to questioning show how far the children can identify and comment on the author's use of language.
• AF7 (W): independent work shows how far the children are able to use effective sentence openers in their own writing.

Session 12

We are learning to ...	Resources
• use the language of possibility • develop success criteria • evaluate plans, ideas, activities or writing using success criteria (PNS Strands 3.3, 9.1) **Assessment Focuses** AF (W): 1, 2	ITP: 3.14, 3.15, 3.16 PCM: 3.15

Shared teaching (1)

• Share the learning objectives and explain that the children are going to write a different mystery story involving Ottoline and Mr Munroe. The audience will be the other children who have enjoyed *Ottoline and the Yellow Cat*.
• Show 'Story ideas' (ITP 3.14) and discuss the success criteria. *What would you expect to find in this story?* (E.g. an interesting puzzle; the same main characters; some new villains; an entertaining story, etc.) Add the children's suggestions to ITP 3.14.
• Explain that first they need an idea for their new mystery stories. Show 'Story starter headlines' (ITP 3.15). Use Think Alouds to model how to use the prompts to discuss possibilities, e.g. *Perhaps this headline will give me an idea for a story. Maybe it was destroyed by ... . They might have wanted to ... .*

Independent and Guided (1)

• The children work in groups, discussing headlines from 'Story starter headlines' (PCM 3.15). Encourage the children to play around with ideas using the prompts and the language of possibility. They collect their favourite ideas in their notebooks. Support the children with an identified need. (T+/ TA+)

Shared teaching (2)

• Ask the children to share their favourite ideas, encouraging others to comment on them. Explain that now they need to develop the ideas and make sure they have all the ingredients of a mystery story.
• Show 'Mix and match story' (ITP 3.16). Demonstrate selecting a villain, a place where they hide out and then a clue that leads Ottoline and Mr Munroe to solve the mystery. Use Think Alouds to show how this might work in the story, e.g. *Perhaps there might be floury pawprints to follow and then they could overhear the villains talking.*
• Discuss how to judge story ideas. *How will we know if it is a good idea?* Refer back to the success criteria on ITP 3.14. Add any new ideas.

Independent and Guided (2)

• The children work independently to develop their own story ideas which they record in their notebooks. Pairs then discuss the story ideas and evaluate them, using ITP 3.14. Support the children with an identified need. (T+/TA+)

Plenary

• Recap the learning objectives. *How have you developed your ideas? What changes did you make after discussing ideas in pairs? How did you use the success criteria to evaluate your ideas? Are you happy with your idea now?*

Assessment pointers

• S&L: group discussion and drama will show how far the children can develop ideas and respond to issues through sustained speaking.
• AF1, 2 (W): group discussion and use of success criteria show how far the children can develop imaginative and appropriate ideas for the task.

Session 13

We are learning to ...	Resources
• evaluate plans, ideas, activities or writing using success criteria • plan the main sequence of events using story planners or storyboards • use time connectives to show time passing (PNS Strands 9.1, 9.2, 10.1) **Assessment Focuses** AF (W): 1, 3	ITP: 3.17, 3.18 PCM: (3.12)

Shared teaching (1)

• Share the learning objectives, explaining that the children will plan out the sequence of events and the stages in the story. *Why is planning important?*
• Show 'Story plan flow chart' (ITP 3.17) and use the headings and events to remind the children of the stages in *Ottoline and the Yellow Cat*. Explain that you are going to follow this to help you plan out your story and they will do the same.
• Model how to adapt the opening event to fit your new idea for a story, e.g. *Mr Munroe noticed an interesting story about wrecked cakes in the newspaper.* Add notes to ITP 3.17.
• Give each child a new copy of 'Story plan flow chart' (PCM 3.12). Ask them to write sentences for an opening event in the first box, using an idea they have already chosen.
• Repeat the process moving onto 'Problem 1', e.g. *Ottoline noticed another report about wrecked cakes and something about a cake competition. They investigated and found a trail of crumbs ... .*
• Ask the children to do the same, again feeding in their own ideas.
• Remind the children about the connectives they added in Session 9 to signal time and place, e.g. 'That afternoon', 'The next morning ... ', 'At the warehouse', etc. Add connectives to the start of each event on your

own plan and ask the children to do the same.
• Repeat the process to complete the flow chart on ITP 3.17.

Independent and Guided (1)

• The children continue to plan independently following the same process, plotting the events on the flow chart and adding time/place connectives. Support the children with an identified need. (T/TA)

Shared teaching (2)

• When the plans are complete, explain the next stage is to try them out.
• Show 'Mystery stories' (ITP 3.18) and discuss the success criteria for the planned stories. Add the children's suggestions to ITP 3.18.
• Model telling the story you have planned and encourage the children to comment using the success criteria.

Independent and Guided (2)

• Pairs use their plans to tell each other the stories they have planned. They use the success criteria to comment on the stories and use the feedback to change and improve their plans. Support the children with an identified need. (T/TA)

Plenary

• Recap the learning objectives. Encourage the children to share some of the changes they have made and explain their reasons. *What time connectives have you used? Did you change the ending of your story?*

Assessment pointers

• S&L: pair work will show how sensitively the children can listen and respond to others.
• AF1, 3 (W): finished plans and revisions made to plans following feedback from pairs, will show how far the children can organise and sequence ideas and produce interesting and appropriate ideas.

<table>
<tr><td>

We are learning to ...
- write an opening that catches the reader's attention
- make the story sound effective by choosing words carefully
- write in complete sentences using some conjunctions (PNS Strands 9.2, 9.4, 11.1)

Assessment Focuses
AF (W): 1, 2, 5, 7

</td><td>

Resources
Ottoline
ITP: (3.17), 3.19, 3.20
PCM: (3.12)

</td></tr>
</table>

Shared teaching
- Recall annotated 'Story plan flow chart' (ITP 3.17). Explain that the children are now going to start writing their own stories following their plans. As the story is going to be quite long, it will need to be divided into chapters and paragraphs. In this session, they will write Chapter 1: their story opening and introduce the problem.
- Share the learning objectives, explaining that the aim is to write an opening that catches the reader's attention. Show 'Story openings' (ITP 3.19) and discuss additional success criteria. *Are there any you would like to add or change?*
- Use Modelled Writing to compose the first few sentences, using Think Alouds to demonstrate how to rehearse sentences orally, reread, check and make changes as you write, e.g. *Mr Munroe was sitting in his chair. Let's add more detail. One day Mr Munroe was sitting in his Beidermeyer armchair.*
- Deliberately write two short sentences and then reread them explaining that it might sound better if you joined them together, e.g. *He was reading the newspaper. Then something caught his eye.* Model joining the sentences with 'when'.

- Explain that you are going to include the newspaper headline to introduce the problem rather than actually writing what caught his eye.
- Compose a few more sentences, this time encouraging the children to suggest ideas for improving word choices or referring to the book to find details to include.
- Show 'Conjunctions' (ITP 3.20) and click to reveal example sentences. Return to the model chapter and begin a sentence, e.g. *He looked at the headline for a long time ...* and then ask for help continuing it. Encourage the children to select a suitable conjunction and then Think-Pair-Share how the sentence might continue.

Independent and Guided
- The children write the opening to their story, using their annotated 'Story plan flow chart' (PCM 3.12) and referring to the earlier modelled text. Pairs then share their writing, focusing on the success criteria on ITP 3.19. Support the children with an identified need. (T+/TA+)

Plenary
- Recap the learning objectives. Encourage pairs to comment on openings that sounded really interesting and effective. *What made it work? What words or conjunctions did they use?* Add good examples to the Learning Wall.

Assessment pointers
- S&L: pair work will show how well the children can express and explain relevant ideas.
- AF1, 2 (W): independent work and peer assessment show how far the children are able to write interesting and appropriate texts.
- AF5, 7 (W): shared teaching and independent work show how far the children can construct and punctuate sentences.

<table>
<tr><td>

We are learning to ...
- write our stories including the problem, build-up, climax and resolution
- use powerful words to create a sense of mystery
- clearly signal changes in time and place
- start a new paragraph for each new event (PNS Strands 9.2, 9.4, 10.1)

Assessment Focuses
AF (W): 3, 4, 7

</td><td>

Resources
Ottoline
ITP: (3.11, 3.17)
PCM: (3.12)

</td></tr>
</table>

Shared teaching (1)
- Recall annotated 'Story plan flow chart' (ITP 3.17). Recap that the children have already written the opening and will now be writing the second part of their story: the build-up focusing on investigating the problem. Explain that in this part of their story, Ottoline and Mr Munroe are going to find the criminal's hideout.
- Share the learning objectives. Remind the children that it will be important to use paragraphs and time connectives to organise their stories to make the progression of events clear.
- Use Modelled Writing to demonstrate following your plan on ITP 3.17 to write the first sentence for each paragraph in this part of the story, e.g. *The next morning Ottoline read the paper very carefully.; After lunch Ottoline and Mr Munroe went out for their afternoon stroll.; That evening Ottoline went to her special disguises wardrobe.*
- Ask the children to highlight the time connectives in your example sentences. *What other time connectives could I have used?* Encourage the children to offer suggestions and if necessary, recall 'Sequence of events' (ITP 3.11).

Independent and Guided (1)
- The children work independently, writing paragraphs following their annotated 'Story plan flow chart' (PCM 3.12). Support the children with an identified need. (T+/TA+)

Shared teaching (2)
- Talk Partners share their stories and then give each other feedback using Two Stars and a Wish.
- Take feedback. *What do you like about your partner's story? What do you think they could improve?*
- Remind the children that in *Ottoline* we get a lot of information from pictures. When they have finished writing their paragraphs for this part of the story, they can add an annotated picture.

Independent and Guided (2)
- The children finish writing the 'Problem' part of the story, taking into account feedback from their partners. The children add an annotated picture to this part of the story. Support the children with an identified need. (T+/TA+)

Plenary
- Recap the learning objectives. *Did you make any changes to your story? What time connectives did you use? When did you start a new paragraph? What picture did you add?*

Assessment pointers
- S&L: pair work will show how sensitively the children can express and respond to opinions.
- AF3, 4, 7 (W): drafting and written outcomes will show how far the children are able to use paragraphs, signal time passing and select words for effect.

We are learning to ...	Resources
• use conjunctions to compose some longer sentences • edit our sentences to choose words with more impact • use speech marks to show which words are spoken (PNS Strands 11.1, 11.2, 11.3) **Assessment Focuses** AF (W): 5, 6, 7	ITP: (3.20), 3.21, 3.22 PCM: (3.12)

Shared teaching (1)

• Share the learning objectives.
• Read 'Text for revision' (ITP 3.21). *What needs to be improved?* Ask the children to suggest which words need to be improved, e.g. 'nice', 'going', 'big', etc. and to provide alternatives.
• Model how to extend some of the short sentences, e.g. by adding more detail to the start of a sentence or a reason to the end of sentences.
• Remind the children how to use conjunctions such as 'when', 'as', 'before', 'until' and 'but' to link sentences. Join two sentences in this way, making the necessary changes in wording. If necessary, recall 'Conjunctions' (ITP 3.20).
• The children Think-Pair-Share a way of joining two sentences in ITP 3.21. Take feedback and alter the text on ITP 3.21.

Independent and Guided (1)

• The children work in pairs to improve words and sentences in their own writing from Session 15, using ITP 3.21 to help them. Support the children with an identified need. (T/TA)

Shared teaching (2)

• Hold a mini-plenary to discuss changes the children have made to their writing. *What suggestions did your partner make?*

• Show ITP 3.21. Focus on the last sentence to introduce the use of speech marks. Model how to add speech marks round the spoken words.
• Show 'Talking heads' (ITP 3.22). Click on the pictures to reveal what the characters say. Use Modelled Writing to write the speech using speech marks, e.g. ' *"I've got a clever plan," said Ottoline.'*
• Click on another picture and ask Talk Partners to write the speech using speech marks and a reporting clause. Continue this for the remaining pictures.
• Use Modelled Writing to compose sentences for the next part of the story on the board using a line of dialogue, e.g. *The grey dog licked his paws. "Mmm, delicious. A pity to destroy a tasty cake like that," he growled.*

Independent and Guided (2)

• The children work independently to write, or revise, the rest of 'Problem' following their annotated 'Story plan flow chart' (PCM 3.12), including some lines of speech. Support the children with an identified need. (T/TA)

Plenary

• Recap the learning objectives. Ask the children to read out a line of speech they have included in their writing, using curled fingers to show where they have put speech marks.

Assessment pointers

• S&L: pair work will show how well the children can express and explain relevant ideas.
• AF5, 6, 7 (W): responses to questioning and independent work will show how far the children are able to construct sentences, use speech marks and choose more adventurous vocabulary.

We are learning to ...	Resources
• clearly signal changes in time and place • decide when to start a new paragraph (PNS Strands 10.1, 10.2) **Assessment Focuses** AF (W): 3, 4	ITP: (3.17) PCM: (3.12)

Shared teaching

• Share the learning objectives and recall annotated 'Story plan flow chart' (ITP 3.17). Recap the stage reached in the children's stories. Explain that they are about to continue the build-up to incorporate a clever plan.
• Read 'Build-up' on ITP 3.17. Point out that there are two parts to the clever plan, so they will probably need two or more chapters.
• Use Modelled Writing and Think Alouds to compose the next chapter of the model text, e.g. *The next day Ottoline came up with a clever plan. But that sounds a bit boring. It might be better to keep the reader guessing and give clues so they can work out the plan.*
• Write an opening sentence to demonstrate this, e.g. *The next day a rather large, well-dressed lady left Apartment 243 of the Pepperpot Building.*
• Ask the children to Think-Pair-Share ideas for the next sentence, giving another small clue about who this lady is, e.g. detailing what she was wearing.
• Use Modelled Writing to create the rest of the paragraph, e.g. describing where she goes.
• Explain that the paragraph ends when the setting changes, e.g. *the next bit is in a different setting and will start: At Grey's cake shop ... .*

Independent and Guided

• The children work independently to write this part of the story, focusing on organising their ideas into chapters and paragraphs, using annotated 'Story plan flow chart' (PCM 3.12).
◦◦◦ Focus on chapters and paragraphs.
◦◦ As above. (TA+)
◦ Focus on dividing writing into clear sections. (T+)

Plenary

• Talk Partners check each other's paragraphs and discuss ideas for ending the chapter with a hook.
• Recap the learning objectives and recall the key points about organising story ideas into paragraphs and chapters. *How do you know when to start a new paragraph or a new chapter? How did you end your chapter(s)?*
• Encourage Talk Partners to offer feedback. *What did you like about your partner's story? Did you make any suggestions for improvements? Do you think your partner ended the chapter with a hook?*

Assessment pointers

• S&L: pair work will show how sensitively the children can express and respond to opinions.
• AF3, 4 (W): written drafts show how far the children can organise ideas and handle movements between paragraphs and chapters.

We are learning to ...	Resources
• use suspense to build up to the most exciting part of our stories • use different types of sentences to make our writing sound effective (PNS Strands 9.2, 11.2) **Assessment Focuses** AF (W): 5, 7	*Ottoline* ITP: 3.23, 3.24, 3.25 PCM: (3.12)

Shared teaching

• Explain that today, the children will be writing the most exciting part of the story – the resolution.
• Share the learning objectives. Show 'Writing story peaks' (ITP 3.23) to establish the success criteria for writing this part of the story. Encourage the children to offer suggestions and add these to ITP 3.23.
• Read 'Text for revision' (ITP 3.24). *Why is this not effective?* Establish that the sentences just describe actions and they need some variety and colour adding.
• Model how to change the structure of the sentences for effect. Use Think Alouds to rehearse sentences, e.g. adding a 'how' or -*ing* starter to make it sound like he's being secretive; using a connecting word to link two actions together, etc. Choose one short sentence to stand alone and explain you have done this for dramatic effect. Highlight the short sentence to emphasise the dramatic change in length.
• Continue to rework the sentence structures on ITP 3.24, encouraging the children to suggest improvements to the choice of words to build up the suspense, e.g. a more powerful verb than 'went', 'got', 'looked'.
• *How could you make the text more effective?* Take feedback and show 'Sentence prompts' (ITP 3.25). Discuss the different sentence types

and openings, then click to see examples from *Ottoline*. Encourage the children to suggest more examples. Make notes on ITP 3.25.

Independent and Guided

• The children write the resolution for their stories referring to their annotated 'Story plan flow chart' (PCM 3.12), using different types of sentences and choosing words for effect.

○○○ Work independently, developing their plans.

○○ Orally compose sentences with a partner and then focus on punctuation. (TA+)

◎ As above. (T+)

Plenary

• Recap the learning objectives. The children underline examples that illustrate their use of different sentence types and powerful words in their work.
• Invite some of the children who are pleased with their work to read it. *What do you think you have done well? Is there anything you would like help with? Does everyone agree that there is a build up of tension? Which sentences or word choices worked really well? Would you change anything to make it even better?*
• (It would be useful to mark stories at this point so you can arrange guided writing groups according to need in Session 19.)

Assessment pointers

• AF5, 7 (W): responses to questioning and independent work show how far the children can vary sentences and choose effective vocabulary.

We are learning to ...	Resources
• write convincing endings where all the puzzles and problems are resolved (PNS Strands 9.2) **Assessment Focuses** AF (W): 1, 3	ITP: (3.17), 3.26

Shared teaching

• Recall annotated 'Story plan flow chart' (ITP 3.17) and explain that this session will focus on the ending of the story. *How do mystery stories usually end? How did* Ottoline and the Yellow Cat *end?* (The Yellow Cat and Cockatoo getting arrested; the postcard from Ottoline's parents.)
• Share the learning objective, establishing that in the ending all loose ends must be tied up.
• Read the notes in the 'Ending' section on ITP 3.17 and ask the children to refer to their own plans. *We need to be clear how the ending will happen. How do the criminals get locked up? How does Ottoline or Mr Munroe put things right for the victims of the crime?*
• Explain that this is a good point to read through their stories so far, to check everything makes sense and to remind them what puzzles and problems need to be resolved.
• Show 'Story endings' (ITP 3.26). *Are there any you would like to add or change?* Model using the success criteria to review one child's story. Read the draft story and model how to respond to the text, asking questions to help clarify parts that are not clear, e.g. *I'm not sure why ... . Was it because ... ? Is this Mr Munroe in disguise? Could there be more of a clue for the reader?*
• Talk Partners discuss what needs to happen to bring this story to a good ending and any good ideas for how to achieve this.

• Take feedback, discussing and developing the suggestions and making a note of 'good advice for the writer'. Use this to focus on the importance of planning for the ending, e.g. *Yes, it would be a good idea to end the last chapter with the bear making a phone call, as that would hint to the reader how the police get there.*

Independent and Guided

• The children work in pairs, using ITP 3.26 to review and give advice on each other's stories and their endings. Work with groups or hold writing conferences to review the children's progress. The children then work independently to write the ending of their story. Support the children with an identified need. (T/TA)

Plenary

• Recap the learning objective. *What have we learned about writing a good ending for a story? Do you think you have written a good ending? If not, what is the problem? Perhaps someone can help you ... .*
• Explain that in the Session 20, the children will be trying out their stories and thinking about how they will present them.

Assessment pointers

• S&L: pair work will show how far the children can listen and respond to others.
• AF1, 3 (W): self-assessment, peer assessment and responses to questioning will show how far the children can develop appropriate ideas and sequence them towards a defined ending.

Session 20

We are learning to ...	Resources
• evaluate plans, ideas, activities or writing using success criteria • present our stories in an interesting way using illustration and layout (PNS Strands 9.1, 9.5) **Assessment Focuses** AF (W): 1, 2	ITP: (3.14, 3.18, 3.19, 3.23, 3.26), 3.27 PCM 3.16

Shared teaching (1)

• Share the learning objectives and explain that now the first draft of the story is complete, the children are going to try out their story on an audience (if possible, a partner from a parallel class) and evaluate it using a marking ladder.

• Show annotated 'Story ideas' (ITP 3.14) and remind the children of the success criteria. Explain that these relate to the overall purpose and effect of their stories. The other success criteria: 'Mystery stories' (ITP 3.18), 'Story openings' (ITP 3.19), 'Story peaks' (ITP 3.23) and 'Story endings' (ITP 3.26), all add to the overall effect.

• Show 'Discussion prompts' (ITP 3.27). Read part of one child's draft story. Use Think Alouds to model how to respond to the text using the prompts, first making positive comments, e.g. *I really liked the part when … ; I liked the way you … ; I wanted to keep reading because … ,etc.* Then suggest where improvements could be made, e.g. *I think it would be better if you end the chapter here, then the reader would really want to read on.*

• Encourage the children to offer more feedback.

Independent and Guided (1)

• The children swap stories with a new partner or a partner from a parallel class, using 'Marking Ladder' (PCM 3.16) to help comment on each other's work, discussing how effective each of the stories is and suggesting improvements. The children then edit and improve their stories. Support the children with an identified need. (T+/TA)

Shared teaching (2)

• Hold a mini-plenary to discuss positive feedback and areas that the children need to work on more.

• Remind the children that one of the things that made *Ottoline and the Yellow Cat* particularly interesting to read was the use of illustration. The children have already drawn one illustration. They can now choose another part of the story to illustrate.

• Discuss how the children would like to present their stories, e.g. as a set of class books to be displayed in the school library or read by another class.

Independent and Guided (2)

• The children draw another illustration and/or work on their final presentation. Support the children with an identified need. (T+/TA+)

Plenary

• Recap the learning objectives. *What changes did you make to your story? How are you going to present your story? What pictures did you add? Why there?*

• Review the unit. *What have you enjoyed about this unit of work? What do you think you are much better at now? What do you think you need to work on more? Did you enjoy the book?*

Assessment pointers

• AF1, 2 (W): finished books will show how far the children can produce imaginative and organised texts.

Character profile

Write about Mr Munroe or Ottoline.

Name: _____
_____

Lives: _____
_____

Friends and family: _____
_____

Likes: _____
_____
_____

Dislikes: _____
_____
_____

Other information: _____
_____
_____

Words to describe character: _____
_____

Crime scenes

Write notes about the crime scenes.

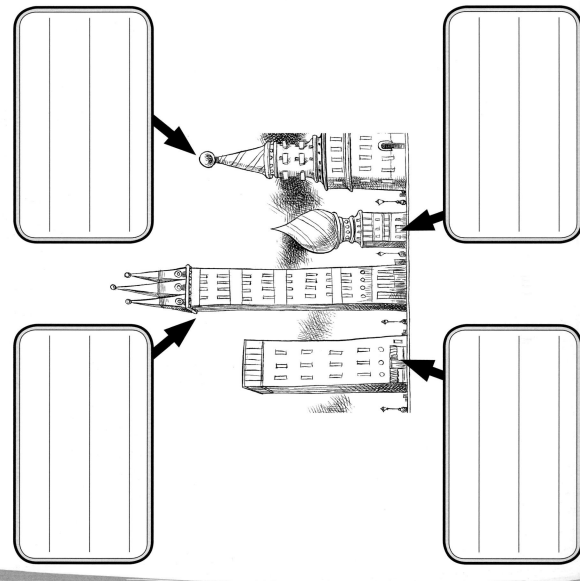

Mr Munroe's feelings

Write how Mr Munroe feels at the different times.

1. MR MUNROE WENT TO HIS ROOM.

2. AT ELEVEN O'CLOCK

3.

4. PRIVATE KEEP OUT

5. AT LUNCH

6. AT TWO O'CLOCK

7. AT FOUR O'CLOCK

8. AT DINNER

Name: _____   Date: _____

Literacy evolve

Mystery clues bookmark

Use the bookmark to record clues.

Mystery clues bookmark

Name: _____

Book title: Ottoline and the Yellow Cat

Chapter: One

Puzzle: Who is Mrs Jansen-Smith?

_____

Page	Clue
_____ :	_____
_____ :	_____
_____ :	_____
_____ :	_____
_____ :	_____

Things to talk about:

1. What's Ottoline's clever plan?
2. How is the plan clever?
3. Is there anything puzzling you?
4. What did you like/dislike about these chapters?

Chapter: _____

Puzzle: _____

_____

Page	Clue
_____ :	_____
_____ :	_____
_____ :	_____
_____ :	_____
_____ :	_____
_____ :	_____

Things to talk about:

_____
_____
_____
_____
_____
_____
_____

Fold

Plot detective cards

1. Put the sentences in order of *most likely, less likely* or *not very likely* to happen. Use clues from the story.

The Yellow Cat could break into Ottoline's apartment.

The other dogs may discover who Mr Munroe really is.

The other dogs could go back to their owners.

Mr Munroe might decide to work for the Yellow Cat.

Mr Munroe might trick Clive the cockatoo.

Ottoline might phone the police.

2. Choose one possibility to discuss in more detail.

a. What would happen next?
b. How might the story end?
c. Would all the problems be solved if this happened?
d. Would any of the characters be happy?

 Literacy evolve

Character cue cards

Take a card each and discuss the questions.

a. What might the Yellow Cat be thinking now?
b. What might she do next?
c. What might happen as a result?

a. What might Ottoline be thinking now?
b. What might she be doing at this moment?
c. What might happen as a result?

a. What might Mr Munroe be thinking now?
b. What might he do next?
c. What might happen as a result?

a. What might Rupe be thinking now?
b. What might he do next?
c. What might happen as a result?

a. How might the story end?
b. How might this happen?
c. Would this be a good ending?

What's the link?

Discuss how the objects and characters play an important part in catching the Yellow Cat and Clive the cockatoo.

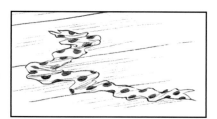

Ottoline's spotted ribbon

a light bulb

the bear from the basement

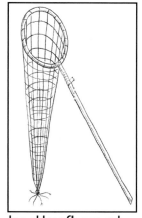

butterfly net (mended)

a door knob

Mr Munroe's drawing

a pillow plumper – Smith and Smith

the Home-Cooked meal company

Literacy Evolve Year 3 © Pearson Education 2009

Book tasters

Read about other mystery stories. Which book would you like to read?

Damian Drooth Supersleuth: Dog Snatchers
by Barbara Mitchelhill

When Mrs Popperwell's dog goes missing, Damian Drooth Supersleuth and his gang of trainee detectives are soon on the trail of the Dog Snatchers. With his clever plan, Damian is sure he will track the criminals down in no time.
But things don't go quite to plan…

The Postbox Mystery
by Robert Swindells

Sam and Laura are sure there is something strange about the postbox on Prospect Street – the one with the initials CR on it. But no one else will believe them. In fact the post office say there shouldn't be a postbox there at all. What is going on? Sam and Laura set about solving the mystery.

Bursting Balloons Mystery
by Alexander McCall Smith

Someone is trying to ruin Mr Helium's hot-air balloon race across America. Even before the race has started gas has been let out, matches have been stolen and lead weights have been strapped to the baskets.

Now top detectives Max and Maddy are in the race and on the case, tracking down the cheat who'll stop at nothing to claim the prize money.

Will they be the next victims of the villain's dirty tricks, or can they blow his plot sky-high?

Letters from a Mouse by Herbie Brennan

S. Mouse takes charge of Joe Hayes' office supply shop when the people go home at night. But when someone demands 'a briefcase big enough to hold half a million pounds in unmarked 5 pound notes', Mouse finds himself right in the middle of a mystery. Can Mouse and his friend Cockroach solve the mystery and stop a gang of thieves?

Read S. Mouse's letters and see if you can crack the case.

Mystery story ingredients

Look at other mystery stories and complete the mind map.

Characters

Good

_____

_____

_____

Bad

_____

_____

_____

Theme

_____

_____

_____

_____

Settings

Safe/familiar

_____

_____

_____

_____

Unsafe/unfamiliar

_____

_____

_____

Mystery stories

Events (what happens)

_____

_____

_____

_____

_____

A puzzle to be solved

_____

_____

_____

_____

_____

Comparing stories

1. Write about a book blurb and front cover.

Title: _____

_____

The story is about: _____

_____

I want to read this story because: _____

_____

2. Write about a different book blurb and front cover.

Title: _____

_____

The story is about: _____

_____

I want to read this story because: _____

_____

The story I prefer is: _____

Sequence of events

Put the main events of *Ottoline and the Yellow Cat* in the correct order. Tell the story.

Mr Munroe noticed something interesting.

The criminals were caught.

Ottoline and Mr Munroe carried out the second part of the plan and set a trap for the criminals.

Ottoline came up with a clever plan to catch the criminals.

The criminals were locked up, everything was put right and everyone was happy.

Ottoline and Mr Munroe went to investigate.

Mr Munroe showed something interesting to Ottoline.

Mr Munroe and the bear carried out the first part of the plan.

Ottoline and Mr Munroe discovered the criminals.

Story plan flow chart

Add notes about the main events from the story.

Opening

_____
_____

Problem

_____
_____

Build-up

_____
_____

Resolution

_____
_____

Ending

_____
_____

Story plan

Write the 'Sequence of events' sentences in the diagram.

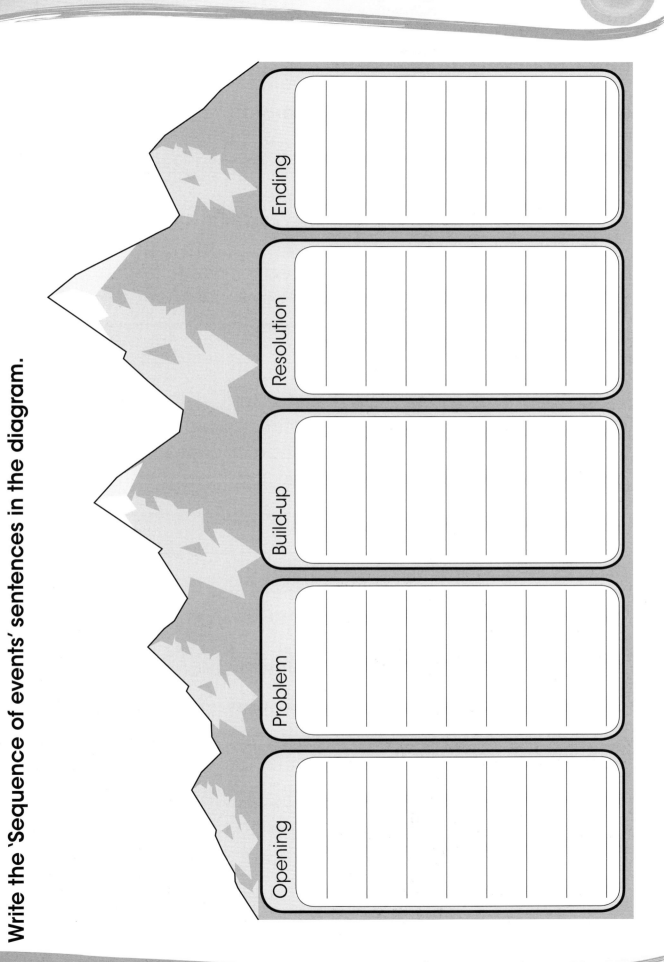

Ending

Resolution

Build-up

Problem

Opening

Discussion prompts

Cut up the questions. Look at the picture(s) and discuss your ideas

---

a. Who can you see in the picture?
b. What can you tell about the characters from how they are drawn?
c. How are the characters placed in the picture?
d. Why are the characters positioned like this?

---

a. What can you see in the picture?
b. What can you tell about the time or place?
c. Why has this time or place been chosen?
d. What is the effect of using this time or place?

---

a. How is colour used in the picture?
b. How is light and dark used?
c. What is the effect of this?
d. How does it add to the effect of the picture?

---

a. How do the pictures differ?
b. What text has the writer included?
c. Why has the author included this text?
d. What effect does this have?

Story starter headlines

Imagine the story behind each headline. Discuss your ideas.

CAKE WRECKER STRIKES AGAIN
Police say 'not a crumb of evidence'

Police in dark over disappearing light bulbs

BAFFLING HAT BURGLARIES
Third robbery in a week

Pets go missing all over Big City: Police say 'it's a mystery'

ART THIEF SWIPES PRICELESS PORTRAIT

Marking Ladder

Use the marking ladder to check your work.

My comments		My partner's comments
	My story is written in chapters.	
	Each chapter is written in paragraphs.	
	I have built up suspense before the most exciting part of my story.	
	I have written complete sentences.	
	I have used time and place connectives.	
	I have included and used speech marks correctly.	

Narrative Unit 4

THE LEGEND OF SPUD MURPHY – novel (Author study)

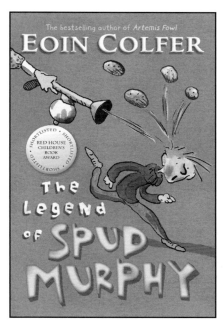

Medium term plan (3 weeks)	
Phase	**Learning Outcomes**
Phase 1: Reading and responding to the story (8 days)	• Children can respond to the author's use of character, plot and narrative style, using evidence from the text. • Children can explain why they like particular books, referring to key features of the text. • Children can use talk to organise a group discussion and a group activity.
Phase 2: Analysing letters (2 days)	• Children can identify the key features of different types of letters. • Children can identify how the style and language of letters can change.
Phase 3: Planning and writing letters (5 days)	• Children can plan a letter for a specific purpose and audience. • Children can draft and proofread letters for a specific purpose and audience.

THE LEGEND OF SPUD MURPHY

Big picture

The children read *The Legend of Spud Murphy* and discuss key aspects of the book: characters, humour, themes, how the story is told. The children research the Eoin Colfer and his other works, watch an interview with the author. They discuss book preferences and nominate their favourites for a book awards ceremony. The children then analyse letters written for different purposes and audiences. They look at sentence structure, and at features relating to layout, organisation and language. Finally the children plan, draft and revise a letter to an author.

Prior learning

This unit assumes that the children can already:

* talk about authors and different types of stories they enjoy reading
* express a personal response or preference and empathise with characters in a story
* work collaboratively, listening to each other and reaching agreement
* use planning to decide what to write, with some awareness of audience and purpose; write, proofread and refine their own work.

Key aspects of learning

Communication: Communicate orally and in writing. Understand the need to vary tone and content for audience and purpose.

Reasoning: Give reasons and use evidence to support their opinions about books and when stating their point of view.

Self-awareness: Reflect on personal response to texts; express preferences; develop a willingness to try something new.

Social skills: Work collaboratively, listen to and respect others' views; take on different roles in the group.

Progression in poetry

In this unit the children will:

* recognise how authors develop plots; understand how language is used to provoke readers' reactions
* identify examples of storytelling in the first person; make deductions about characters' feelings, behaviour and relationships
* recognise the features and conventions of letter-writing; develop ideas for their own letters. Draft, revise and proofread letters.

Cross-curricular links

Geography: The children could write an email to a child in another school about the area where they live.

ICT: The children could use websites to find out about books and authors; use word processing to prepare and present information.

PSHE: The children could write a letter to a child in the year below welcoming them to their new class.

Reading time

50 minutes

PHASE 1: READING AND RESPONDING TO THE STORY (8 DAYS)

Session 1

We are learning to …	Resources
• share our opinions about a story (or poem) and give reasons for our views • write in the role of a character (PNS Strands 1.3, 8.2) **Assessment Focuses** AF (R): 2, 6, 7	*The Legend of Spud Murphy* *Author reading* (film) ITP: 4.1, 4.2 PCM: 4.1

Shared teaching

* Ask the children to explore the front cover of *The Legend of Spud Murphy. Who is the author? Have you read any of their other books?*
* Share the learning objectives.
* Show 'What type of story?' (ITP 4.1). Ask the children to use information from the cover to Think-Pair-Share predictions about what type of story it might be. Invite the children to move the words on ITP 4.1, explaining their choices.
* Read Chapter 1 with the children following in their own books. Additionally, watch Eoin Colfer read an extract from this unit in *Author reading*.
* Talk Partners respond to the story. *Is there anything you liked or disliked? Did anything puzzle you? Does it remind you of your family, anything that has happened to you or any other stories you have read?*
* Discuss whether the children want to change their predictions about the type of story it is. *Why? How do you know for sure that it is that type of story?*
* Read 'The Legend of Spud Murphy' (ITP 4.2). *Who is telling the story? How do we know?* Explain the term 'first person'. Highlight first person statements and the pronouns 'I' and 'me' in the extract.

* Discuss what we know about the characters. *What does Will tell us?* Highlight Will's comments.
* Discuss the effect of telling the story in the first person. *Do you like the story written like this? How does it change how we feel about the characters?* (E.g. it sounds like Will is talking directly to us; it has a personal/informal style; we feel close to Will and share his thoughts.)
* Now discuss the effect of telling the story in the third person, e.g. *Will had one big brother, Marty, and three little brothers Donnie, Bert and HP.*
* Organise a whole-class Hot-Seating activity. Ask one child to take on the role of Marty and one child to take the role of Will.

Independent and Guided

* The children explore the use of first person, writing in the role of characters, using details from the text and the hot-seating activity.
  * Use 'Email to Will' (PCM 4.1).
  * As above. (T+)
  * Write character statements in the form of 'Who am I?' clues. (TA+)

Plenary

* Recap the learning objectives. Ask the children to share first person sentences and add to the Learning Wall. *Whose sentence do you like? Who has chosen good details to include?*

Assessment pointers

* S&L: hot-seating will show how well the children can sustain roles to explore characters.
* AF2 (R): response to questioning shows how far the children can make effective references to the text.
* AF6, 7 (R): response to questioning and pair work will show how far the children can relate the text to its genre and understand the effect on the reader of writing in the first person.

<table>
<tr><td>

We are learning to ...

- explore characters using evidence from the text
- judge a character's behaviour using evidence from the text
(PNS Strands 7.2, 8.2)

Assessment Focuses

AF (R): 2, 3

</td><td>

Resources

The Legend of Spud Murphy
ITP: 4.3, 4.4
PCM: 4.2, 4.3

</td></tr>
</table>

Shared teaching

- Recap Chapter 1. *What do you think will happen at the library? What have we been told about the librarian, Mrs Murphy?*
- Read Chapter 2. Encourage the children to share their impressions of Spud Murphy. *What do you think of her? Do you feel sorry for Will?*
- Share the learning objectives. Focus on how the author builds up our expectations of Spud Murphy. *What are we told about Spud Murphy before we meet her? Where does this information come from? Does this affect how we feel about her?*
- Show *'The Legend of Spud Murphy'* (ITP 4.3) and focus on Will's first meeting with the librarian. *Which words and phrases help you picture her?* Highlight examples of descriptive phrases, e.g. 'elderly woman', 'grey hair was tied back so tightly ... '.
- Discuss why the author has included particular similes and comparisons: '(ink stamps) hooked into her belt like six-shooters'; 'knuckles bigger than acorns'. *What impression do these create?*
- Read ITP 4.3 again. *What else apart from her appearance makes Spud Murphy scary?* Use a different colour to highlight details about: the way she acts, e.g. 'banging the desk with an ink stamp'; her voice, e.g. 'like two pieces of rusted metal ... '; and what she says, e.g. 'What do you want?'.
- Show 'Spud Murphy character rating' (ITP 4.4). Talk Partners discuss

how to describe Spud Murphy. Invite the children to drag the markers on the rating scales on ITP 4.4 and explain their decisions by referring to the story. *What makes you think that?*
- Explain that the children will look for more evidence during independent work.

Independent and Guided

- In pairs, the children identify parts of the text that influence the reader's view of Spud Murphy.
- ⬤⬤⬤ Complete 'Spud Murphy' (PCM 4.2), focusing on her actions, dialogue and what others say about her.
- ⬤⬤ Annotate 'Spud Murphy speech bubbles' (PCM 4.3) with words and phrases to show what she says in Chapter 2. (TA+)
- ⬤ Use words from ITP 4.4 to write sentences beginning 'Spud Murphy is/is not ... '. (T+)

Plenary

- Recap the learning objectives. Summarise how the author has created a sense of Spud Murphy's character through descriptive language of her appearance and actions and how other characters describe her.
- Discuss additional evidence gathered and add examples to the Learning Wall. *What new information did you find about Spud Murphy? Has your opinion of her changed? How would she describe herself?*

Assessment pointers

- AF2, 3 (R): responses to questioning and independent work show how well the children can select relevant information from the text and make inferences about a character.

<table>
<tr><td>

We are learning to ...

- say what we like or dislike about a story, explaining and giving reasons
- explore how authors create humour
(PNS Strands 8.1, 8.3)

Assessment Focuses

AF (R): 2, 5, 6

</td><td>

Resources

The Legend of Spud Murphy
ITP: 4.5, 4.6

</td></tr>
</table>

Shared teaching

- Recap Chapter 2 and encourage predictions. *It doesn't sound like much fun. I wonder what Will and Marty will do?*
- Ask the children to visualise events as you read Chapter 3. Use expression to convey the humour in the text.
- *What did you like best about this chapter? Do you think Marty and Will thought it was funny? How would you feel? What will happen the next time they go to the library?*
- Share the learning objectives and discuss which bits of the story the children thought were funny. Talk Partners look through Chapter 3 and choose two or three funny moments.
- Take feedback and encourage the children to explain their choices. Choose the children's top five favourite moments and record these on 'Funniest moments' (ITP 4.5). Give each event a title, e.g. 'Marty the crocodile'. Ask the children to order the events according to how funny they think they are.
- Read *'The Legend of Spud Murphy'* (ITP 4.6). *Which bits made you smile? What makes this funny?* Highlight the parts identified and discuss features and techniques, such as the use of language; Will's comments on the action; humorous descriptive details, e.g. 'Spud stood, slippered feet apart'; funny mental images; humorous phrases, e.g. 'ninja librarian'; short sentences, e.g. 'It was Spud.'

- Discuss the illustrations and how they contribute to the humour. *Which is the funniest illustration? Which sentence does it illustrate?*

Independent and Guided

- Small groups focus on another extract; deciding what makes it funny and responding to the humour in different ways.
- ⬤⬤⬤ Select a 'funniest moment', read the appropriate incident and create a Freeze Frame to convey the event and humour. (TA+)
- ⬤⬤ Practise reading aloud the 'hand-stamping incident' (pages 41–44). Use sticky notes to record funny moments. (T+)
- ⬤ Role Play the scene of 'Marty's trick' (pages 31–32), using sentences from the text as dialogue.

Plenary

- Recap the learning objectives. Watch and discuss the Freeze Frames, readings and role plays.
- Encourage the children to explain what made their extracts funny. *Was it the situation, how it was described, particular words and phrases or the dialogue?*

Assessment pointers

- S&L: drama pieces will show how far the children can sustain roles and scenarios to explore the text.
- AF2 (R): responses to questioning and independent work will show how far the children are able to retrieve information from the text and use quotations to support views.
- AF5, 6 (R): responses to questioning will show how far the children can explain as well as identify a humorous moment or humorous language from the story.

Session 4

We are learning to ...	Resources
• discuss the text giving reasons for our views • understand how and why chracters change • explore how authors surprise us (PNS Strands 1.3, 7.2, 8.3) **Assessment Focuses** AF (R): 2, 3	*The Legend of Spud Murphy* ITP: 4.7, 4.8 PCM: 4.4, 4.5

Shared teaching

• Use Babble Gabble to recap the story so far. In pairs, the children take turns to retell the story so far, prompting each other if details of the plot or funny events are missed out.
• As a class, discuss what might happen next. *Do you think Will and Marty will be looking forward to going to the library again?* Focus on the two problems: Spud Murphy and being bored.
• Read Chapter 4. Encourage the children to respond to the events. *That's interesting. Did anything surprise you? Has the story taken an unexpected route?*
• Share the learning objectives and explain that one of the themes in this story is Will and Marty's attitude to books and reading.
• Show 'What Will says' (ITP 4.7). Click on each option to explore Will's views. Discuss what they show about his attitudes and feelings. *Why do you think he feels like this? Do you think these views might be beginning to change? What evidence is there?*
• Show '*The Legend of Spud Murphy*' (ITP 4.8). Read until '... just another couple of sentences.' *What are the signs that Will is changing his attitude?* Focus on changes in Will's behaviour, e.g. reading rather than pretending to read; finding a sentence interesting; reading more. *Will says: 'I wouldn't read the whole book, no way.' Why does he say this?*
• Read and discuss the second part of ITP 4.8. *What does Will mean by*

'I was lost in the tale' and 'It was another world'*? What has happened? Have you ever felt like this?*
• Discuss reasons for the change in Will's behaviour and attitude. *Why does Will carry on reading? Why does this particular book interest him?*

Independent and Guided

• Pairs look for further evidence from the chapters they have read so far, discussing the thoughts of the different characters at the end of Chapter 4.
• 🔗 Read paragraph 1 of Chapter 5 before completing 'What the characters say' (PCM 4.4). (TA)
• 🔗 Record ideas and evidence on 'Will and books' (PCM 4.5).
• 🔗 Guided reading focusing on evidence of the characters' thoughts, e.g. their speech. (T+)

Plenary

• Recap the learning objectives. Recall ITP 4.7. *What might Will say now?* Encourage responses in first person, as if Will is speaking.
• Discuss how the story might continue. *Are all the problems solved? What might happen next? I wonder if there will be any more surprises?*
• If time, continue reading Chapter 5 as far as page 72 ('Or was I?').

Assessment pointers

• S&L: group work will show how far the children can organise and sustain collaboration and discussion.
• AF2 (R): paired work and responses to questioning will show how far the children understand the story so far.
• AF3 (R): responses to questioning and independent work shows how far the children can make deductions about Will's feelings, supported by reference to the text.

Session 5

We are learning to ...	Resources
• use the language of possibility to discuss characters' feelings and relationships • judge a character's behaviour using evidence from the text • explore how authors surprise us (PNS Strands 3.3, 8.2, 8.3) **Assessment Focuses** AF (R): 2, 3, 6	*The Legend of Spud Murphy* ITP: (4.4), 4.9 PCM: 4.6

Shared teaching

• If you have not already done so, read Chapter 5 as far as page 72 ('Or was I?') before the session.
• Share the learning objectives and ecap the story so far. *What might happen next?*
• Read to the end of the book. Encourage the children to respond. *Is it a good ending? Was it what you expected? How did the author build up the surprise and make it funny?*
• Recall 'Spud Murphy character rating' (ITP 4.4) annotated in Session 2. *Would you choose the same scores now? Has your opinion of Spud changed?* Think-Pair-Share ideas. Take feedback, encouraging reference to Spud's actions and comments at the end of Chapter 5.
• Explain that because the story is told in the first person we see all the other characters through Will's eyes. *But what if we could see events through Spud's eyes? What might she say?* Invite some suggestions using the language of possibility.
• Talk Partners discuss questions to ask Spud Murphy, focusing on her behaviour, e.g. *Why did you ... ? What were you thinking when ... ?*
• Set up a Teacher-In-Role activity. Take the role of Spud Murphy and answer the children's questions. Use your answers to present her

actions in a more sympathetic way, e.g. *I had to work until eight o'clock the other night to sort out the mess someone had made.*
• Discuss whether the drama activity has changed their opinion of Spud.
• Show 'Character links' (ITP 4.9) and focus on the character relationships at the end of the story. Click on Spud's links to Will and Marty. *What might Spud say about Will? What might she say about Marty?* Allow pairs Think Time, encouraging the children to look back at the end of the chapter. Add suggestions to ITP 4.9.
• Discuss how and why the relationship between Spud and Will has changed. *I wonder whether Spud has changed or whether Will sees her differently.*

Independent and Guided

• Small groups explore character relationships further, referring to the text.
• 🔗 Explore the relationship between Will and Marty through guided reading. (T+)
• 🔗 Complete 'Character relationships' (PCM 4.6).
• 🔗 Complete a Role on the Wall activity for Spud. Write what others might say about her outside the character outline; write what Spud might say about herself inside the character outline. (TA+)

Plenary

• Recap the learning objectives. Add more information to ITP 4.9.
• Discuss why the book is called *The Legend of Spud Murphy*.

Assessment pointers

• S&L: group work will show how well the children can adopt group roles and express opinions.
• AF2, 6 (R): responses to questioning show how far the children understand events in the story and are aware of the effect the text has on the reader.
• AF3 (R): independent work shows how far the children are able to make inferences about relationships.

Session 6

We are learning to ...
- share our opinions about a story (or poem) and give reasons for our views
- work together effectively in groups, including all group members
- say what we like or dislike about a story, explaining and giving reasons
(PNS Strands 1.3, 3.2, 8.1)

Assessment Focuses
AF (R): 6

Resources
The Legend of Spud Murphy

ITP: 4.10

Shared teaching
- Share the learning objectives. Introduce the idea of book groups for discussing a shared book. Explain that the groups will be discussing *The Legend of Spud Murphy*.
- Begin with a general discussion about the book to encourage confidence in expressing opinions. *What did you like best? Was there anything you disliked?* Encourage a child to talk at length about aspects of the text that appealed or didn't appeal to them. *Why do you say that? Tell me more about ... .* Encourage the children to express a personal opinion rather than simply agreeing with everyone else.
- Use 'Discussion starters' (ITP 4.10) to introduce features that might be discussed in a book group. Explain that these are not questions to be answered briefly, but prompts to start a discussion. Click to reveal.
- Begin modelling how a book group discussion works by clicking on one of the prompts, e.g. characters. *Who do you think was the best character? Why do you think that?* Ask the children to Think-Pair-Share responses in groups, as preparation for a whole-class discussion.
- In the class discussion, develop responses and encourage the children to make reference to the text as much as possible. Encourage discussion between the children, e.g. *Why do you say Marty is funny? Can you give an example? What do you think ... ? Do you agree that Marty is the funniest character?*
- Repeat the process with other prompts on ITP 4.10. Increase the time given to group discussion as the children become more confident. Circulate, encouraging discussion and modelling how to include all members of the group. Prompt children to provide further explanation and refer to the book where necessary.

Independent and Guided
- The children work in book groups, discussing and selecting their 'best bits' from the story. They discuss reasons for choices and prepare evidence to present to the class, e.g. a selection of quotes capturing favourite moments, annotated sections of text, or a collage of drawings with quotations. The children decide within the group how they will present their discussions and organise roles accordingly. Support the children with an identified need. (T/TA)

Plenary
- Recap the learning objectives. Invite different groups to present the outcomes of their discussions. Add any supporting materials the groups have prepared to the Learning Wall. Encourage the children to explain their choices. *To sum up, would you recommend this book to other children of your age?*

Assessment pointers
- S&L: group discussion and drama will show how far the children can develop ideas and respond to issues through sustained speaking.
- AF6 (R): responses to questioning and group work shows how well the children are able to discuss personal opinions about the book, referring to key aspects of the text.

Session 7

We are learning to ...
- find out more about authors and the types of books they write
- compare books by an author, looking for similarities and differences
- use knowledge about authors to help us choose new books to read
(PNS Strands 8.1)

Assessment Focuses
AF (R): 7

Resources
The Legend of Spud Murphy

Interview with Eoin Colfer (film)

ITP: 4.11

PCM: 4.7

Shared teaching
- Use the Learning Wall to recap what the children enjoyed about *The Legend of Spud Murphy. Do you know any other books by Eoin Colfer?*
- Share the learning objectives. Explain that you will read the opening of two stories: one by Eoin Colfer and one by another author.
- Show 'Other stories' (ITP 4.11) Click next to reveal the authors and titles. *Which do you think is by Eoin Colfer? What clues are there? Can you guess who the other author is?*
- Focus on the extract by Eoin Colfer. Highlight familiar features, e.g. the characters, use of the first person, the personal/informal style, humour, the theme of family relationships, etc. Explain that this is the sequel to *The Legend of Spud Murphy* so it uses the same characters but in a different setting. *I wonder why the author chose a similar title?*
- Compare the style of the two extracts. Highlight features in the text, e.g. use of the third person, longer sentences, the formal style of language.
- Discuss what the children know about Eoin Colfer. *Where can we find information about him?*
- Ask the children to imagine that they could interview the author. *What questions would you ask him about the characters or events in The Legend of Spud Murphy?*
- The children Think-Pair-Share ideas and write three questions. Add the questions to the Learning Wall.
- Watch *Interview with Eoin Colfer: Part 1.* The children listen to see if their questions are answered.
- Discuss what the children learnt. *What was the most interesting? Did he answer your questions? Do you have any new questions to ask?*

Independent and Guided
- The children work in pairs or groups to collect and present more information about Eoin Colfer and his books.
- **(OOO)** Use copies of Eoin Colfer's books (or the Internet if other books aren't available) to find out about the different series he has created. Write a summary to explain what each series is about. (TA+)
- **(OO)** Use the Internet to research other books by Eoin Colfer. (T+)
- **(O)** Use *The Legend of Spud Murphy* and the Internet to complete 'Other books' (PCM 4.7).

Plenary
- Recap the learning objectives. Ask groups to share their information with the class. *What did you find out? What types of books does Eoin Colfer write? Do they sound interesting? Would you like to read another of his stories?* Add to the Learning Wall.

Assessment pointers
- S&L: group work will show how far the children can engage with others, draw ideas together and promote discussion.
- AF7 (R): responses to questioning show how far the children can relate the text to others in the series and to talk about different types of story.

We are learning to ...	Resources
• use rules to help us speak, listen and respond to other group members • organise and take part in a group discussion of books we have read • talk about our favourite books, explaining our choices by referring to key aspects of the text (PNS Strands 3.2, 8.1) **Assessment Focuses** AF (R): 6, 7	Interview with Eoin Colfer (film) ITP: (4.10), 4.12, 4.13 PCM: 4.8

Shared teaching

• Show 'Will's favourite books' (ITP 4.12). *Do you remember how Will suddenly discovered some great books? These were some of his favourites. What sort of books did Will like? Do you think you would like these books?* Click to reveal information about the books.
• Remind the children that in previous sessions, they learnt about Eoin Colfer's books but they didn't find out about his favourite books and why he likes writing.
• Watch *Interview with Eoin Colfer Part 2. What were his favourite books?*
• Allow Think Time for the children to consider their favourite books.
• Introduce the idea of book awards and explain that they are awarded each year to outstanding books, e.g. *Storm* won a Carnegie Medal; *Ottoline and the Yellow Cat* won the 2007 Nestlé Children's Book Prize; and Eoin Colfer has won numerous awards including the British Book Awards Children's Book of the Year in 2002.
• Explain that the children are going to present their own awards. They will form judging panels, discussing which books they think are 'outstanding' and deserve an award. *What categories could we have?* (E.g. funniest story, most exciting story, best character, best illustration)

• *Can you think of books to nominate for these categories? You will need to put forward a convincing argument for your favourite books, explaining what makes them outstanding or memorable.*
• Recall 'Discussion starters' (ITP 4.10) and focus on features of stories that make them memorable. *What qualities are important? What makes a book a good read?* (E.g. an interesting, exciting plot; memorable moments; how the story is told, etc.) Remind the children to refer to these features when giving reasons for their choices.
• Show 'Rules for discussion' (ITP 4.13). Discuss why the rules are important and how to keep to them. *Why shouldn't you interrupt people? How can you make sure everyone is included? How can you respond to what someone says? Are there any you would like to add?*

Independent and Guided

• The children work in groups, thinking of different categories for book awards, discussing nominated books and giving reasons for their choices. Complete 'Book award' (PCM 4.8) for each chosen book. Support the children with an identified need. (T+/TA+)

Plenary

• Encourage groups to share their nominations and reasons. Add completed certificates to the Learning Wall and encourage the children to select a new book to read based on the recommendations.
• Recap the learning objectives and ask for feedback on the discussions. *How well did you stick to the rules? Did you explain their choices?*

Assessment pointers

• S&L: group work will show how far the children can adopt group roles and express relevant ideas.
• AF6 (R): the group activity will show how far the children can work with others, listening and responding effectively.
• AF7 (R): responses to questioning will show how far the children can understand genre and types of stories.

PHASE 2: ANALYSING LETTERS (2 DAYS)

We are learning to ...	Resources
• identify how the style and language of letters can change • identify different purposes for writing letters (PNS Strands 7.3, 7.5) **Assessment Focuses** AF (R): 5, 6	ITP: 4.14 PCM: 4.9

Shared teaching

• Share the learning objectives. Explain that in later sessions the children will be writing letters to authors, so they need to learn how to write in an appropriate way.
• Read Screen 1 of 'Letters' (ITP 4.14). *Who is the letter to? Who has sent it? Why was it sent?* Make sure the children appreciate the link with the story *The Legend of Spud Murphy. Who is Martin? Why don't they call him Marty? Does it remind you of a part of the story?*
• Ask the children to identify which parts of the letter told them who it was from and to, and the purpose of the letter.
• Discuss reasons why schools write letters home to parents, e.g. giving information about events or trips; explaining decisions; requesting help; sending congratulations, etc. Begin a list of different purposes for writing letters on the Learning Wall.
• Read Screen 2 of ITP 4.14. *Who is this letter from?* Again, ensure the children appreciate the link with the story. *Who is Angela? What clues link it to the story? Does the letter surprise you? What is the purpose of the letter? Do you think Jean is a friend? What makes you say that?*
• Discuss other reasons for writing letters to friends and add suggestions to the list of purposes on the Learning Wall.
• Compare the two letters, focusing on the different audiences and

purposes, and how this affects the style of the letter. Focus on Screen 1 again. *This is a very formal letter. Which parts of the letter or which words and phrases tell you that?* ('Dear Mr and Mrs Woodman', 'Yours sincerely', 'Martin' not Marty, 'I regret to inform you … ') *Why is the letter written in this way?*
• Focus on Screen 2 again. *This is an informal, friendly letter. Which parts of the letter or which words and phrases tell you that?* ('My dear Jean', 'Fondest wishes', exclamations, 'P.S.') *Why is the letter written like this?*

Independent and Guided

• The children work in pairs reading letters and discussing purpose, audience and style.
• **ooo** Complete 'Letters' (PCM 4.9). If appropriate, extend to write a reply to the letter on Screen 1 of ITP 4.14.
• **oo** Complete PCM 4.9. (TA+)
• **o** Guided reading. (T+)

Plenary

• Recap the learning objectives, reinforcing the link between audience, purpose and style. Take feedback on the letters read. Discuss examples of formal and informal language. *Of all the letters you read, which are the most formal and most informal? What makes you say that?*

Assessment pointers

• S&L: pair work will show how well the children can express and explain relevant ideas.
• AF5 (R): responses to questioning and independent work show how far the children can understand the author's use of language.
• AF6 (R): responses to questioning show how far the children are able to identify the author's purpose.

We are learning to ...
- identify the layout and key features of letters
- use paragraphs to organise information in letters
- use conjunctions to compose some longer sentences (PNS Strands 7.3, 10.2, 11.1)

Resources
ITP: (4.14), 4.15, 4.16
PCM: (4.9), 4.10

Assessment Focuses
AF (R): 4; AF (W): 5

Shared teaching (1)

- Share the learning objectives and show 'Features of a letter' (ITP 4.15). Ask the children to move the labels to identify key features of the letter. Discuss why each feature is important. *Why should the sender put his or her address? Why is the name needed here?*
- Focus on the layout of the letter, e.g. the position of the address, date, greeting, sign off and signature, each on a separate line.
- Recall Screen 1 of 'Letters' (ITP 4.14), discussing similarities in the layout, greeting, and sign off. Focus on the use of paragraphs. *Look at the main part of the letter. How is this set out?*
- Read the letter one paragraph at a time, asking the children to make notes to summarise the main point for each paragraph. Annotate ITP 4.14 to show that each paragraph makes a different point.

Independent and Guided (1)

- The children explore the organisation and layout of letters.
- **ooo** Use 'Letter jigsaw' (PCM 4.10). The children reassemble the pieces of the letter into the correct order.
- **oo** As above. (T+)
- **o** Annotate Screen 2 of 'Letters' (ITP 4.14) and 'Letters' (PCM 4.9) with similar labels to ITP 4.15. (TA)

Shared teaching (2)

- Discuss the activities. *Did all the letters have the same features? How did you reorder the sections of the letter? How did you know which section or paragraph went first or last?*
- Recall Screen 1 of ITP 4.14 again and focus on sentence structures. *Look at the second paragraph. Can you find some long sentences that use joining words other than 'and'?* Ask the children to read the complete sentences aloud. Highlight the conjunctions: 'when', 'while', 'though', 'so'. Start a list of conjunctions on the Learning Wall.
- Show 'Conjunctions' (ITP 4.16). Read the sentence starter. Talk Partners choose one of the conjunctions then complete the sentence. Take feedback commenting on appropriate use of conjunctions to link clauses together. Add annotations to ITP 4.16.

Independent and Guided (2)

- The children work in pairs to write more sentences about why they like reading. Encourage the children to refer to ITP 4.16 and use a range of conjunctions. Support the children with an identified need (T/TA).

Plenary

- Recap the learning objectives and summarise the learning in this phase. *What have you learnt about writing letters and their layout? How should a letter be organised? How can conjunctions help you write good letters?*

Assessment pointers

- S&L: pair work will show how far the children can listen and respond to others.
- AF4 (R): responses to questioning show how far the children understand the structure and organisation of letters.
- AF5 (W): independent work will show how far the children are able to use varying sentences and conjunctions.

PHASE 3: PLANNING AND WRITING LETTERS (5 DAYS)

We are learning to ...
- think about who we are writing for and why (our audience and purpose)
- develop ideas for writing
- group our ideas into sections according to subject (PNS Strands 9.1, 10.2)

Resources
ITP: (4.10)

Assessment Focuses
AF (W): 2, 3

Shared teaching (1)

- Explain that the children will write letters to the authors they chose for book awards in Session 8. *Why might you write to an author?* (E.g. to tell them about the award, to say why you enjoyed the book, to ask questions, etc.)
- Share the learning objectives. Explain that as a class, the children will write a letter to Eoin Colfer.
- Talk Partners discuss what they want to say in the class letter. Encourage the children to look at book awards certificates on the Learning Wall and think back to book group discussions. Recall 'Discussion prompts' (ITP 4.10) to remind them of different ideas.
- Invite responses, commenting on the ideas and demonstrating how to make short notes, e.g. enjoyed your story, the award, funny characters, Spud Murphy – scary, etc.
- Ask the children to suggest quality questions to ask Eoin Colfer.

Independent and Guided (1)

- The children work in pairs to choose a book from the list of book awards on the Learning Wall, then plan a letter to the author. They

record each idea or question on a separate sticky note. Support the children with an identified need. (T/TA).

Shared teaching (2)

- Return to the notes for the class letter to Eoin Colfer. Explain that the children are going to group their notes into sets. Use Think Alouds to model grouping points on similar subjects, e.g. *These notes are all about the characters.*
- Discuss how to sequence the ideas, e.g. opening with 'how much we enjoyed it', before saying 'what we liked', then 'asking questions'.

Independent and Guided (2)

- The children work in pairs to sort their sticky notes into groups, then decide how to order the groups. The children should discuss reasons for organising ideas in different ways. Support the children with an identified need (T+/TA+).

Plenary

- Recap the learning objectives. Ask some of the children to explain how they have grouped their ideas and why.
- Save the shared plan for the letter to Eoin Colfer for future reference.

Assessment pointers

- S&L: pair work will show how well the children can recount ideas and listen and respond to others.
- AF2, 3 (W): responses to questioning and independent work will show how far the children are able to think about the audience and purpose of a letter and to organise ideas.

<table>
<tr><td>

We are learning to ...
- choose words and phrases that give a letter a suitably formal style
- organise letters into simple paragraphs
- change our notes into complete sentences using conjunctions
- type and change text on a word processor (PNS Strands 9.4, 10.2, 11.1, 12.2)

Assessment Focuses
AF (W): 2, 5, 7

</td><td>

Resources
ITP: (4.16), 4.17, 4.18
PCM: 4.11

</td></tr>
</table>

Shared teaching

- Share the learning objectives. *What do we need to remember when writing a letter? What about the style?* Discuss success criteria and add any additional points to 'Writing letters' (ITP 4.17).
- Review the sticky note plan for the class letter to Eoin Colfer. Discuss how related ideas were grouped together. *How will this help us to write our letter in paragraphs?*
- Show 'Letter writing frame' (ITP 4.18) and explain that the sentence and paragraph starters will help us write the letter and that we can change them to fit our own ideas.
- Discuss how to begin the class letter using Think Alouds, e.g. *I can't begin 'Hi there' or 'Dear Eoin' because I don't know him and I'm writing a formal letter. I'll begin: 'Dear Mr Colfer'. That sounds polite and formal.*
- On ITP 4.18, use Modelled Writing to compose the first sentence, rehearsing it orally before writing, e.g. *I am writing to tell you how much we have enjoyed your story* The Legend of Spud Murphy.
- Demonstrate referring to your notes to decide how to continue the opening paragraph, e.g. *Yes, I must tell him about the award.* Model

changing the note into a complete sentence, e.g. *In fact, we enjoyed it so much that ... .*
- Explain that you need to start a new paragraph when you move onto a new subject, e.g. the next set of notes. Choose a suitable paragraph starter from ITP 4.18, e.g. 'I particularly liked ... '. Model changing 'I' to 'We' as you are writing the letter on behalf of the class.
- Focus on expanding a sentence using a conjunction, e.g. *We particularly liked the characters in your story ... .* Recall 'Conjunctions' (ITP 4.16) to remind the children of different linking words. Encourage Talk Partners to rehearse some conjunctions orally, before inviting suggestions to complete the sentence.

Independent and Guided

- The children draft the main body of their own letters to authors, focusing on the content, not the layout. If possible, allow the children to use computers to write their letters.
  - **ooo** Write independently, choosing and adapting paragraph starters from ITP 4.18 or 'Letter to an author' (PCM 4.11). (T+)
  - **oo** As above. Focus on changing notes into complete sentences. (TA+)
  - **o** Use PCM 4.11 to structure the letter.

Plenary

- Recap the learning objectives and discuss the children's progress. *How have you started each paragraph? What conjunctions have you used? Does your letter sound formal?*

Assessment pointers

- AF2, 5, 7 (W): letters show how far the children are able to write for audience and purpose using longer sentences with conjunctions and choosing words and phrases to achieve a formal tone.

<table>
<tr><td>

We are learning to ...
- edit writing to make it more effective
- use synonyms rather than repeating a word
- use conjunctions to join sentences
- type and change text on a word processor (PNS Strands 9.1, 9.4, 11.1, 12.2)

Assessment Focuses
AF (W): 2, 5, 7

</td><td>

Resources
ITP: (4.16), 4.19

</td></tr>
</table>

Shared teaching

- Share the learning objectives. Explain that in this session, the children will check the letters they wrote in Session 12 and make improvements. When doing this they should think about who the letter is for (the audience) and why they are writing it (the purpose).
- Show 'Letter for redrafting' (ITP 4.19). Explain that you will read the letter aloud one paragraph at a time. This is a good way to check that the letter makes sense, that the sentences flow together, and that it sounds suitably formal.
- Read the first paragraph and use Think Alouds to evaluate it, e.g. *This paragraph starts off well, but I'm not sure about the ending. What do you think?* Encourage the children to comment, developing their responses. *You're right. It doesn't sound very formal. Why is that? Why does the last sentence sound odd?*
- Use Modelled Writing to rework the last two sentences of paragraph 1, explaining how the changes will improve the formal tone and flow of the sentences.
- Read the second paragraph aloud. *This doesn't sound quite right. Why not?* Allow Think Time before asking the children to comment. Develop responses, focusing on improving sentence structure, e.g. *Yes, it is all short sentences. What's wrong with that? How can we improve it?*

- Show 'Conjunctions' (ITP 4.16). Discuss which conjunction could be used to join two sentences. Ask Talk Partners to orally rehearse the sentence before you model making the changes, e.g. *We laughed out loud when our teacher read it to us.* Repeat to join other short sentences into longer ones.
- Draw attention to the end of the letter (the closing statement and signing off). *What is wrong here? How should the letter end?*
- Reread the letter from the beginning. Point out that the word 'funny' is used a number of times. *What other words could we use?* (E.g. hilarious, amusing, humorous, comical, etc.) Model trying out these words in different positions and making changes.

Independent and Guided

- In pairs, the children read their letters aloud and follow the revision process modelled in the shared session.
  - **ooo** Focus on whether the formal style is maintained and look for any words that are overused. Use a thesaurus to find alternative words.
  - **oo** Focus on checking for sense and whether the sentences flow. (TA)
  - **o** As above. (T)

Plenary

- Recap the learning objectives. *What changes have you made to your letters? Why? How did that improve your letter?*

Assessment pointers

- S&L: pair work will show how far the children can listen and respond to others.
- AF2 (W): responses during the plenary will show how far the children are aware of the task, reader and purpose.
- AF5, 7 (W): independent work shows how far the children are able to use varied sentences and appropriate vocabulary.

We are learning to ...
- edit writing to ensure we have used correct punctuation and spelling
- set out a letter correctly
- use a keyboard to type, edit and redraft
(PNS Strands 9.1, 9.5, 12.2)

Assessment Focuses
AF (W): 2, 6, 3

Resources
ITP: (4.15, 4.17), 4.20

Shared teaching (1)

- Share the learning objectives. Explain that all letters must be checked very carefully before they are sent, as a letter with no punctuation and lots of spelling mistakes doesn't look very good and is difficult to read.
- Show 'Letter for proofreading' (ITP 4.20). Explain that proofreaders have to read carefully and be good punctuation detectives.
- Read aloud, starting at paragraph 3, as the children follow the text. *Did you spot any mistakes with capital letters, full stops or question marks?* Discuss and make the changes needed. Encourage the children to give reasons for changes, e.g. capital letters for names and book titles; commas before a conjunction, etc.
- Explain that proofreaders also have to be good spelling detectives. Discuss common errors, e.g. when adding *-ing*.
- Review success criteria using 'Writing letters' (ITP 4.17). Add any relevant points about using accurate spelling and punctuation.

Independent and Guided (1)

- The children work with a proofreading partner to check their letters for punctuation and spelling errors.

∞ Refer to ITP 4.17. Evaluate and improve letters. (T)

∞ As above. Check and change any errors.

◉ As above. (TA+)

Shared teaching (2)

- Encourage pairs to feed back. *Are you happy with your letter? Can you tick all the success criteria?*
- Explain that the final stage is to present the letters, using the correct layout for a formal letter. Refer to the Learning Wall or recall 'Features of a letter' (ITP 4.15) to remind the children of the correct layout.
- Annotate ITP 4.20 to model the correct layout, e.g. *I need to add the school address and date at the top. I must make sure that 'Dear ... ', 'Yours sincerely' and the signature are all on separate lines.*

Independent and Guided (2)

- The children write neatly, or use computers to present their letters in the correct layout. If using a word processor, encourage the children to use the spell check function. Support the children with an identified need. (T/TA)

Plenary

- Recap the learning objectives. Discuss what the children have learnt about writing letters. *What will you need to work on next time you write a letter? Do you think the author will be pleased to receive this letter? What makes you say that? What are you most pleased with?*

Assessment pointers

- S&L: pair work will show how well the children can express and explain relevant ideas.
- AF2, 6, 8 (W): written outcomes will show how well the children can produce letters suited to the task, reader and purpose, using an appropriate style, accurate grammar and syntax and correct spelling.

Session 15

We are learning to ...
- think about who we are writing for and why (our audience and purpose)
- choose the form and style to suit the audience
- set out a letter correctly
- use paragraphs to organise information in letters
(PNS learning objectives 9.1, 9.5, 10.2)

Assessment Focuses
AF (W): 2

Resources
ITP: (4.17), 4.21
PCM: (4.8), 4.12

Shared teaching

- Share the learning objectives. Recall the formal letters the children wrote to an author and explain that they are now going to write a letter for a different purpose and audience.
- Show and read 'Letter from Will' (ITP 4.21). *You are going to write a reply to Will. What will be the purpose of your letter?* (to answer a query; give information) *What sort of things might you say in your letter?* (suggested books; information about them)
- Discuss the style to use. *Should it be formal like the letter to the author?* Refer to Will's letter and identify examples of informal greetings and language.
- Discuss what the children need to remember when writing the letter. The children Think-Pair-Share success criteria for their letter to Will.
- Invite feedback and amend 'Writing letters' (ITP 4.17) to suit an informal letter. Reinforce particular success criteria to focus on identified needs.
- Remind the children that the first stage in writing the letter to an author was planning it. *How did you plan your letter?* (making short notes; sorting and sequencing ideas)

- Use 'Letter plan' (PCM 4.12). Ask the children to work individually or in pairs to gather and note ideas for their letters. Recall 'Book award' (PCM 4.8) on the Learning Wall for ideas of books and qualities to mention. Circulate and support the children as necessary.
- As a class discuss how to proceed. *How will your plan help you write your letter?* (using paragraphs) Discuss possible paragraph starters. *Thank you for ... ; I am writing to ... ; I would like to recommend ... ; I think you will like ... ; Another book you might like ... .*

Independent and Guided

- The children write letters to Will, referring to the agreed success criteria.

∞ Write independently.

∞ As above. (T)

◉ Use paragraph starters to support writing. (TA)

Plenary

- Talk Partners check their letters against the success criteria. *Are you pleased with your letter? Do you think Will will be pleased with it?* Ask for feedback using thumbs up, down, or halfway.
- Recap the learning objectives. Ask the children to reflect on the process of writing letters. Make a list of next steps that the children suggest for improving their writing skills.
- Recap the unit as a whole. *What did you enjoy most? What did you find hard? Did you enjoy the book? Will you read more of his books?*

Assessment pointers

- AF2 (W): written letters and self-assessment show how well the children can write to suit the task, reader and purpose, using the main features of letters and an appropriate style.

Email to Will

Write a reply to Harry's email, imagining you are Will. Write about his family and the things he likes.

```
From: Harry
To: Will
Subject: All about me

Hi Will,

Thanks for letting me write to you.
My name is Harry.

I live with my Mum, my cat and my big
sister Jess. Jess is the clever one,
or that's what everyone says. Do you
have any brothers or sisters?

I like reading and watching cartoons.
What do you like?

Please write back.

Bye,

Harry
```

```
From: Will
To: Harry
Subject: RE: All about me.

Hi Harry,
_____
_____
_____
_____
_____
_____
_____
```

Spud Murphy

Complete the mind map about Spud Murphy.

What she says (or how she says it) _____

What other people say about her

Her behaviour

What Will says about her (or how he describes her)

Spud Murphy speech bubbles

Write what Spud Murphy says into the speech bubbles.

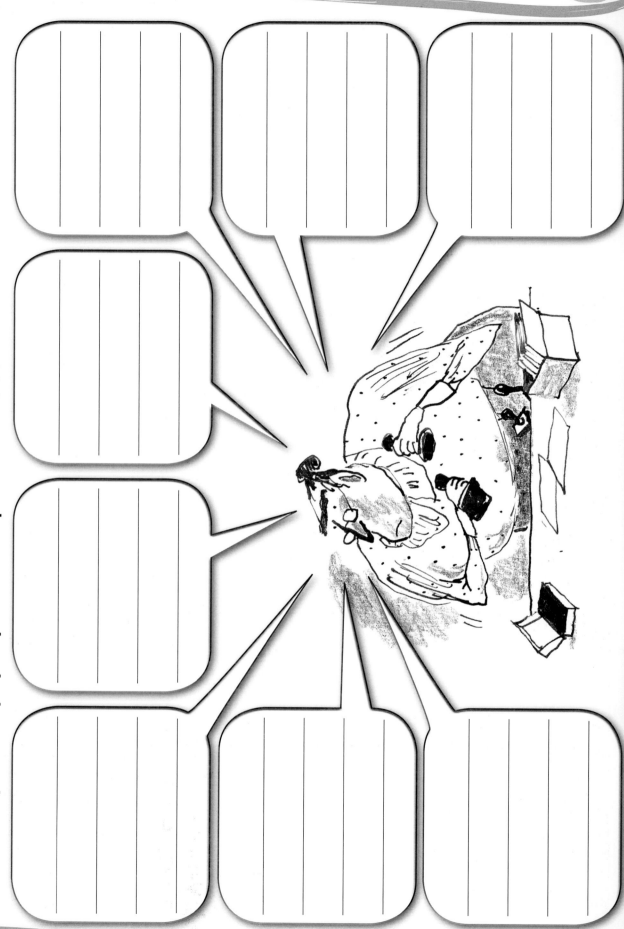

Literacy Evolve Year 3 © Pearson Education 2009

What the characters say

Write what the characters would say about books, reading and libraries now.

Will and books

1. Highlight what Will thinks about books at the start of Chapter 4.

boring   magical   exciting   imaginative

fun

fascinating   unexciting   gripping   entertaining

dull   educational   interesting

How do you know this? _____

_____

_____

2. Highlight what Will thinks about books at the end of Chapter 4.

magical   educational   fascinating   imaginative

exciting   entertaining   unexciting

dull   fun   gripping   boring   interesting

How do you know this? _____

_____

_____

Character relationships

1. Write what these characters might say about Spud Murphy.

Will

Marty

Mum

2. Write what Spud Murphy says about herself.

Spud Murphy

Other books

Write about two of Eoin Colfer's other books.

Title: _____

Age of reader: _____

Description: _____

Title: _____

Age of reader: _____

Description: _____

Book award

Complete a book award for your chosen book.

Book Awards 20____

This certificate is awarded to:

_____ [name of author]

author of: _____ [book title]

The above title has been voted:

_____ [category]

by: _____ [child/class name]

What the judges said:

_____

_____

Best Book

Literacy Evolve Year 3 © Pearson Education 2009

Letters

Read the letters and complete the information. Highlight clues in the letters

Dear Mr Wilson,

We are writing to inform you that you have won third prize in our painting competition.

The judges thought your painting of a cottage by the sea was quite charming. They particularly liked the way you caught the sunlight shining on the sea.

We would also like to take this opportunity to invite you to an exhibition where all the paintings entered in our competition will be on show. The exhibition will be at the Town Hall from June 1st.

Congratulations from all the competition judges and we look forward to seeing you at the Town Hall in June.

Yours sincerely,

A. J. Hunter

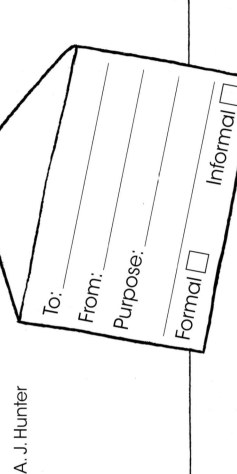

To: _____
From: _____
Purpose: _____

Formal ☐   Informal ☐

Hi there Jimbo!

Guess what? It's my birthday next Saturday and I'm having a party. Can you come?

It's going to be great. We're all going to dress up. Cool, eh?

Email me if you can come.

See you!

Marty

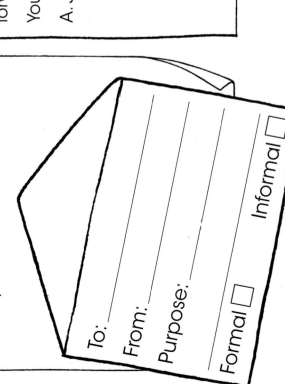

To: _____
From: _____
Purpose: _____

Formal ☐   Informal ☐

Letter jigsaw

Cut up and order the letter.

Both my fish are goldfish but one of them has white patches. I am keeping them in a bowl and giving them goldfish food from the pet shop.

5 Newhall Street
Hamley
OX1 4AB

Thank you for your help.

I am writing to ask for some information about how to look after fish. I have just been given two fish for my birthday but I am not sure how to take care of them. I was told that the Children's Pet Club has lots of information to help new pet owners like me.

Yours faithfully,

What I want to know is should they have a bigger tank and how often do I need to change their water? Can you give me some advice? I am enclosing an envelope and a stamp so you can send some information to me.

Dear Sir or Madam,

Letter to an author

Use the writing frame to write a letter to an author.

_____
_____
_____
_____

Dear _____ ,

I am writing to _____
_____

I thought the story was _____
_____

I particularly liked the _____
_____

My favourite part was _____
_____

I wanted to ask you _____
_____

Yours sincerely,

_____

Letter plan

Plan a letter to Will.

| Write the start to your letter. | _____
_____
_____
_____ |

| Write something to help Will answer the question. | _____
_____
_____
_____
_____ |

| Write more information you want to tell Will. | _____
_____
_____
_____ |

| End your letter. | _____
_____
_____ |

Literacy Evolve Year 3 © Pearson Education 2009

DRAGON SLAYER – film (Play and film scripts)

Medium term plan (4 weeks)	
Phase	**Learning Outcomes**
Phase 1: Familiarisation with the genre (4 days)	• Children can recognise the features of a traditional tale. • Children can orally retell a traditional tale. • Children can identify the differences between a play script and a narrative version of a story. • Children can write and punctuate reported speech. • Children can recognise and understand how a play script is laid out. • Children can read aloud with expression.
Phase 2: Capturing ideas (7 days)	• Children can understand how film techniques convey character. • Children can use drama techniques to explore a character. • Children can empathise with a character in a film and explain their actions. • Children can write and perform dialogue expressively.
Phase 3: Planning and writing the play script (9 days)	• Children can write a script using appropriate layout and directions. • Children can write dialogue for a script. • Children can perform a script expressively. • Children can use gestures in a dramatic performance. • Children can extend a story.

Narrative Unit 5

DRAGON SLAYER

Big picture

The children read a story and a play version of *Hansel and Gretel*. They recognise features of the traditional tale and identify differences between narrative stories and play scripts, focusing on presentation, settings, dialogue and character. They watch the film *Dragon Slayer* (previously watched in Unit 2), and use talk and drama techniques to analyse characters, thoughts, feelings and relationships. They then write and perform a play script of the story. They go on to write and perform a new scene, focusing on inventing a suitable plot, effective directions, expressive dialogue and appropriate props and gestures.

Prior learning

This unit assumes that the children can already:
• understand and respond to a story told in film
• infer character motivations and feelings from visual clues
• use drama techniques to explore character and feelings
• identify and describe the purpose and effect of film techniques
• improvise dialogue to explore characters
• work collaboratively to explore a shared text.

Key aspects of learning

Communication: Interpret a character's thoughts and feelings from a visual medium and express them in words; work collaboratively in a group; give and respond to feedback.

Creative thinking: Improvise and write dialogue; write effective stage directions including expression, gesture and props.

Empathy: Understand a character's dilemma; describe, respond to and portray a character's feelings expressively.

Social skills: Work in groups; offer constructive feedback; cooperate to prepare a group performance.

Progression in poetry

In this unit the children will:
• identify how different texts appeal to readers
• use appropriate technical language and layout to write a script
• write expressive dialogue to convey character, motivation, dilemmas and relationships.

Cross-curricular links

Art and Design: The children could create posters, tickets or programmes to accompany their performances.

Citizenship: The children could explore themes of dilemmas; personal responsibility.

Design and Technology: The children could create props for the performance.

ICT: The final performances could be filmed and edited.

Viewing time

8 minutes 10 seconds approx.

PHASE 1: FAMILIARISATION WITH THE GENRE (4 DAYS)

Session 1

We are learning to ...	Resources
• explore characters using evidence from the text • recognise features of traditional tales • explore how the features of traditional tales appeal to readers (PNS Strands 7.2, 7.3, 7.5) **Assessment Focuses** AF (R): 2, 3	ITP: 5.1, 5.2 PCM: 5.1

Shared teaching

• Explain that the 'Big Picture' for this unit will be exploring how play scripts are set out.
• Share the learning objectives.
• Talk Partners discuss features of traditional tales. *What kind of characters/setting do traditional tales have? What kinds of problems happen? What special words, phrases or objects do you find in traditional tales?* Take feedback and scribe responses.
• Explain that the children are going to read *The Tale of Hansel and Gretel. What is the story about? Who are the main characters?*
• Read 'The Tale of Hansel and Gretel' (ITP 5.1), modelling good expression and intonation. The children follow the text on the screen, focusing particularly on what the characters say and do.
• After reading the story, Talk Partners identify how the reader knows whether characters are 'good' or 'bad' (by what they say and do). Take feedback.
• Show 'Describing the characters' (ITP 5.2) and focus on one of the characters, e.g. the stepmother. *What is she like? Which of these adjectives would you use to describe her? Which bit of the story makes*

you choose that word? Remind the children of the significance of zones and drag the words into place.

Independent and Guided

• The children work in groups to complete 'Target board' (PCM 5.1). Allocate a character secretly to each group so that the other groups don't overhear. *What is your character like? Which adjectives would you use to describe your character? Which bit of the story makes you choose those words?* When the group has agreed, the words should be written on the target board. Encourage early finishers to add extra adjectives of their own. Support the children with an identified need. (T+/TA+)

Plenary

• Recap the learning objectives. Show ITP 5.2 again and ask the first group to reveal their chosen adjectives one at a time, starting with one that could describe more than one character and saving the adjective that would easily identify the character until last.
• Drag the adjectives onto the target board one at a time. *Who could this describe? Who couldn't it describe? Which bit of the story makes you think that?* Continue until the character has been identified, and repeat with all of the groups.

Assessment pointers

• S&L: group work will show how well the children can organise and sustain collaboration and discussion.
• AF 2, 3 (R): responses show how far the children can describe characters from the things they say and do and can identify information from the text to support their views.

Session 2

<table>
<tr><td>We are learning to ...
• use other words instead of 'said' to show how characters speak
• use speech marks to show which words are spoken
(PNS Strands 9.4, 11.3)
Assessment Focuses
AF (W): 6, 7</td><td>Resources
ITP: (5.1), 5.3
PCM: 5.2, 5.3, 5.4</td></tr>
</table>

Shared teaching (1)

• Share the learning objectives and remind the children that they were first introduced to speech marks in Unit 3. Explain that they are now going to look at speech marks in more detail.
• Show 'Talking heads' (ITP 5.3). *How do you think the stepmother speaks?* (Click to hear her speak.) Explain that this is direct speech. *How would you write this? What punctuation do you need to use?* Point out the speech marks.
• Click on the stepmother again. *How does she speak? Which word from the list best describes this?*
• Drag the words to form the stepmother's direct speech.
• Play the speech of the other characters. Talk Partners discuss how to write these words as direct speech. Take feedback and drag the words into place. Encourage the children to explain their choice of verbs.

Independent and Guided

• The children rewrite speech bubbles as direct speech. Encourage the children to use ITP 5.3 for help.

[OOO] Complete 'Writing speech 1' (PCM 5.2), adding in the character's name and a verb other than 'said'.

[OO] Complete 'Writing speech 2' (PCM 5.3), adding the character's name and an appropriate verb from the list. (T)

[O] Complete 'Writing speech 3' (PCM 5.4). (TA)

Shared teaching (2)

• Take feedback. *What was in the speech bubble? How did you change this into direct speech?*
• Write some more speech from the story in speech bubbles. *How could you rewrite this with speech marks? Who might have said this in the story? How might they have said it?* Scribe ideas.
• Talk Partners Role Play reading the speech to each other as different characters.

Plenary

• Recap the learning objectives.
• Play a quick game with the children. One child retells or invents speech from *The Tale of Hansel and Gretel* while Talk Partners race to write this as direct speech.
• Encourage pairs to share their answers with the class. *Which character was speaking? What word do you think describes how it was said?*

Assessment pointers

• S&L: role plays will show how well the children can convey ideas about characters through speech.
• AF6, 7 (W): completed PCMs and response to questions will show how far the children are able to set out and punctuate direct speech and to use appropriate verbs.

Session 3

<table>
<tr><td>We are learning to ...
• read a script with expression
• learn how a play script is set out
(PNS Strands 1.1, 7.3)
Assessment Focuses
AF (R): 1</td><td>Resources
ITP: 5.4</td></tr>
</table>

Shared teaching

• Talk Partners play Just a Minute, taking it in turns to retell *The Tale of Hansel and Gretel*. Take feedback, encouraging the class to retell the story as a whole.
• Share the learning objectives and explain that today, the children are going to look at how a play script is written. They are going to try to read the play with expression, to show what the characters are feeling.
• Show 'Hansel and Gretel: a play' (ITP 5.4). Introduce some of the written conventions and specific vocabulary associated with play scripts, e.g. the layout, cast list, scene headings, characters' names etc. *Why is a narrator needed? What information do they give us?*
• Point out the words in brackets before the father's second speech. *What are these?* (character directions) *Why is this information included?* (to explain how the play should be acted)
• Explain that when we read a play, we don't say the character's name or any stage directions aloud, only the words the character says. Highlight some of this direct speech.
• Read Scene 1, modelling appropriate expression, intonation and volume.
• Talk Partners try reading the first four lines after the narrator. Remind them to pay attention to the character directions and to only read the direct speech, using expression and the correct intonation.

• Ask a few pairs to read the lines for the class. Encourage the class to comment on the performances. *What did you like about their performance? How well do you think they read the lines?*
• Divide the class into three groups and allocate each group a character from Scene 2 (excluding the narrator). Remind the children to read only the direct speech. Then read Scene 2, taking the part of the narrator with the groups reading the part of the character that they have been allocated.
• Allow Think Time for the class to evaluate Scene 2. *What did you do well? What could you improve?*

Independent and Guided

• The children work in groups to read Scenes 1 and 2. They discuss how the characters feel and practise reading the parts with appropriate expression, intonation and volume. Support the children with an identified need. (T+/TA+)

Plenary

• Recap the learning objectives and explain that they are going to listen to how expressively the different groups can read their scenes.
• Invite groups to read one or both of the scenes. During each reading the class make notes of good use of expression, tone, volume and good interpretation of any character directions. *What did you like? What improvements could be made?*

Assessment pointers

• S&L: oral readings will show how far the children can interpret the text through speech.
• AF1 (R): group work indicates how far the children understand the conventions of the play script and how to read following directions.

Session 4

We are learning to ...	Resources
• read a script with expression • compare a story with a play script (PNS Strands 1.1, 7.3) **Assessment Focuses** AF (R): 4	ITP: (5.4), 5.5 PCM: 5.5, 5.6

Shared teaching (1)

• Share the learning objectives and recap Session 3. *Where did we stop in the play? What do you think will happen in Scene 3?* Take feedback.
• Recall 'Hansel and Gretel: a play' (ITP 5.4) and read Scene 3, trying to use different voices for the different parts.
• Talk Partners discuss what might happen in the last scene. *How do you think the next scene will begin? What do you think the different characters might say? How do you think they will say it?*
• Read Scene 4. *Did any of your guesses match the play script? Would you have said anything differently?*
• Remind the children that it is important to use different voices for the characters so that the audience knows more about the characters and what they are like.
• Focus on some of the lines from Scenes 3 and 4 and invite the children to suggest different ways of saying them. Encourage the class to comment on which they think sounds the most effective.

Independent and Guided (1)

• The children work in groups to perform Scenes 3 and 4. Encourage them to think carefully about the different emotions they have to convey. Support the children with an identified need. (T/TA)

Shared teaching (2)

• Discuss how well the children worked together. *What did you like about your performance? What do you think could be improved? Did you work well as a group?*
• *Do you think there are any differences between the story and the play of* The Tale of Hansel and Gretel*?* Allow Think Time before taking responses.
• Show 'Stories and plays' (ITP 5.5). Highlight a couple of differences between the story and the play, e.g. the different tense, the different information given about the characters.

Independent and Guided (2)

• The children work in groups to analyse the difference between the story and play versions of *The Tale of Hansel and Gretel*.
  OOO Compare Scene 3 of the play with pages 3–8 and complete 'Making comparisons' (PCM 5.5).
  OO Compare Scene 2 with pages 1–3 and complete PCM 5.5. (T+)
  O Compare Scene 4 with page 8 and complete 'Plays and stories' (PCM 5.6). (TA+)

Plenary

• Take feedback from each group and highlight the differences between the story and the play script on ITP 5.5.
• Recap the learning objectives.

Assessment pointers

• S&L: oral readings will show how far the children can interpret the text through speech.
• AF4 (R): group work, plenary and PCMs show how far the children can comment on the structure and organisation of texts.

PHASE 2: CAPTURING IDEAS (7 DAYS)

Session 5

We are learning to ...	Resources
• understand how and why characters change • explore how film directors use film techniques to tell us about characters (PNS Strands 7.2, 8.3) **Assessment Focuses** AF (R): 3, 5	*Dragon Slayer* (film) ITP: 5.6, 5.7, 5.8 PCM: 5.7

Shared teaching

• Explain that the children have been studying how play scripts are set out, in order to write their own scenes based on *Dragon Slayer*.
• Explain that they first need to explore the characters and their relationships in more detail. Share the learning objectives and explain that they will be focusing on how the thoughts and feelings of the dragon slayer, the horse and the baby dragon change through one scene, and how the director helped us to know this.
• Watch the film *Dragon Slayer*.
• Show 'Story hand' (ITP 5.6) to recall the main points of the film. The children can follow along on their own hands.
• Discuss how the film told the story. *Was there any dialogue in the film? How did we know what was happening? What techniques did the director use to help us?* (pictures at the beginning and the use of camera shots to reveal characters' actions, thoughts and feelings)
• Remind the children of the work done earlier in Unit 2. *What different camera shots can you remember?* Show 'Camera shots' (ITP 5.7) and review the different terminology.
• Show 'Actions and feelings' (ITP 5.8) and explain the headings.
• Watch the film from the beginning to Marker 1. Talk Partners discuss the dragon slayer's actions and feelings and how they know what his

feelings are, e.g. what techniques the director uses to tell us, such as particular camera shots. Encourage the children to share their ideas and use Modelled Writing to show how to fill in information about 'Clip 1' on ITP 5.8 for the dragon slayer.

Independent and Guided

• The children work in groups, each focusing on a different character to complete 'Actions and feelings' (PCM 5.7). Within the groups the children work in pairs, one focusing on actions and the other on feelings. Both pairs think about the film technique, e.g. close-up shots, music, etc. Show the film from Marker 1 to Marker 3, Marker 3 to Marker 5 and Marker 5 to Marker 7, allowing time after each clip for pairs to make notes.
  OOO Complete PCM 5.7 for the baby dragon. The baby dragon doesn't feature in Clip 2.
  OO Complete PCM 5.7 for the dragon slayer. (T+)
  O Complete PCM 5.7 for the horse. (TA+)

Plenary

• Recap the learning objectives. *What have you learnt about your character? How did the film director help you know this? How did your character's feelings change through the scenes? Did all the characters change through the scenes? Who changed the least and who changed the most?*
• Create Role on the Walls for the characters.

Assessment pointers

• AF3 (R): responses in group work and completed PCMs will show how far the children can make inferences about characters' emotions.
• AF5 (R): responses also show how far the children can engage with the use of film techniques and the effect on the audience.

Session 6

We are learning to ...
- discuss the text, giving reasons for our views
- understand how and why characters change
- write brief character profiles
  (PNS Strands 1.3, 7.2)

Assessment Focuses
AF (R): 3

Resources
Dragon Slayer (film)
ITP: (5.8) 5.9
PCM: (5.7), 5.8

Shared teaching (1)
- Recall 'Actions and feelings' (ITP 5.8) to recap the key points, focusing on the thoughts and feelings in the three clips from Markers 1 to 7.
- Share the learning objectives. Show 'Character ratings' (ITP 5.9) and explain that we're going to focus on the dragon when we first see it. Tick 'Beginning'. Encourage the children to suggest where to mark on each scale, explaining their ideas with reference to the film.
- Explain that most of the pairs of adjectives are opposites and that sometimes both could describe a character at different times, e.g. the dragon happily scratching its back, then fighting the dragon slayer.
- Refer back to ITP 5.8 and explain that it is important to justify choices by referencing the film in the space below each pair of words. Use Modelled Writing to write this for the dragon slayer.

Independent and Guided (1)
- The children work in the same pairs as in Session 5 to complete 'Character ratings' (PCM 5.8) for their character. Encourage the children to refer to completed 'Actions and feelings' (PCM 5.7).
  - **ᴏᴏᴏ** Pairs complete PCM 5.8 twice for the baby dragon: once for the scene from Marker 2 to Marker 4 (Beginning) and again from Marker 4 to Marker 7 (End), either doing one each, or working jointly on both.
  - **ᴏᴏ** As above but for the dragon slayer. (T+)

- **ᴏ** As above but for the horse. (TA+)

Shared teaching (2)
- Encourage pairs to share their ideas with the class. *What ratings did you give your character?*
- Use Modelled Writing to show how to turn the information on the charts into sentences showing how a character has experienced a range of emotions in the scene, e.g. *At the beginning the dragon slayer was very brave because he fought the huge dragon. After he had killed the dragon he seemed sad because he went quiet and stared at it for a long time.*
- Draw attention to the use of conjunctions such as 'because' and connectives like 'after'.

Independent and Guided (2)
- The children use completed PCM 5.8 to write character profiles showing the range of emotions their character has experienced.
  - **ᴏᴏᴏ** Write a brief character profile using conjunctions and connectives.
  - **ᴏᴏ** As above. (T+)
  - **ᴏ** Write simple sentences about their character. (TA+)

Plenary
- Set up a whole-class Hot-Seating activity, inviting the children to take on the roles of the dragon slayer, horse and baby dragon. Encourage the other children to ask questions using their character profiles.
- Recap the learning objectives. *Which character changed the most?*

Assessment pointers
- S&L: hot-seating will show how far the children can sustain roles and recount ideas.
- AF3 (R): completed PCMs and response to questions will show how far the children are able to understand implied feelings.

Session 7

We are learning to ...
- listen and respond to others
- explore the relationships between characters
  (PNS Strands 2.1, 7.2)

Assessment Focuses
AF (R): 3

Resources
Dragon Slayer (film)
ITP: 5.10
PCM: 5.9, 5.10

Shared teaching
- Share the learning objectives, reminding the children that in Session 6 they looked at the characters' thoughts and feelings. Explain that today, they are going to look at the characters and what they think about each other.
- Show 'Character relationships' (ITP 5.10) and focus on Screen 1. Divide the class in two and within that into Talk Partners. One group discusses what they think the dragon slayer thinks about the horse and the other group discusses what the horse thinks about the dragon slayer.
- Take feedback and choose two thoughts to add to ITP 5.10.
- Scribe a few sentences to sum up thoughts at this point, e.g. *The dragon slayer hopes that his horse will watch the battle and be impressed with his strength. However, the horse is not really interested and prefers to eat grass instead. This makes the dragon slayer annoyed.*
- Go to Screen 2. Talk Partners discuss what the dragon slayer and the horse think about each other at this point. Encourage the children to suggest ideas and add to the thought bubbles. Again scribe sentences to summarise the characters' thoughts about each other.

Independent and Guided
- The children watch the film from Marker 1 to Marker 7. Pause at key points to allow the children time to complete the PCMs. Then the children Think-Pair-Share their completed PCMs.
  - **ᴏᴏᴏ** Complete 'Character relationships' (PCM 5.9). (T+)
  - **ᴏᴏ** Complete 'What are they thinking?' (PCM 5.10).
  - **ᴏ** As above. (TA+)

Plenary
- Recap the learning objectives.
- Role Play the moment when the dragon slayer tries to push the horse, asking either a child or teaching assistant to take one of the roles, e.g. dragon slayer: *Whatever is the matter with this animal? Come on, move!;* horse: *He can push all he likes. I'm not budging!*
- Encourage pairs to act out different moments in the last scene, using their work on the characters' thoughts.

Assessment pointers
- S&L: role plays will show how well the children can convey ideas about characters through speech and gesture.
- AF3 (R): responses to questions and PCMs show how far the children can make inferences about characters and their relationships.

We are learning to ...	**Resources**
• listen and respond to others • use hot-seating to explore characters' views and feelings • put ourselves in the role of a character to help us understand their feelings, thoughts and actions (PNS learning objectives 2.1, 4.2, 8.2) **Assessment Focuses** AF (R): 3	PCM: (5.9, 5.10)

Shared teaching (1)

• Share the learning objectives and explain that the children are going to explore the character of the dragon slayer. *What can you remember about the dragon slayer? Do you have any questions about him?* (E.g. *Why didn't he seem pleased when he had killed the dragon?*)
• Talk Partners discuss any puzzles about the dragon slayer they would like to know the answers to. If necessary, refer the children to completed 'Character relationships' (PCM 5.9) or 'What are they thinking?' (PCM 5.10) for ideas. Take feedback and scribe some responses.
• Demonstrate the difference between open questions ('why', 'what', 'how') and closed questions (those with yes/no answers).
• Use Modelled Writing to show a few possible open questions about the dragon slayer, e.g. *How long have you been a dragon slayer? Who taught you to fight?* Encourage the children to formulate their own open questions.

Independent and Guided (1)

• The children work in pairs to think of at least three questions to ask the dragon slayer. They check to make sure that they are 'open' questions

and write them down on separate pieces of paper. Support the children with an identified need. (T/TA)

Shared teaching (2)

• Act as Teacher in Role and explain that you will be taking the role of the dragon slayer. Use a prop (helmet, toy sword, etc.) to show when you are in role and when you are yourself again.
• Step into role. Encourage the children to ask their questions and model answering in role.

Independent and Guided (2)

• The children work in the same pairs to discuss possible answers that the dragon slayer could give to their questions and write these on the back of the questions. They then use Hot-Seating, taking it in turns to be the dragon slayer and the questioner. Encourage the children to use all their knowledge of the dragon slayer so far to inform their role play. Support the children with an identified need. (T/TA)

Plenary

• Explain that the children are now going to find out even more about the character of the dragon slayer.
• Invite pairs who worked particularly well together to perform their hot-seating.
• Recap the learning objectives. *What do you think were good questions? What have you learned about the dragon slayer?*

Assessment pointers

• S&L: drama activites will show how far the children can sustain roles and understand the characters.
• AF3 (R): hot-seating activity will show how far the children can make inferences about characters and their feelings.

We are learning to ...	**Resources**
• listen and respond to others • use hot-seating to explore characters' thoughts and feelings • put ourselves in the role of characters to help us understand their feelings, thoughts and actions (PNS Strands 2.1, 4.2, 8.2) **Assessment Focuses** AF (R): 3	PCM: (5.9, 5.10)

Shared teaching

• Share the learning objectives. Explain that in Session 8 the children explored the character of the dragon slayer, but today they are going to think about the horse and the baby dragon. *Is there anything you would like to know about these characters?*
• Talk Partners discuss any puzzles they have about the horse, e.g. *How and when did the horse first meet the dragon slayer? What does the horse think about killing dragons? Why did the horse refuse to move when the dragon slayer wanted to leave? Had he ever been stubborn before?* If necessary, refer the children to completed 'Character relationships' (PCM 5.9) or 'What are they thinking?' (PCM 5.10) for ideas. Remind the children to ask open questions. Take feedback and scribe some possible questions.
• Talk Partners discuss puzzles about the baby dragon, e.g. *How did it feel when it couldn't wake its mother up? Where is its father? What did it think about riding on a horse?* Take feedback and scribe a few possible questions.
• Focus on the list of questions. Encourage the children to think of possible answers. *How would the character answer the question?*

What might they say? How do you think they would say it? Encourage the children to use their knowledge from the *Dragon Slayer* film and previous sessions to support their ideas.

Independent and Guided

• Divide the class into two groups: one focusing on the baby dragon and the other on the horse. In pairs within the groups, the children plan and write questions to ask the other group about that group's character. They then discuss how their own character might respond to questions the other group might ask. Place pairs together, one from each group to do a Hot-Seating activity, taking it in turns to answer questions in role. Support the children with an identified need. (T+/TA+)

Plenary

• Recap the learning objectives and encourage pairs to give feedback. *What interesting questions did they ask you? What interesting answers did they give you? Is there anything still puzzling you about the characters? Which character interests you the most?*

Assessment pointers

• S&L: hot-seating will show how far the children can sustain roles to explore ideas and listen and respond to others.
• AF3 (R): written questions and answers will show how far the children can make inferences about how characters think and feel.

We are learning to …
- use drama to explore characters' thoughts and feelings
- understand a character's thoughts and feelings (PNS Strands 4.2, 7.2)

Assessment Focuses
AF (R): 3

Resources
Dragon Slayer (film)
PCM: 5.11

Shared teaching

- Share the learning objective and explain that the children are going to explore what the characters might have said to one another at different points in the film.
- Go to *Dragon Slayer* Marker 3 and pause the film. Talk Partners discuss the dragon slayer at this point in the film. *What do you think he is feeling? What do you think he might have said?*
- Return to the paused screen of *Dragon Slayer*. Encourage pairs to suggest dialogue for the dragon slayer and use it to annotate the image on the screen.
- Invite the children to speak the words as the dragon slayer might have said them, discussing tone and expression. *How did the dragon slayer feel? How would he have said the line?* Take suggestions and demonstrate how to scribe this.
- Pairs Freeze Frame the scene: one child positions the other child as the dragon slayer. On the command *Freeze!* the 'dragon slayers' hold their positions as the 'sculptors' form a circle around them and move clockwise around the group to look at all of them.
- Ask the 'sculptors' to stand still. Thought Track the dragon slayer, asking the 'sculptors' for suggestions as to what the dragon slayer could be thinking at this moment in time, and what he would say. Scribe the children's ideas. *How would the dragon slayer say this?*

- Go to Marker 4 and pause the film. Talk Partners discuss how to Freeze Frame this scene and what the characters might be thinking.
- Invite four children to create the Freeze Frame and encourage the children to Thought Track the characters, with one child as sculptor.

Independent and Guided

- The children work in groups of three to Freeze Frame scenes from *Dragon Slayer*. Explain that the picture is a starting point and they should think about what the other characters, the baby dragon, the horse and the dragon slayer, are doing at each point. Encourage the children to think about the characters' thoughts.
- 🔵🔵🔵 Use Part A of 'Freeze!' (PCM 5.11). (TA+)
- 🔵🔵 Use Part B of 'Freeze!' (PCM 5.11).
- 🔵 As above. (T)

Plenary

- Recap the learning objective. *What new things did you learn about the character? How well did you work as a group?*
- Ask groups to show their freeze frames and explain their characters' thoughts and what they might say. Encourage the children to offer feedback. *What did you like about their freeze frame? Do you agree with what the characters are thinking? Is there anything you think could be improved?*

Assessment pointers

- S&L: freeze frames will show how far the children can create roles to explore different viewpoints and comment constructively on each other's performances.
- AF3 (R): performances and evaluation discussions will show how far the children can make inferences about characters through freeze frame and thought tracking.

We are learning to …
- prepare and rehearse scripts for performance
- include dialogue, stage directions and sound effects
- perform dialogue with expression and actions to engage the audience (PNS Strands 1.1, 4.1)

Assessment Focuses
AF (R): 3

Resources
Dragon Slayer (film)
PCM: 5.12, 5.13

Shared teaching (1)

- Share the learning objectives and explain that today, the children will think about dialogue and stage directions for *Dragon Slayer*.
- Go to Marker 1 of *Dragon Slayer*. Explain that in plays, characters often think aloud so the audience know what they are thinking. Talk Partners discuss what the dragon slayer might think aloud at this moment.
- Take feedback and scribe ideas in speech bubbles on the paused screen. Encourage the children to speak the words as the dragon slayer might say them, focusing on tone of voice and expression.
- Use Modelled Writing to add stage directions. Encourage the children to offer suggestions. *What powerful verbs can you think of?* (E.g. 'strode' instead of 'walked'.)

Independent and Guided (1)

- The children work in small groups to complete 'The dragon slayer' (PCM 5.12). Encourage the children to think about expression, character actions (using powerful verbs) and sound effects. The children then take turns to Role Play the scene.
- 🔵🔵🔵 Complete Question 1 on PCM 5.12. (TA+)
- 🔵🔵 Complete Question 2 on PCM 5.12.

- 🔵 As above. (T+)

Shared teaching (2)

- Watch *Dragon Slayer* and pause at 3 mins 3 s. *What would the dragon slayer say at this point?* Take feedback and add suggestions to the paused screen.
- *How would the dragon slayer say these lines?*. Take ideas and use Modelled Writing to add stage directions. *What sound effects could we add?*
- Watch from Marker 3 to Marker 4. Remind the children of the dilemma the dragon slayer faces as discussed in Unit 2.

Independent and Guided (2)

- The children work in groups to complete 'A dilemma' (PCM 5.13). They then Role Play the dilemma. Support the children with an identified need. (T/TA)

Plenary

- Invite groups to perform their scenes. During each performance ask the other children to make notes, focusing on dialogue and expression.
- Take feedback after each performance. *What did you like most about their performance? What do you think they could improve?*
- Recap the learning objectives.

Assessment pointers

- S&L: role plays will show how well the children can convey ideas about characters through speech and gesture.
- AF3 (R): talk partner work, group work and performances will show how far the children are able to interpret characters' thoughts and feelings, based on what they know about the text.

Session 12

We are learning to ...	Resources
• include dialogue, stage directions and sound effects • write a play script • use play script conventions (PNS Strands 1.1, 9.2, 9.5) **Assessment Focuses** AF (W): 2, 3, 5, 7	*Dragon Slayer* (film) ITP: (5.5), 5.11, 5.12 PCM: (5.13), 5.14

Shared teaching

• Share the learning objectives.
• Remind the children of the work they did in Session 4. *What are the features of a play script? How is it different to a story?* (E.g. there is much more dialogue in a play.) Allow Think Time before taking responses. If necessary, recall 'Stories and plays' (ITP 5.5).
• Show 'Writing a play' (ITP 5.11) and discuss the success criteria. Add the children's suggestions for further success criteria.
• Watch *Dragon Slayer* from the beginning to Marker 1. Show 'Writing a play script' (ITP 5.12) and use Modelled Writing to turn this scene into a play script. Include the title of the scene, e.g. Scene 1; character names, a narrator to briefly sum up the background to the scene, dialogue and strong verbs.
• Watch *Dragon Slayer* from Marker 1 to Marker 2. Talk Partners discuss how to set this out as a play script. *What might the dragon slayer say to the horse? How might he say it? What stage directions are needed?*
• Take feedback and scribe ideas for the next part of the script on ITP 5.12. Remind the children of the key features of a script as you write. Encourage the children to suggest improvements as you work through the script. *What stage direction could we add here? What powerful verbs could we use? Have we done everything on the list of success criteria?*

Independent and guided

• The children work independently, using annotated 'A dilemma' (PCM 5.13) and 'A play script' (PCM 5.14) to begin writing their own play script for *Dragon Slayer*. Encourage the children to refer to the success criteria on ITP 5.11. Support the children with an identified need, e.g. with the use of powerful verbs or the incorporation of stage directions, actions, sound effects, etc. (T/TA)

Plenary

• Recap the learning objectives.
• Remind the class of the agreed success criteria for writing plays. *Are there any new points you would like to add to this now?*
• Talk Partners share their plays and evaluate these against the success criteria. They write Two Stars and a Wish about their own plays in light of their partner's feedback.
• Take feedback. *What do you think is effective about your play? What would you like to change? What feedback did your partner give you?*
• Take in the children's work and note positive points and any areas for improvement.

Assessment pointers

• S&L: pair work will show how well the children can express and explain relevant ideas.
• AF2, 3 (W): response to questions, play scripts and evaluation using success criteria show how far the children can organise and produce texts appropriate to task.
• AF5, 7 (W): play scripts and response to questions show how far the children are able to construct varied sentences using effective vocabulary.

Session 13

We are learning to ...	Resources
• work with an editing partner to improve our writing • edit writing to make it more effective (PNS Strands 9.1) **Assessment Focuses** AF (W): 2, 3	ITP: (5.11) PCM: (5.14)

Shared teaching

• Recap Session 12 and remind the children of their two stars and a wish.
• Share the learning objectives and explain that today, the children are going to use feedback to improve their scripts.
• Display one of the children's play scripts from Session 12 that contains positive points and some areas for development.
• Recall 'Writing a play' (ITP 5.11) and remind the children of the success criteria. *Are there any points you would like to add to the list or change?*
• Talk Partners refer to the success criteria and identify one positive point in the child's play script you have shown them and one area that could be improved.
• Take feedback and encourage the children to explain their comments, offering ideas for how to improve the play scripts. Emphasise positive and constructive feedback and model how to give it, e.g. *You have set out the play very well but you have forgotten to start each speech on a new line.*
• Use Modelled Writing to improve aspects of the play script. *Is there any punctuation we need to add? Could we use more powerful verbs anywhere? Is there any dialogue we could add? How do you think the character would say that?*

Independent and Guided

• The children work independently, using the feedback from Session 12 to make changes to their annotated 'A play script' (PCM 5.14). Encourage the children to refer to the success criteria on ITP 5.11 when revising their text. Pairs then share the changes they have made and discuss further improvements. Allow the children time to make more alterations to their play scripts. Support the children with an identified need. (T+/TA+)

Plenary

• Recap the learning objectives and invite the children to give feedback. *What changes did you make to your play? How has this improved your play script? What feedback did your partner give you?*
• Ask the children to set a target for improvement in Session 14.

Assessment pointers

• S&L: pair work will show how sensitively the children can express and respond to opinions.
• AF2, 3 (W): play scripts and evaluation show how far the children can organise and produce texts appropriate to task.

We are learning to ...	Resources
• prepare and rehearse scripts for performance • investigate the impact of using props, gesture and dialogue • use talk to organise roles and action • perform dialogue with expression and actions to engage the audience (PNS Strands 1.1, 3.1, 4.1) **Assessment Focuses** AF (W): 3	ITP: (5.12), 5.13

Shared teaching (1)

• Share the learning objectives and explain that the children are going to prepare plays for performance, focusing on dialogue, actions, gesture and use of props.
• Show 'Performing a play' (ITP 5.13) and discuss the success criteria. *Can you think of any other criteria to add to the list?* Save annotations.
• Recall annotated 'A play script' (ITP 5.12). Divide the class into groups and allocate parts for a first read-through. Encourage the children to read expressively, using the stage directions.
• Encourage the children to comment on their performance. *What did you think you read well? Are there any improvements you could make?*

Independent and Guided (1)

• The children work in small groups to develop the script from ITP 5.12. Half of the groups focus on how the dialogue could be spoken and the other half on the actions, gesture and use of props (real or imaginary), that could be used. Support the children with an identified need. (T/TA)

Shared teaching (2)

• Show ITP 5.13 and focus on the criteria referring to dialogue.

• Select a 'dialogue' group to perform for the class. The audience listen for performances that convey the appropriate emotions. Model how to give feedback, e.g. *I could tell that the dragon slayer was feeling a little bit tired and sad because you made their voice sound really weary.*
• Explain that tone of voice is important because it conveys a lot of information to the audience and keeps them interested.
• Repeat the process with a group that focused on gesture, action or props and invite feedback. This time the audience look for performances that use effective gestures, actions or props. E.g. *Your face told us that he was surprised and I liked the way you shrugged your shoulders to show that you were sad but it had to be done.*
• Explain that facial expression is also very important when performing. *What does your face do when you are sad, happy or angry?*

Independent and Guided (2)

• Small groups use one of their play scripts from Sessions 12 and 13. They allocate roles, think about appropriate gestures, facial expressions and actions, decide on props and prepare their performance. Support the children with an identified need. (T/TA)

Plenary

• Recap the learning objectives. *What have you learnt about developing a performance?*
• Talk Partners identify one area (dialogue, gesture, props) that they feel they have used successfully to convey emotion and one area in which they feel they could improve. Take feedback and save responses.

Assessment pointers

• S&L: group work will show how well the children can adopt group roles, drawing together and promoting effective planning.
• AF3 (W): play scripts will show how well the children can organise and structure their writing to aid their performances.

We are learning to ...	Resources
• prepare and rehearse scripts for performance • investigate the impact of using props, gesture and dialogue • use talk to organise roles and action (PNS learning objectives 1.1, 3.1, 4.1) **Assessment Focuses** AF (R): 3; AF (W): 3	ITP: (5.13)

Shared teaching (1)

• Share the learning objectives and explain that groups will complete the preparation of their play scripts in order to perform for the class or a parallel class.
• Recall 'Performing a play' (ITP 5.13) and remind the children of the success criteria.
• Recap the plenary of Session 14. *What do you think you did well? What did you find hard?*
• Talk Partners discuss the things they found difficult, e.g. expressing the horse's emotions, and try to think of solutions to the problems.
• Take feedback and encourage the children to offer suggestions for possible solutions, e.g. *The horse doesn't always have to speak but he could use his face to show that he is cross, or toss his head up and down.*

Independent and Guided

• Working in the same groups as Session 14, the children make final changes to their script and then act it out. As the children work through the script, Freeze Frame and explore the characters' thoughts and feelings. Circulate looking for evidence that children are trying out

and discussing the effectiveness of various techniques. Support the children with an identified need. (T/TA)

Shared teaching (2)

• The groups perform their plays. Remind the class of the success criteria and assign groups particular things to look for during the performance, e.g. use of expressive dialogue, actions, gesture, props (if used).
• Model how to give positive and constructive feedback, e.g. *I like the way you ... ; I wonder if you have thought of ... ; I thought you showed how they were feeling very well; I'm not sure the prop was really helpful.*
• Encourage the class to offer feedback on the performances, balancing positive and constructive criticism.

Plenary

• Recap the learning objectives and encourage the children to identify good points and one or two things that could be improved, referring to the success criteria on ITP 5.13.
• Discuss the evaluations. *What positive comments were most useful? How did you feel when someone said that something could be improved about your performance? What do you think is the best way of making a constructive comment?*

Assessment pointers

• S&L: group work will show how far the children can manage discussion and feed back with sensitivity.
• AF3 (R): group work will show how well the children are able to infer characters' feelings from what they know about a text.
• AF3 (W): play scripts will show how well the children can organise and structure their writing to aid their performances.

Session 16

<table>
<tr><td colspan="2">

We are learning to ...
- develop ideas for writing
- plan the main events using storyboards
  (PNS Strands 9.1, 9.2)

Assessment Focuses
AF (W): 1, 2

</td><td>

Resources
Dragon Slayer (film)
ITP: 5.14, 5.15
PCM: 5.15

</td></tr>
</table>

Shared teaching

- Share the learning objectives and explain that the children are going to think about what might happen next in the dragon slayer's story.
- Watch *Dragon Slayer* from Marker 7 to the end of the film. Discuss what ideas this gives them about what might have happened next.
- Talk Partners discuss other things that could happen, both good things and possible problems. *How might the dragons be helpful? What problems could they cause? What training or care might they need?* Take feedback and add responses to the Learning Wall.
- Show '*Tracking and Taming Dragons*' (ITP 5.14). Explain any unfamiliar words, e.g. 'dominance', 'fatality', 'stock-in-trade', etc. Pay particular attention to the diagram showing dragon-training equipment.
- Talk Partners discuss any further ideas that this extract has given them about how the dragon slayer's story might continue. Take feedback and add any new ideas to the Learning Wall.
- Explain that the children are going to use these ideas and their own ideas to create storyboards of what might happen next. This will help them to write a final scene for their play script.
- Show 'Storyboard' (ITP 5.15). *What might the previous picture have been?* (E.g. the dragon slayer buying the forge with the money raised from dragon slaying.) *What might the next picture be?* (E.g. customers buying items made at the forge and no longer fearing dragons.)

Encourage the children to offer suggestions and add notes to ITP 5.15. Explain that you have written notes to describe the scene, but that the children will draw pictures.

Independent and Guided

- Using 'Storyboard' (PCM 5.15) the children work independently to plan a continuation of the dragon slayer's story, focusing only on drawing the scenes.
- **∞** Complete all five squares.
- **∞** Complete four squares. (TA+)
- **◉** Complete three squares. (T+)

Plenary

- Recap the learning objectives.
- Talk Partners share their storyboards and describe what is going to happen next. *How successful are your partner's ideas? Are the ideas clear? Will they interest the audience? Is there anything that surprised or puzzled you?*
- If there is time, the children reflect on their own storyboards, thinking about what has worked well and what might need to be altered.

Assessment pointers

- S&L: pair work will show how sensitively the children can express and respond to ideas.
- AF1, 2 (W): group work and PCMs show how far the children can plan imaginative texts, thinking about audience and purpose.

Session 17

<table>
<tr><td colspan="2">

We are learning to ...
- use a storyboard to develop ideas
- annotate our storyboards with dialogue, stage directions and sound effects
  (PNS Strands 9.5)

Assessment Focuses
AF (W): 7

</td><td>

Resources
ITP: (5.11, 5.15)
PCM: (5.15)

</td></tr>
</table>

Shared teaching

- Share the learning objectives and explain that in this session, the children will begin to plan play scripts based on their storyboards from Session 16.
- Recall annotated 'Writing a play' (ITP 5.11) and remind the children of the success criteria.
- Recall 'Storyboard' (ITP 5.15). *What do you think the characters are saying in the middle picture?* Allow Think Time before taking feedback and adding dialogue in the box under the picture.
- Encourage the children to speak the words as the characters might say them, focusing on tone and expression. Use Modelled Writing to add this detail to ITP 5.15, e.g. *The dragon slayer bellowed happily.* Remind the children to think of powerful verbs for characters' actions.
- Use Modelled Writing to show how to indicate an action, e.g. (*Striking his hammer against the horseshoe.*)

Independent and Guided

- The children work independently to develop 'Storyboard' (PCM 5.15) to continue the story, focusing on adding notes about dialogue, character actions (using powerful verbs) and sound effects. Support the children with an identified need. (T/TA)

Plenary

- Recap the learning objectives. *Have you used appropriate dialogue for your characters? Have you included stage directions? Have you used powerful verbs?*
- Talk Partners share their storyboards and offer positive and constructive feedback, referring to the success criteria.
- Invite pairs to share their storyboards and to discuss the comments they gave each other.

Assessment pointers

- S&L: pair work will show how far the children can listen and respond to others.
- AF7 (W): storyboard annotations show how far the children can select appropriate vocabulary for dialogue and stage directions.

Session 18

<table>
<tr><td colspan="2">

We are learning to ...
- write a play script
- choose powerful verbs and adjectives
- use play script conventions
  (PNS Strands 9.2, 9.4, 9.5)

Assessment Focuses
AF (W): 2, 3, 7
</td><td>

Resources
ITP: (5.11, 5.12, 5.15)
PCM: (5.14, 5.15)
</td></tr>
</table>

Shared teaching

- Share the learning objectives and remind the children of the feedback they discussed in the plenary of Session 17. Explain that today, they are going to turn their storyboards into play scripts incorporating their feedback from Session 17.
- Remind the children of what needs to be included in the play script, using annotated 'Writing a play' (ITP 5.11) and 'A play script' (ITP 5.12).
- Recall 'Storyboard' (ITP 5.15) and use Modelled Writing to turn the notes under the picture into a full play script, e.g. *Scene 1: The New Blacksmith's Forge. Narrator: After travelling far and wide, the dragon slayer and the baby dragons found a new home. The forge needed a lot of work but with his dragon slaying money they soon had the place looking wonderful.* Include a cast list at the beginning.
- Use Think Alouds to model orally rehearsing ideas to encourage the children to remind you of the correct formatting, e.g. characters' names on the left followed by a colon; stage directions and sound effects in brackets, etc. Also encourage them to suggest ideas for what the characters might say and do.
- Draw attention to the use of powerful verbs, e.g. *dragon slayer: (striking his hammer against the horseshoe).* Save the modelled script.
- Talk Partners discuss how to set out the next part of the play script.

What might the baby dragon say to the dragon slayer as it breathes fire to heat the metal? What stage directions are needed? (E.g. A loud roaring is heard as the flames heat up the metal.)

Independent and Guided

- The children work independently to write a play script based on their completed 'Storyboard' (PCM 5.15). Supply the children requiring additional support with a new copy of 'A play script' (PCM 5.14) to help them structure their writing. Support the children with an identified need. (T/TA)

Plenary

- Recap the learning objectives and remind the children of the success criteria on ITP 5.11.
- Talk Partners work together to evaluate their work against the success criteria, commenting on what is particularly effective and what could be improved or developed further.
- Encourage pairs to give feedback. *What do you like most about your partner's play script? What parts of the success criteria do they need to work on? Are there any problems you need help with?*
- Take in the children's work and review it in order to choose samples to display in Session 19.

Assessment pointers

- S&L: pair work will show how sensitively the children can express and respond to opinions.
- AF2, 3, 7 (W): play scripts show how far the children can organise texts appropriately, use effective vocabulary and produce texts appropriate to purpose.

Session 19

<table>
<tr><td colspan="2">

We are learning to ...
- evaluate writing using a marking ladder
- edit writing to make it more effective
  (PNS Strands 9.1)

Assessment Focuses
AF (W): 2, 3, 6, 7
</td><td>

Resources
ITP: 5.16
PCM: 5.16
</td></tr>
</table>

Shared teaching

- Share the learning objectives and explain that today, the children are going to use marking ladders to evaluate their work. Explain that the points on the marking ladder are taken from the success criteria, so if they have referred to the success criteria, the children should be able to tick a lot of the points on the marking ladder.
- Choose a sample of the children's work from Session 18 that contains positive points and areas for development and display so that all the children can view it.
- Show 'Marking ladder' (ITP 5.16). Model giving positive and constructive criticism, e.g. *They have included a title and cast list which is good but they have forgotten to use colons in the right place.* Use Modelled Writing to demonstrate adding notes to ITP 5.16.
- Talk Partners use the marking ladder to identify one positive point from the sample of writing and one area that could be improved.
- Take responses from the children and use several of their suggestions (choosing the most appropriate ideas) to model how to improve aspects of the writing.

Independent and Guided

- The children work with a partner to edit and improve their work using 'Marking ladder' (PCM 5.16) and their completed play scripts. Part way

through this activity, run a mini-plenary to discuss changes that the children are making, e.g. using a more powerful verb or adding a stage direction, action or sound effect and how this has improved the script. Support the children with an identified need. (T+/TA+)

Plenary

- Recap the learning objectives. Identify certain pairs to explain to the rest of the group how they have edited their work. *What areas do you think you have done well? What area did you decide needed improving? How have you improved it?*
- Encourage the rest of the class to evaluate the improvements against the marking ladder. *Has this improvement been successful? Are there any problems you need help with? Can anyone think of a way to resolve this?*

Assessment pointers

- S&L: pair work will show how well the children can express and explain relevant ideas.
- AF2, 3, 6, 7 (W): play scripts show how far the children can organise texts appropriately, use effective vocabulary, write accurately and produce texts appropriate to purpose.

We are learning to ...	Resources
• prepare and rehearse scripts for performance • use talk to organise roles and action • perform dialogue with expression and actions to engage the audience • discuss and evaluate each other's performance (PNS Strands 1.1, 3.1, 4.1, 4.3) **Assessment Focuses** AF (W): 3	ITP: (5.12, 5.13)

Shared teaching (1)

• Share the learning objectives and explain that today, the children are going to prepare to perform their play script for the rest of the class or a parallel class.
• Recall 'A play script' (ITP 5.12) or alternatively, display a script by one of the children as a shared model. *How might we perform this?* As in earlier sessions, focus on dialogue, expression, gesture and action, and the use of props.
• Recall 'Performing a play' (ITP 5.13) and remind the class of the success criteria. Focus on the use of dialogue first.
• Divide the class into groups and give each group a character to play. Read together, encouraging the children to think about expression and tone of voice as the groups read in unison.
• Encourage the children to evaluate the performance. *Do you think we read that well? How could we improve our performance?*

Independent and Guided

• The children work in groups of four to act out one of their play scripts. They work cooperatively to allocate roles, think about appropriate gestures, facial expression and actions, decide on props and prepare their performance. Support groups as necessary or work in a guided session with groups who would benefit from additional support. Support the children with an identified need. (T/TA)

Shared teaching (2)

• Assign groups of children different things to look for during the performances, e.g. the use of dialogue, actions, gesture, props.
• Remind the children of how to give both positive and constructive feedback, e.g. *I like the way you ... ; I thought you showed how they were feeling; Perhaps you could consider ... .*
• Organise the groups to present their performances.
• After each performance, ask the children to identify Two Stars and a Wish for the group. Encourage the children to make constructive comments referring to the success criteria.
• Scribe responses under headings according to the focuses of the group, e.g. dialogue, actions, etc.

Plenary

• Recap the learning objectives.
• Prompt the class to think about the evaluations made about the performances. *What positive comments were the most useful? How did you feel when someone said that something could be improved about your performance? What do you think is the best way of making a point about something that could be improved?*
• Recap the unit as a whole. *What did you enjoy most about this unit? What did you find hard at the beginning that is easier now? Are there still things you find hard?*

Assessment pointers

• S&L: group work and dramatisations will show how well the children can adopt group roles, create and sustain characters and listen and respond to others.
• AF3 (W): play scripts will show how well the children can organise and structure their writing to aid their performances.

Target board

Write the words to describe your character on the target.

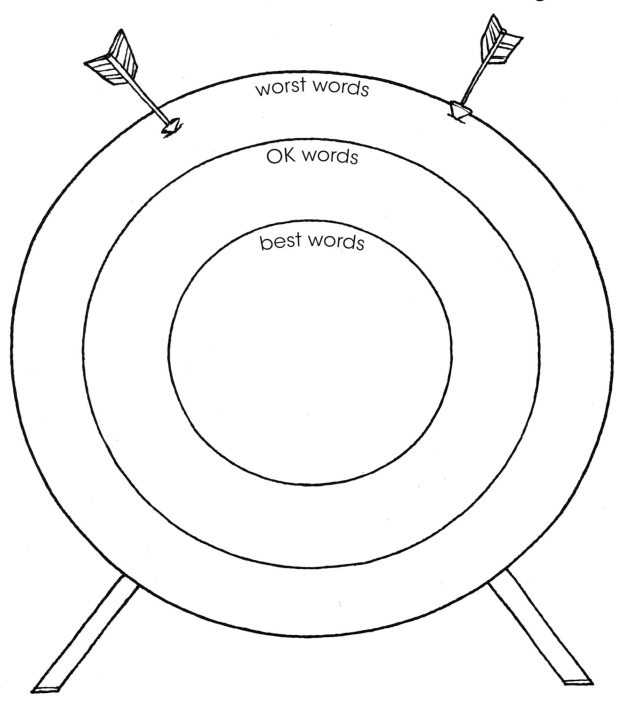

worst words

OK words

best words

| poor | rich | greedy | wicked | kind |
| sad | happy | frightened | clever | brave |

Writing speech 1

Re-write the words as direct speech, adding who is speaking and how.

I'm always so hungry!

"I'm always so hungry!" moaned the

stepmother. _____

Then there will be more food for us!

_____
_____

You have to get *into* the oven to check how hot it is.

_____
_____

I have a plan!

_____
_____

Don't worry. I left a trail of breadcrumbs behind us.

_____
_____

Now all our troubles are over.

_____
_____

Oh no! You're not a kind old woman after all!

_____
_____

Come inside, children, I will feed you properly, and then you can rest.

_____
_____

Writing speech 2

Re-write the words as direct speech, adding who is speaking and how. Use the verbs to help you.

said	moaned	sighed	whispered
exclaimed	replied	shouted	cried

I'm always so hungry!   _____

_____

Then there will be more food for us!   _____

_____

Now all our troubles are over.   _____

_____

Don't worry. I left a trail of breadcrumbs behind us.   _____

_____

Oh no! You're not a kind old woman after all!   _____

_____

You have to get *into* the oven to check how hot it is.   _____

_____

Writing speech 3

Re-write the words as direct speech, adding who is speaking and how. Use the words to help you.

| cried Gretel | whispered Hansel | moaned step-mother | laughed father | cackled wicked witch |

I'm always so hungry!

_____

_____

_____

I have a plan!

_____

_____

_____

Now all our troubles are over.

_____

_____

_____

Oh no! You're not a kind old woman after all!

_____

_____

_____

Making comparisons

Compare the story and the playscript. Complete the table.

	Hansel and Gretel story	Hansel and Gretel playscript
Point 1	*Speech marks are used.*	*Speech marks are not used.*
Point 2		
Point 3		
Point 4		
Point 5		
Point 6		
Point 7		

Plays and stories

Tick whether the statements are true for the story or the play script of *Hansel and Gretel*.

	Story	Playscript
The names of the characters are written on the left-hand side.		✓
Speech marks are not used.		
A list of all the characters is included.		
A narrator explains things that happen.		
Information about how the character speaks is included in brackets.		
Information about what the character does is included in brackets.		
Speech marks are used to let the reader know the character is speaking.		
The name of the character is usually added after the speech marks.		
Description is used to let the reader know what is happening to a character or to describe the setting.		
Words like *said, shrieked, whispered,* are used after the speech marks to show how something is said.		

Actions and feelings

Complete the table about your character.

Character's name: _____

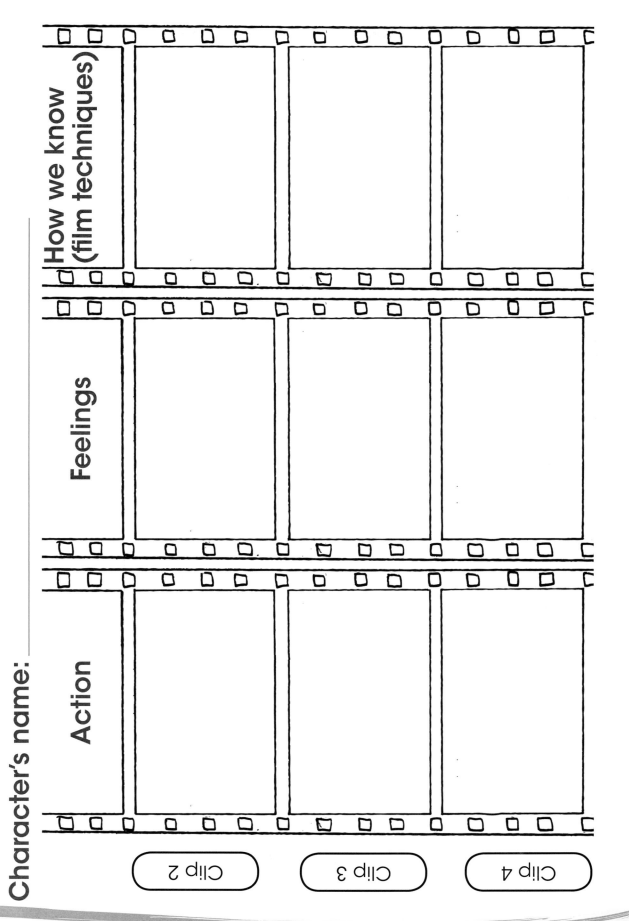

Action	Feelings	How we know (film techniques)

Clip 2

Clip 3

Clip 4

Character ratings

Tick your chosen character. Put a cross on each bar to describe them.

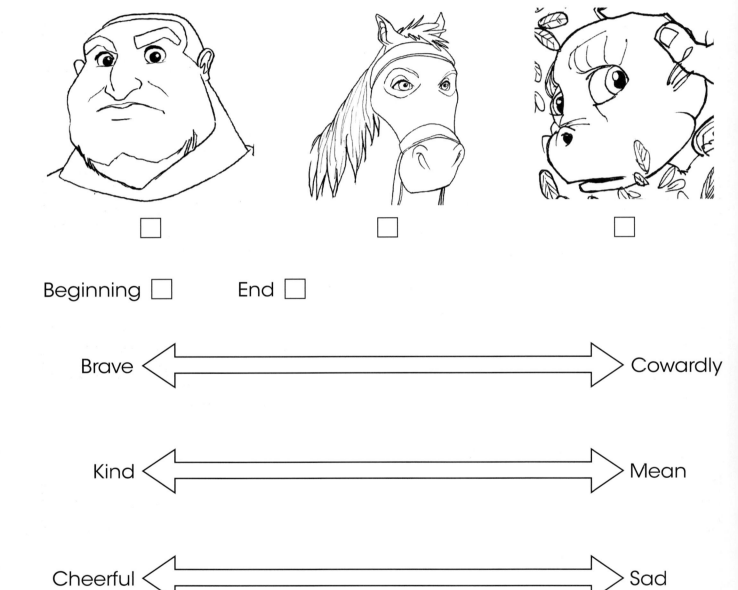

☐   ☐   ☐

Beginning ☐   End ☐

Brave ⟵————————————————————⟶ Cowardly

Kind ⟵————————————————————⟶ Mean

Cheerful ⟵————————————————————⟶ Sad

Surprised ⟵————————————————————⟶ Puzzled

Character relationships

1. Write what the characters think about each other during scene.

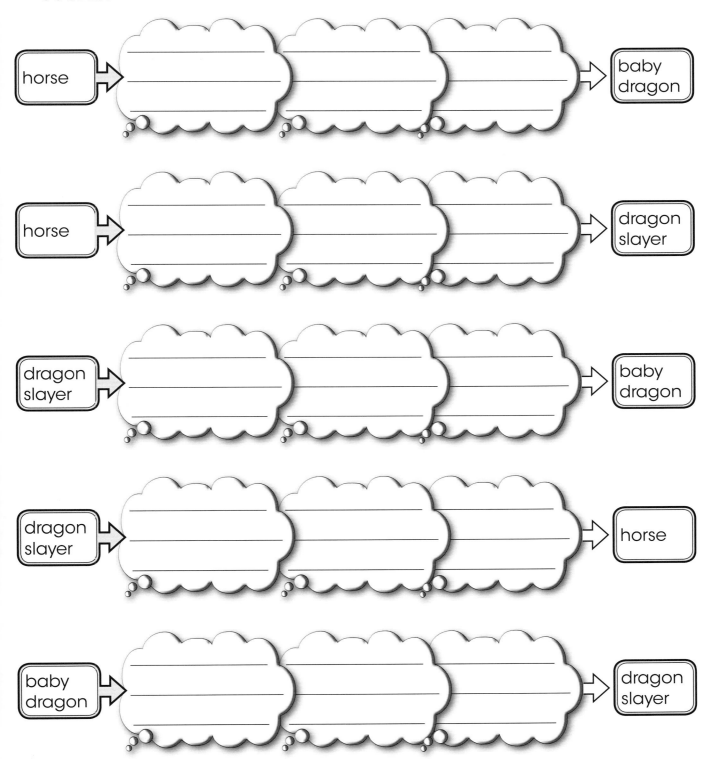

2. Whose thoughts changed the most? Why?

What are they thinking?

1. Write the dragon slayer's thoughts about the horse.

The horse eating the grass.
_____
_____
_____

The dragon slayer pushes the horse. _____
_____
_____

The dragon slayer puts the baby dragon on the horse's back.
_____
_____

Write your own idea for another moment here. _____
_____
_____

2. Write the horse's thoughts about the dragon slayer.

The dragon slayer hears a noise in the bushes. _____
_____
_____

The dragon slayer tries to frighten away the baby dragon. _____
_____
_____

The dragon slayer holds the Baby Dragon. _____
_____
_____

Write your own idea for another moment here. _____
_____
_____

Literacy Evolve Year 3 © Pearson Education 2009

Freeze!

Use the pictures to plan a freeze frame.

A

B

Name: _____ Date: _____

The dragon slayer

1. Write what he is thinking.

The dragon slayer has just killed the dragon and is weighing the gold.

2. Write what he is thinking.

The dragon slayer hears a noise.

A dilemma

Write what the characters might say and how they might say it.

Action	Speech	Stage directions
The dragon slayer hears a noise.	What was that?	He stops and turns round quickly.
The dragon slayer sees the baby dragon.		
The dragon slayer tries to scare the baby dragon away.		
The dragon slayer tries to leave but the horse won't move.		
The horse pushes the dragon slayer towards the baby dragon.		
The dragon slayer tries to be nice to the baby dragon.		
The baby dragon burns the dragon slayer.		
The baby dragon likes the dragon slayer.		

Literacy evolve

A play script

Use the frame to write your play script.

Title: _____

Cast

_____ : _____

_____ : _____

_____ : _____

Scene: _____

Narrator: _____

_____

_____

_____ : _____

_____ : _____

_____ : _____

_____ : _____

_____ : _____

_____ : _____

_____ : _____

_____ : _____

Storyboard

Draw pictures to continue the story. Add dialogue and stage directions.

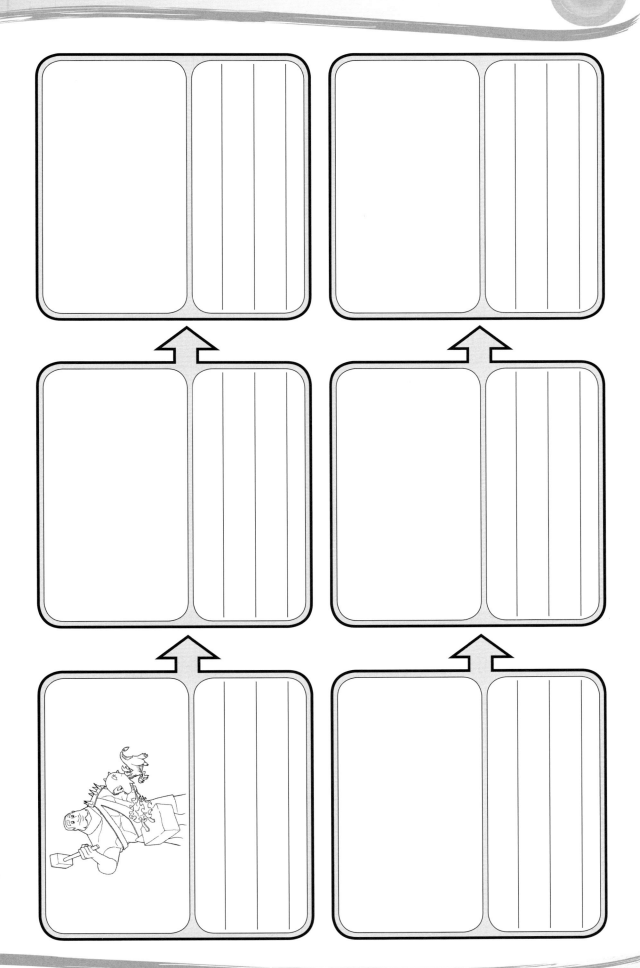

My play script

Use the marking ladder to check your work.

My comments		My partner's comments
	My playscript has got a title.	
	I have included a cast list.	
	I have written character names followed by a colon (:)	
	I have included stage directions.	
	I have used powerful verbs.	
	I have started each new speech on a new line.	

Poetry Unit 1

ROGER MCGOUGH/GINA DOUTHWAITE (Performance)

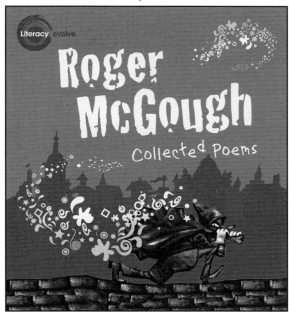 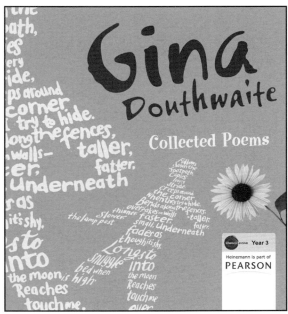

Medium term plan (1 week)	
Phase	**Learning Outcomes**
Phase 1: Familiarisation with the genre (2 days)	• Children can identify what makes a good performance poem. • Children can identify what makes a good performance of a poem. • Children can discuss and create different interpretations of how poems might be performed.
Phase 2: Capturing ideas: planning a performance poem (1 day)	• Children can develop ideas for a good performance poem. • Children can use their own experiences to create a performance poem.
Phase 3: Writing and performing a poem (2 days)	• Children can draft and refine their own performance poem. • Children can rehearse and participate in a performance of a poem, and can evaluate that performance.

ROGER MCGOUGH/GINA DOUTHWAITE

Big picture

The children explore the idea of performance poetry, watching and performing poems for themselves. Class discussion and modelled annotation of the poems helps draw together thoughts about how different poems can be performed. The children establish success criteria for performance poems and work in small groups to create their own, using a poem by Roger McGough as a model. They rehearse their final versions before performing them to the rest of the class.

Prior learning

This unit assumes that children can already:

• read poems for an audience, speaking with clarity and appropriate intonation
• work as a group to achieve a common task; listen to others; contribute ideas and reach agreement
• comment on the impact of particular words and phrases on the audience, with some awareness of how poets can vary these for different effects
• create their own poems, planning what to write and making choices about the words and phrases they use.

Key aspects of learning

Communication: Express themselves through group dialogue, writing and performance.

Creative thinking: Create their own interpretations of how poems could be performed. Write own poems, using language and performance techniques.
Self-awareness: Express preferences, likes and dislikes; be aware of themselves as performers, and as part of a group performance.
Social skills: Work collaboratively in small groups to create a performance. Plan together; decide roles; listen to others and resolve conflicts.

Progression in poetry

In this unit the children will:

• discuss the choice of words and their impact, noticing how the poet creates 'sound effects' by using alliteration, rhythm or rhyme and creates pictures using similes
• create own poems, using powerful adjectives and verbs
• perform individually or chorally; vary volume, experimenting with expression and use pauses for effect
• use actions, voices, sound effects and musical patterns to add to a performance.

Cross-curricular links

ICT: The children could use ICT to write and present their performance poems; they could film and review their poetry performances.

PHASE 1: FAMILIARISATION WITH THE GENRE (2 DAYS)

Session 1

We are learning to ...	Resources
• prepare and perform a poem • use talk to organise roles and action • understand what makes a good performance poem (PNS Strands 1.1, 3.1, 7.5) **Assessment Focuses** AF (R): 5	The Fight of the Year (film) Year 3 Poetry Collection ITP: P1.1

Shared teaching

• Explain that the children are going to be reading some performance poetry in this unit. *What do you think a performance poem is?* (A poem that needs to be read aloud or acted out in an interesting way to be fully enjoyed.) Discuss the differences between written and performance poems.
• Share the learning objectives.
• Watch *The Fight of the Year. What did you like about the performance?*
• Read *The Fight of the Year* by Roger McGough (page 7), with the children following in their own books.
• Check the children's comprehension. *What kind of sports commentary is the poem meant to sound like? What words or phrases give us clues that this is a boxing match? Why is the poem called* The Fight of the Year*? Why are there twelve rounds in this fight?* (12 months in the year) *Which round is this one?* (the third month: March)
• Talk about the lists of words and phrases used in the poem. *What title would you give to each list? Is the number of items in each list significant? Why are there ten in the final list?* (When the count gets to ten, as in a boxing match, winter is counted out and has lost the fight.)
• *What other things connected with spring could the poet have included*

in each list? What are 'bobtail clouds', 'scallywaggy winds' and 'a pavement artist'?
• Discuss performance poetry. *What features make this a good performance poem?* (E.g. the use of a sports commentator voice, the momentum created by the short words and phrases associated with spring, the occasional use of rhyme ('hounds'/'rounds', 'town'/'down', 'dinner'/'winner'.)
• Ask the children to read the poem again themselves. Think-Pair-Share how it could be performed by a small group rather than an individual person. Encourage the children to use 'Performance poetry' (ITP P1.1) to develop ideas.

Independent and Guided

• Small mixed ability groups rehearse a performance of *The Fight of the Year*. All group members should be involved in acting out or speaking the words. Stress that there must be no contact in the performances. If possible, make audio or video recordings to be played back to the class during the plenary. Support the children with an identified need. (T+/TA+)

Plenary

• Recap the learning objectives.
• Ask the groups to present their performances. If audio recordings or videos were made, review these as a group.
• Ask the children to use Two Stars and a Wish to evaluate their own performance and those of the other groups.

Assessment pointers

• S&L: group work and poetry performances will show how well the children effectively collaborate and understand the poem.
• AF5 (R): oral responses to the poem will show how far the children understand the poet's use of language.

We are learning to ...	Resources
• prepare and perform a poem • discuss and evaluate each other's performances • understand what makes a good performance poem (PNS Strands 1.1, 4.3, 7.5) **Assessment Focuses** AF (R): 5	*Bully Night* (film) *Year 3 Poetry Collection* ITP: (P1.1), P1.2

Shared teaching

• Share the learning objectives.
• Talk Partners share things they like and don't like about the night time.
• Take feedback. Watch *Bully Night*. What did you like about this performance? How did it make you feel?
• Read *Bully Night* by Roger McGough (page 6). *Why is the night like a bully? Why has the poet used repetition in the last six lines?* (to build up tension) *What does the phrase 'fast awake' mean? Why is this an example of word play? Why does the poem stop suddenly after 'the'? What effect does this have on the reader?* Encourage the children to refer to the poem to explain their views.
• Show 'Bully Night' (ITP P1.2). Discuss the poem's features, e.g. sound patterns such as rhyme, alliteration ('burglars'/'bogeymen', 'slink'/'sleep'), assonance ('creaking'/'shrieking'), and a refrain ('Bully night' / 'I do not like'), as well as repetition.
• Ask the children to refer back to *The Fight of the Year* by Roger McGough (page 7). *What similarities are there to* Bully Night? *Are there any differences?* (*Bully Night* doesn't use speech, such as a sports commentator's voice.)
• Discuss how *Bully Night* could be performed as a choral reading by the whole class. *How could the sound patterns be brought out? Where could pauses or silence be included? How can we divide the poem into parts for different groups to read? What kind of voice should be used for the different parts? How fast or slow, loud or soft should they be read? Who will conduct the 'choir' and how?* Annotate ITP P1.2.
• Rehearse a choral reading of the poem with the whole class. If possible, record the choral reading. Discuss improvements that could be made and then perform the poem again.

Independent and Guided

• The children, working in the same groups from Session 1, choose another poem from the *Year 3 Poetry Collection* to perform as a choral reading. (*The Sound Collector* by Roger McGough, pages 2–3, should not be used as this is covered in Session 3.) Remind the children to read the poem several times and discuss ideas of how to present it. Recall 'Performance poetry' (ITP P1.1) to prompt discussion. Support the children with an identified need. (T/TA)

Plenary

• Recap the learning objectives.
• Organise a 'Poetry Show'. Each group introduces and performs their poem. Encourage the children to discuss their group work. *Why did you choose this poem? Why did you perform it in this way? What do you think about your performance? What do you think you could improve? How?*

Assessment pointers

• S&L: group work and choral readings will show how well the children adopt group roles and understand the poem.
• AF5 (R): oral responses to the poem will show how far the children understand the literary features of the poem.

PHASE 2: CAPTURING IDEAS: PLANNING A PERFORMANCE POEM (1 DAY)

We are learning to ...	Resources
• explore how authors use poetic techniques • develop ideas for writing • collect suitable words and phrases before we write (PNS Strands 8.3, 9.1, 9.4) **Assessment Focuses** AF (W): 1, 7	*Year 3 Poetry Collection* ITP: P1.3 PCM: P1.1

Shared teaching

• Ask the children to be quiet for two minutes and write a list of any sounds they hear inside and outside the classroom. After two minutes, Talk Partners share their lists.
• Ask partners to feed back some of the sounds they heard.
• Share the learning objectives.
• Read *The Sound Collector* by Roger McGough (pages 2–3). Talk about what happens in the poem. *Why is the stranger dressed in black and grey?* (to make him seem sinister) *What kind of sounds does he take away – unusual or everyday sounds? Which sounds are pleasant? Which are unpleasant? Why doesn't the stranger leave his name? I wonder what life would be like without any sounds at all.*
• Show '*The Sound Collector*' (ITP P1.3) and discuss the structure of the poem. Highlight the repeated line of the first and last stanzas and discuss how they provide a frame for the list of sounds in the middle part of the poem.
• *What do you notice about the sounds described?* Highlight on the screen that they usually follow the same format, i.e. 'the whistling of the kettle', 'the turning of the lock', etc.
• Discuss performing the poem. *How could you divide the poem between speakers? Should you include sound effects, mime or both? Where should there be pauses and silence?*
• Tell the children they are going to develop ideas for their own version of *The Sound Collector*. They will keep the first and last stanzas but write their own lists of sounds to go in the middle.

Independent and Guided

• The children discuss in groups which everyday sounds they wouldn't want the Sound Collector to take. On a large piece of paper they list the best examples, using the structure: 'the whistling of the kettle'. They do not need to use rhyme.
  - ●●● List at least eight sounds.
  - ●● List at least six sounds. (T+)
  - ● Complete 'Sounds to collect' (PCM P1.1). (TA+)

Plenary

• Read the opening stanza of the poem. Ask groups to share some of the sounds they have chosen in the independent activity . Then read out the final stanza. *Which sounds did you think were good? Which would be good for performing?*
• Recap the learning objectives and add the children's lists of sounds to the Learning Wall in preparation for Session 4.

Assessment pointers

• S&L: group work will show how far the children can engage with others, draw ideas together and promote discussion.
• AF1, 7 (W): group work and lists created show how far the children can produce imaginative writing, using effective vocabulary.

Session 4

We are learning to ...	Resources
• write performance/shape poems, focusing on descriptive language (PNS Strands 9.4) **Assessment Focuses** AF (W): 1, 7	*Year 3 Poetry Collection* ITP: (P1.3), P1.4 PCM: (P1.1), P1.2, P1.3, P1.4

Shared teaching

- Share the learning objective.
- Show 'Everyday sounds' (ITP P1.4). Ask the children to close their eyes and listen. Click to play the sounds. *Can you guess what the sounds are? How would you describe them?* Drag the question marks to reveal what the sounds are beneath.
- Read *The Sound Collector* by Roger McGough (pages 2–3) again. Explain that the children are going to use their lists of sounds from Session 3 to write their own version of the poem.
- Discuss other possible ideas for sounds which could be included. *What words or phrases could we use to describe them?* Scribe ideas for the children to refer to during independent work.
- Recall '*The Sound Collector*' (ITP P1.3) and highlight key words in the poem, e.g. 'whistling', 'purring', 'popping', etc. *Why did the poet choose these sounds? What do they add to the poem?* If appropriate, explain the term onomatopoeia (words that sound like the object or action they describe). *Can you think of any more words like this?* Again scribe ideas for the children to refer to during independent work.

Independent and Guided

- The children work in groups to draft their new versions of the poem, starting and finishing with the first and last stanzas of the original

poem. Encourage the children to develop their lists of sounds from Session 3. If appropriate, the children could use ICT to write their new poems. Remind the children that their poems will eventually be performed and to think about this when developing their ideas.

- Use 'The Smell Collector' (PCM P1.2) to create a new poem using the same framework as *The Sound Collector*. (T+)
- Complete 'The Sound Collector 1' (PCM P1.3) including different sounds and rhyme. Use rhyming dictionaries, including online ones, to develop ideas.
- Complete 'The Sound Collector 2' (PCM P1.4) using ideas from 'Sounds to collect' (PCM P1.1). (TA+)

Plenary

- Recap the learning objective.
- Join groups together to share their poems and think about how they could be performed. *What sound effects would you use? How would you change your voice; loud, soft, quick, slow? Would you use any actions?*
- Ask groups to feed back. *What did you like about the other group's poem? Did you suggest any changes? How do you think it could be performed?* If ICT was used, show some of the poems on the whiteboard as you discuss them.
- End the session by asking the children to imagine all the sounds have been stolen from the classroom. *How silently can you move on to the next activity?*

Assessment Pointers

- S&L: group work will show how well the children can organise and sustain collaboration and discussion.
- AF1, 7 (W): the children's poems will show how far they can write imaginatively, choosing interesting vocabulary.

Session 5

We are learning to ...	Resources
• investigate the impact of using sound effects • prepare and perform a poem • evaluate each other's performances using success criteria (PNS Strands 1.1, 4.3) **Assessment Focuses** AF (W): 1, 7	*The Fight of the Year* (film) *Bully Night* (film) *Year 3 Poetry Collection* ITP: P1.5 PCM: (P1.2, P1.3, P1.4)

Shared teaching

- Share the learning objectives.
- Watch or read again the previous poems used in this unit, e.g. *The Fight of the Year, Bully Night, The Sound Collector,* etc.
- If appropriate, watch or listen to other poets performing their own work.
- The children Think-Pair-Share what makes a good performance poem. *What brings the poem to life for the audience? How does the poet change his voice? Does he use sound effects, mime or silence?*
- Take feedback and use 'Performance poems' (ITP P1.5) to develop success criteria for effective poetry performances. *Are there any you would like to add or change?*

Independent and Guided

- The children work in the same groups as Session 4 to practise performing their versions of *The Sound Collector* or 'The Smell Collector', using completed 'The Smell Collector' (PCM P1.2), 'The Sound Collector 1' (PCM P1.3) or 'The Sound Collector 2' (PCM P1.4). Remind the children to refer to ITP P1.5 to check their performance against the success criteria. When the groups are ready, pair different groups together. Each group takes it in turns to perform while the other

uses ITP P1.5 to evaluate the performance. The groups then make changes to their performance in light of the feedback.

- Use musical instruments to accompany the performance. (T+)
- Experiment using solo voices and a chorus at different times.
- Use simple sound effects created from classroom materials. (TA+)

Plenary

- Recap the learning objectives.
- Ask the children to perform their own versions of *The Sound Collector* or 'The Smell Collector' to the class. If possible, film or record the performances.
- Ask each group to evaluate its own performance. *What did you like about your performance? Did you make any changes to your performance using the success criteria? Would you make any more changes now? How well do think you worked as a group?*
- Encourage the class to give feedback on the performances. *Which versions of the poem did you like?*
- Discuss the work done over the unit as a whole. *Which poems did you like? Which poems made good performances? Would you like to read more of the poet's work?*

Assessment Pointers

- S&L: group work and poetry performances will show how well the children adopt group roles, collaborate and vary talk according to purpose.
- AF1, 7 (W): the children's poems show how far they can write imaginatively, choosing interesting and appropriate vocabulary.

Sounds to collect

Write a list of objects that make sounds.

	The singing of the birds.
	The laughing of my friends.

The Smell Collector

Write a new poem about a Smell Collector. Use the same features as *The Sound Collector*.

_____

_____

_____

_____

_____

_____

_____

_____

_____

_____

_____

The Sound Collector 1

Write your own version of the poem. Use rhyming dictionaries to help you.

A stranger called _____

_____

_____

_____

_____

_____

_____

_____

_____

_____

_____

A stranger called _____

_____

_____

_____

The Sound Collector 2

Complete the lines to create your own version of the poem.

A stranger called this morning

Dressed all in black and grey

Put every sound into a bag

And carried them away

The _____ of the _____

The _____ of the frog

The _____ of the _____

The _____ of the dog

The _____ of the _____

The _____ of the car

The _____ of the _____

The _____ of the guitar

A stranger called this morning

He didn't leave his name

Left us only silence

Life will never be the same.

ROGER MCGOUGH/GINA DOUTHWAITE (Shape)

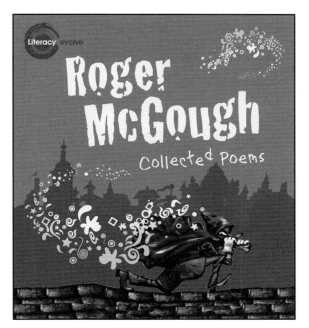

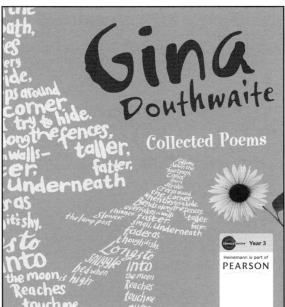

Medium term plan (2 weeks)	
Phase	**Learning Outcomes**
Phase 1: Exploring calligrams and shape poems (4 days)	• Children can create their own calligrams. • Children can discuss how words and shapes combine to make effective shape poems. • Children can use different shape poems as models for their own work.
Phase 2: Capturing ideas; shared composition of shape poems (3 days)	• Children can contribute ideas to create, edit and refine a class poem. • Children can work in groups to trial and develop ideas about writing shape poems.
Phase 3: Drafting and revising shape poems (3 days)	• Children can create their own shape poems, based on shared success criteria. • Children can reflect on the creative process and use drafting to improve their work.

ROGER MCGOUGH/GINA DOUTHWAITE

Big picture

The children are introduced to the idea of calligrams. They discuss what makes a good calligram and experiment with creating some of their own. They then look at several different types of shape poem, exploring how the poet uses the language and layout to create an effective poem. The children identify success criteria for shape poems. They then work as a class to develop a class poem, evaluating it against the success criteria. Finally, they create their own shape poems, working with each other to draft and improve them ready for a class display.

Prior learning

This unit assumes that children can already:
- respond to poems in different formats, with some experience of shape poems and word art
- explore imagery and features of the poet's use of language to describe events, places or feelings
- use drama strategies to explore texts and characters
- work collaboratively to share ideas, create first drafts and edit and improve their poems
- use presentational techniques to develop their work.

Key aspects of learning

Creative thinking: Choose words, images, shapes and presentational styles for their own poems, responding to different stimuli.

Evaluation: Evaluate poems in terms of the success criteria and the impact it has on the reader.

Social skills: Work collaboratively in small groups and with the whole class to generate ideas and shape these into poems; offer constructive criticism while working with a partner.

Progression in poetry

In this unit the children will:
- describe the effect a poem has on the reader and suggest possible interpretations
- discuss the choice of words and their impact, noticing how the poet creates 'sound effects' by using alliteration, rhythm or rhyme and creates imagery by using similes
- explain the pattern of different simple forms and experiment with these in their own work.

Cross-curricular links

Art: The children could present words and poems in different shapes, using different fonts and illustrations.
ICT: The children could use word processing or design software to present their shape poems and calligrams.

PHASE 1: EXPLORING CALLIGRAMS AND SHAPE POEMS (4 DAYS)

Session 1

We are learning to ...	Resources
• understand what makes a good calligram • write calligrams (PNS Strands 7.5, 9.5) **Assessment Focuses** AF (R): 5; AF (W): 1	*Year 3 Poetry Collection* ITP: P2.1, P2.2 PCM: P2.1

Shared teaching

- Share the learning objectives.
- Show 'Calligrams' (ITP P2.1) and click to reveal the calligrams. *What is a calligram?* (A word or phrase written in a way that reflects its meaning.) If possible, demonstrate how you can make calligrams using computer software, or draw out shapes.
- Read *Circus of Shapes* by Gina Douthwaite (page 3) as an example of calligrams linked together by a theme. Discuss how the different words have been presented. *What do the calligrams represent? Why has the poet presented the words in different ways?*
- Show 'Creating calligrams' (ITP P2.2) and encourage the children to add their own criteria.
- Briefly explain that adjectives are words that describe things. Give the children a list of suitable adjectives, e.g. cloudy, shaky, spiky, scary, etc. Ask them to choose one and write it as a calligram and to hold it up when they have finished. Share some good examples with the class.
- Explain that it isn't just adjectives that can be made into calligrams: verbs, nouns and adverbs can also be made into shapes. Mind Map a list of words that would make good calligrams, e.g. frown, long, fiery, explode, etc. Try to include examples from all the four word classes mentioned. Add to the Learning Wall, organised into four word classes.

Independent and Guided

- The children create their own calligrams, either by hand or using ICT. (If using ICT, save them for use in the plenary.) Encourage them to experiment and to redraft their work, using different shapes and colours to bring out the meaning of the words more effectively. Pairs evaluate each other's calligrams using ITP P2.2. The children then prepare a final draft for presentation.
- **OOO** Choose their own words. (T+)
- **OO** Choose words from the Learning Wall.
- **O** Complete 'Calligrams' (PCM P2.1). (TA+)

Plenary

- Recap the learning objectives.
- View any calligrams which have been saved using ICT. Ask the other children to hold up handwritten examples.
- Recap the success criteria. Invite one or two children to feed back on their partner's calligrams. *Which examples are the most effective? Did you suggest any changes? Do the calligrams meet the success criteria?*
- Create a classroom display of calligrams or scan into a computer for presentation as a slideshow.

Assessment pointers

- S&L: pair work will show how sensitively the children can give and respond to opinions.
- AF5 (R): response to the poem will show how far the children understand the poet's use of language at word level.
- AF1 (W): the children's word choices will show how far they are able to produce thoughtful and imaginative work.

We are learning to …
• identify how different kinds of shape poems are written (PNS Strands 7.5)

Assessment Focuses
AF (R): 4; AF (W): 1

Resources
Year 3 Poetry Collection
ITP: P2.3
PCM: P2.2, P2.3, P2.4

Shared teaching
• Share the learning objective.
• Ask the children to close their eyes. Read *Milking Time* by Gina Douthwaite (page 4) and ask them what pictures the poem creates in their minds. Encourage the children to share their ideas with the class.
• Read 'Milking Time' (ITP P2.3). *What do you like or dislike about the poem?*
• Discuss the language used, e.g the use of precise adjectives that appeal to different senses, e.g. 'dark', 'hot', 'misty', 'crisp'; the use of vivid images, e.g. 'white patches of jigsaw', 'misty ghosts'; and no use of rhyme.
• Compare ITP P2.3 with *Milking Time* (page 4). Think-Pair-Share what is different about the poem. *Which version do you prefer?*
• Take feedback and encourage the children to give reasons for their preferences, referring to the poem.
• Discuss how the poem has been made into a shape poem by writing inside the image of the animal described. *Why are the words of the poem written in white on the dark patches of the cow?* Explore how this adds to the meaning of the words and explain that in the dark yard it's only the white, jigsaw shaped patches that would show up. Also draw attention to the upside down 'i' which creates a drop of milk.
• Explain that the children are going to create their own shape poems about an elephant or a butterfly. The poems will be written inside the

shape of the creature and will not use rhyme. Mind Map some words to describe either or both of these creatures that appeal to the different senses. Add to the Learning Wall.

Independent and Guided
• The children create their own animal shape poems, using ICT if possible. Encourage them to think about how to divide up the poem and write it inside the image. Remind them not to use rhyme.
  Complete 'Butterfly' (PCM P2.2) or 'Elephant' (PCM P2.3). Encourage them to use precise adjectives that appeal to different senses to describe their chosen animal. (T)
  Use words from the Learning Wall to complete PCM P2.2 or PCM P2.3.
  Use 'Word bank' (PCM P2.4) to complete PCM P2.2 or PCM P2.3. (TA)

Plenary
• Recap the learning objective.
• Talk Partners share their poems. *Which ones do you think are particularly effective as shape poems?*
• Ask partners to feed back on poems they think are particularly good. Encourage them to explain their reasons. *How do the shapes add to the meaning of the words?*

Assessment pointers
• S&L: pair work will show how well the children can express and explain relevant ideas.
• AF4 (R): shared teaching and the plenary will show how far the children understand the structure and organisation of the poem.
• AF1 (W): the children's shape poems will show how far they are able to make good word choices and group ideas.

We are learning to …
• identify how different kinds of shape poems are written
• share our opinions about a story (or poem) and give reasons for our views (PNS Strands 7.5, 8.1)

Assessment Focuses
AF (R): 4, 6

Resources
Year 3 Poetry Collection
ITP: P2.4
PCM: P2.5

Shared teaching
• Share the learning objectives and explain that the children are going to explore different ways to write shape poems.
• Share the title of the poem, *CARtoon* by Gina Douthwaite (page 10), and explain it is about a family travelling back from holiday in their crowded car. *How do you think it might be written?*
• Read and enjoy the poem. *Was it written how you thought it would be?*
• Discuss any unfamiliar vocabulary, e.g. 'migraine', 'cones', 'congestion', 'Bumper Bonzer Break-A-Way'. *Why is the title written the way it is?* (The poem is shaped like a cartoon picture of a car.).
• Look back at *Milking Time* (page 4). *How is CARtoon different?* (E.g. it includes alliteration and rhyme.). Recap or explain alliteration (the use of similar sounds at the beginning of two or more words together, e.g. 'boot-a-bulging', 'roof rack rocking', etc.)
• Talk Partners discuss how many different sounds they can find in the poem that use alliteration. Take feedback and underline the different sounds on 'CARtoon' (ITP P2.4).
• Ask the children where the rhyme words are in the poem and highlight them on ITP P2.4. *Is there a difference between where the rhymes are in the four short lines and in the four longer ones?*
• Talk about other differences between *Milking Time* and *CARtoon*, e.g the way the words are written in a shape instead of being written

inside an image, and the way the 'O's in the last line are the car's wheels.
• Think-Pair-Share which of the two kinds of shape poem the children enjoyed most. *How did the poems make you feel? What different images did they paint in your mind?* Encourage the children to refer to the poems to support their views.

Independent and Guided
• The children work in groups to read, enjoy and discuss other shape poems by Gina Douthwaite in the *Year 3 Poetry Collection*.
  Read and discuss *Fruit Salad* (page 2) and *Handy to Have* (page 9). Use 'Discussion checklist' (PCM P2.5) and encourage the children to refer to the texts of the poems to support their views. (T+)
  Read and discuss *Fruit Salad*, using PCM P2.5.
  Read and discuss *Handy to Have*, using PCM P2.5. (TA+)

Plenary
• Recap the learning objectives and ask the groups to feed back on the poems. *Which poems did you like or dislike?* Encourage them to refer to the texts to support their views.
• Discuss shape poems. *Is it easy to tell where to start reading these poems and in which direction to read them? Can you start reading* Handy to Have *and* Fruit Salad *from different places without spoiling the poems?*

Assessment pointers
• S&L: group work will show how far the children can express and respond to opinions.
• AF4, 6 (R): shared and group discussions show how far the children understand the features and organisation of shape poems and the effects this has on the reader.

We are learning to ...	Resources
• identify how different kinds of shape poems are written (PNS Strands 7.5) **Assessment Focuses** AF (R): 4; AF (W): 3	*Year 3 Poetry Collection* ITP: P2.5, P2.6 PCM: P2.6, P2.7

Shared teaching

• Share the learning objective.
• Show and read 'Downhill Racer / Uphill Climb' (ITP P2.5).
• Talk partners discuss how to make this into a shape poem. *Could you write it inside a shape like* Milking Time? *Could you make the words into a shape like* CARtoon? *Could you write it in a different way?*
• Discuss the children's ideas for making the plain text into a shape poem. Then read *Downhill Racer / Uphill Climb* by Roger McGough (pages 8–9). *Was the poem written the way you predicted?*
• Discuss the features of this poem. *What does the layout remind you of?* (The words zig-zag down the page like a skier and then climb back up the next page like a person plodding back up the ski slope.) *How does the downhill part of the poem create the impression of skiing downhill?* (It has rhymes and short sentences, so you read it quickly.) *What is different about the uphill part of the poem?* (It only has one word on each line with big spaces between each word at the beginning, so you read the poem more slowly until you get near to the top, when it speeds up again.) *Why is 'Wheeeeee' printed sloping downwards?* (It is like the skier, ready to set off again.)
• Show 'Comparing shape poems' (ITP P2.6). Use the chart to talk about the similarities and differences between the three shape poems the children have read. *Are there any other similarities or differences?*
• Discuss shape poems. *Is it easy to tell where to start reading poems like* Downhill Racer / Uphill Climb? *Which direction do you read them? Can you start reading poems like this from different places like with* Handy to Have *and* Fruit Salad?

Independent and Guided

• The children work in pairs to explore how to create shape poems using *Downhill Racer / Uphill Climb* as a model. If appropriate, use ICT to write the poems.
 ∞ Use 'Shape poem frame' (PCM P2.6) to create a shape poem. (T+)
 ∞ Use 'Shape poem words' (PCM P2.7) to write the text as a shape poem. (TA+)
 ◉ Place the text on PCM P2.7 on to PCM P2.6.

Plenary

• Recap the learning objective and ask pairs to share their shape poems. Discuss the different ways of setting out the same text. *Which versions are more effective?*

Assessment pointers

• S&L: pair work will show how far the children can listen and repsond to others.
• AF4 (R): responses to questioning show how far the children understand the presentational features of the text.
• AF3 (W): the children's shape poems show how far they are able to sequence material effectively.

PHASE 2: CAPTURING IDEAS; SHARED COMPOSITION OF SHAPE POEMS (3 DAYS)

Session 5

We are learning to ...	Resources
• write different kinds of shape poems (PNS Strands 9.5) **Assessment Focuses** AF (R): 5, 6; AF (W): 3	*Year 3 Poetry Collection* ITP: P2.7

Shared teaching

• Share the learning objective.
• Explain that the children are going to write some shape poems on the theme of animals. First, they are going to look at another poem by Gina Douthwaite. Then they will write some poems as a class.
• Read *Blackbird* by Gina Douthwaite (page 5). *What is it about? How does it make you feel?*
• Look back at *Milking Time* by Gina Douthwaite (page 4). *How is* Blackbird *similar to* Milking Time? (The poem is also written inside an image.) *How is it different?* (Rhyme and rhythm are used; the poem is addressed to the blackbird.)
• Show 'Animals' (ITP P2.7). *Which of these would be a good choice for writing a shape poem?* As a class, choose one animal to focus on.
• Ask the children to mime how the creature would move and behave.
• Mind Map words, phrases, similes and metaphors to describe how the creature moves, e.g. *Squirrel you move so quickly through the trees.*
• Focus on the chosen animal on ITP P2.7 again. Mind Map language to describe how the creature looks. Add to the Learning Wall.
• Draft a shared poem in plain text form, describing the chosen animal. Encourage the children to offer suggestions. The poem can be addressed to the creature, as in *Blackbird*. It does not have to rhyme, e.g. *You move so quickly / We can only see you when you pause / With your feathery tail sticking up / And black eyes darting,* etc.

Independent and Guided

• Ask the children to work in groups to make the draft of the class poem into a shape poem like *Milking Time* or *Blackbird.* The children can use the photos from ITP P2.7 to create outlines for their poems.
 ∞ Draft another short, non-rhyming shape poem about the same animal. (T).
 ∞ Edit and revise the class poem to improve it and make it fit inside the outline.
 ◉ Write the class poem inside the outline. (TA)

Plenary

• Recap the learning objective.
• Show the image of the chosen creature from ITP P2.7 again. Click on the picture and write the class poem inside the image. Take suggestions from the children for how to edit the draft of the class poem to make it fit inside the image.
• Save and print off the final version of the class shape poem and add to the Learning Wall.

Assessment pointers

• S&L: group work will show how well the children can organise and sustain collaboration and discussion.
• AF5, 6 (R): class discussion shows how far the children understand an author's use of language and the effect on the reader.
• AF3 (W): the whole-class poem and independent work will show how far the children are able to organise ideas, present poems effectively and write imaginatively.

Session 6

<table>
<tr><td>We are learning to ...
• write different kinds of shape poems
(PNS Strands 9.5)
Assessment Focuses
AF (R): 4; AF (W): 3</td><td>Resources
Year 3 Poetry Collection
ITP: (P2.6), P2.8</td></tr>
</table>

Shared teaching

• Share the learning objectives and explain that in this session, the children are going to write another shape poem about an animal.
• Ask the children to look back at *CARtoon* (page 10), *Handy to Have* (page 9), and *Fruit Salad* (page 2) by Gina Douthwaite.
• Read *Bathroom Bug* (page 6) by Gina Douthwaite for another example of this kind of shape poem. Discuss responses to this poem and what it is about.
• Recap how, in this kind of shape poem, the words are made into the shape of the creature being described, unlike *Blackbird* and *Milking Time* where the poem is contained by the outline shape. The letters also make part of the creature, e.g. 'IT' makes the antennae of the Bathroom Bug. Sometimes features are added outside the shape like the legs of the bug. Ask the children to find similar poems to *Bathroom Bug* in the *Year 3 Poetry Collection*, e.g. *Guess What*.
• Explain that this is the type of shape poem the children will be writing. Recall 'Comparing shape poems' (ITP P2.6) if needed.
• Show 'Insects' (ITP P2.8). Choose one insect and drag the image onto the screen.
• Mind Map ideas and language to describe what the insect looks like and how it moves. Emphasise strong verbs and adjectives, as used in *Bathroom Bug*. Add to the Learning Wall.

• Develop a draft of a shared poem describing the chosen insect and encourage the children to offer suggestions, e.g. *It hums as it moves / furry with black and yellow stripes / that say 'Danger! Don't touch'*.
• Add a text box over the insect outline on ITP P2.8. Write the class poem in the insect. It does not have to rhyme. Encourage the children to suggest how to fit the poem in the shape. Then drag the shape away, leaving only the text box.

Independent and Guided

• Groups develop the class shape poem. They draw a faint outline of the insect to write their poems into. (If necessary, print off copies of the image from ITP P2.8 for the children to trace around.) At the end they should remove the pencil lines to leave only the poem visible.

ooo Use any of the letters from the poem as features of the creature.

oo Add any features to the creature inside the poem. (T+)

o Add arms or legs, a head, eyes or ears, etc. on the outside of the poem. Change the colours of the text to help represent the animal. (TA+)

Plenary

• Recap the learning objectives. Encourage groups to feed back on their changes and incorporate their suggestions onto ITP 2.8 where appropriate. Print off the final version and add to the Learning Wall.

Assessment pointers

• S&L: group work and poems will show how well the children collaborate to explore and discuss ideas.
• AF4 (R): class discussion and response to questions will show how far the children understand the structure of different shape poems.
• AF3 (W): the whole-class poem and groups' revisions show how far the children are able to organise and present poems effectively.

Session 7

<table>
<tr><td>We are learning to ...
• choose powerful verbs and adjectives
• write different kinds of shape poems
(PNS Strands 9.4, 9.5)
Assessment Focuses
AF (R): 4; AF (W):3</td><td>Resources
Year 3 Poetry Collection
ITP: (P2.6)</td></tr>
</table>

Shared teaching

• Share the learning objectives. Explain that the children are going to write a third kind of shape poem as a class. Remind them of *Downhill Racer / Uphill Climb* by Roger McGough (pages 8–9) and recall 'Comparing shape poems' (ITP P2.6) if needed.
• Before the children see the poem, read *The Allivator* by Roger McGough (page 5). *What do you think this shape poem looks like?*
• Reread the poem with the children following in their books. *Did you like the poem? What is it about? What is an Allivator a mixture of?*
• Discuss how the poem has to be read from bottom to top like *Uphill Climb* and how, when you read the poem, it is like walking up an escalator.
• Explain that the children are going to create a shape poem like *The Allivator* about a real creature with a distinctive shape that moves in a distinctive way: a snake.
• Ask the children to improvise how a snake would move using their hands.
• Take feedback and Mind Map the children's descriptions of what a snake looks like and how it moves. Emphasise powerful adjectives and verbs. Add to the Learning Wall.
• Talk Partners think of ideas for a shared poem describing the snake. The poem could begin *Beware the snake . . . .*

• Encourage the children to suggest ideas and use these to develop a draft of a plain text poem, not in a shape, at this stage. Collate and edit the children's suggestions on the whiteboard.
• Leave the draft on the whiteboard so that the children can refer to it during the independent and guided activity.

Independent and Guided

• The children work in groups to develop ways of writing the draft poem to mirror the movement of the snake, e.g. in zig-zags like *Downhill Racer*. Encourage them to refer to the draft of the class poem.

ooo Experiment with other shapes that the snake poem could be set out in, e.g. a coil or spiral shape, including a way to show the snake's eyes and forked tongue. (T+)

oo Improve the draft of the poem by adding alliterative 's' sounds to suggest the sound the snake makes.

o Write the draft poem in a zig-zag shape. (TA+)

Plenary

• Take suggestions from the groups as to how to set out the shape poem. Incorporate these suggestions to transform the plain text version of the class poem into a shape poem. Display the final version.
• Recap the learning objectives.

Assessment pointers

• S&L: group work will show how far the children can engage with others, draw ideas together and promote discussion.
• AF4 (R): class discussion shows how far the children understand the structure and organisation of different poems.
• AF3 (W): the whole-class poem and the groups' revisions will show how far the children are able to organise and present poems effectively.

Session 8

We are learning to ...	Resources
• work with an editing partner to improve our writing • choose powerful words and adjectives • write performance/shape poems, focusing on descriptive language (PNS Strands 9.1, 9.4) **Assessment Focuses** AF (R): 2; AF (W): 7	*Year 3 Poetry Collection* ITP: (P2.7, P2.8), P2.9 PCM: P2.8

Shared teaching

• Show 'Shape poems' (ITP P2.9). Discuss ideas with the children as to what makes a good shape poem. *Are there any you would like to add or change?*
• Turn to the centre page of the *Year 3 Poetry Collection* and read 'How I wrote my favourite poem: *Pheasant*' by Gina Douthwaite. *How does Gina start a poem?* (with notes and ideas) *What does she do with her ideas?* (She writes a draft.) *What does she do with her drafts?* (She tests them and changes words.) *Why does she call her early poem a 'flat' pheasant?* (because it isn't a shape poem) *How does she create a shape poem?* (She takes a 'flat' poem and writes it into a shape.)
• Share the learning objectives.
• Explain that the children are going to copy how Gina writes a poem. In this session, they are going to develop ideas and write a draft of a poem; a 'flat' poem. In Session 9 they are going to turn their 'flat' poem into a shape.

Independent and Guided

• Recall either 'Animals' (ITP P2.7) or 'Insects' (ITP P2.8) and ask the children to choose an image to write about. They describe the image using interesting language, especially powerful verbs and adjectives.

Encourage the children to focus on the details of the photographs. When the children have made notes of their ideas, Talk Partners turn their descriptions into a non-rhyming poem. Remind the children that this should be a 'flat' poem and not in the shape of the creature.

⊙⊙⊙ Experiment with using images and comparisons to describe their creature, thinking about what it reminds them of and what it looks or moves like. Try including some similes. (T+)

⊙⊙ Use all their five senses to describe their creature.

⊙ Use the word bank of adjectives and verbs on 'Sense word banks' (PCM P2.8) to create a poem. (TA+)

Plenary

• Recap the learning objectives.
• Recap the first of the success criteria for the shape poems: the words must be interesting and powerful. *Who thinks their partner has written a particularly good draft? What interesting and powerful language did they use?*
• Ask some of the children to read their drafts. Encourage the class to comment on the poem. *What is good about it? What changes could be made?*
• Discuss how, in Session 9, the children will begin to make their drafts into shape poems.

Assessment pointers

• AF2 (R): response to questions will show how far the children are able to retrieve information from the text.
• AF7 (W): the draft poems will show how far the children can use relevant vocabulary with some adventurous word choices.

Session 9

We are learning to ...	Resources
• use success criteria to give each other feedback • write different kinds of shape poems (PNS Strands 9.1, 9.5) **Assessment Focuses** AF (W): 1, 2, 3	*Year 3 Poetry Collection* ITP: (P2.6, P2.7, P2.8, P2.9)

Shared teaching

• Recall 'Shape poems' (ITP P2.9) and remind the children of the criteria for creating a good shape poem.
• Recap how Gina Douthwaite creates shape poems and explain that in this session, the children will be turning the drafts they wrote in Session 8 into a shape that matches their creature, so the focus will be on the layout of the poem.
• Recap the different shape poems covered in the unit. *What was your favourite poem? What different types of shape poems have we looked at?* (words written inside an image, words written to make a shape and words that act out movement)
• Recall annotated 'Comparing shape poems' (ITP P2.6). *Can you find more examples of these types of poems in the* Year 3 Poetry Collection*?* Read one type of each poem and ask Talk Partners to discuss how the different poems are set out.
• Take feedback and discuss as a class.

Independent and Guided

• The children rework their draft poem to make it into a shape poem. If needed, print images from 'Animals' (ITP P2.7) or 'Insects' (ITP P2.8) for the children to draw around or write over. Encourage the children

to use the *Year 3 Poetry Collection* for ideas of how to arrange their poems.

⊙⊙⊙ Choose which type of shape poem to create and apply this to their 'flat' poem. (T+)

⊙⊙ Draw a pencil outline based on a photograph from ITP P2.7 or ITP P2.8. Experiment with writing their draft inside the outline and revise the draft so that it fits well. They then carefully rub out the pencil outline so that the text is in the shape of the chosen creature.

⊙ Using a photograph from ITP P2.7 or ITP P2.8, experiment with writing their draft poem on top of the image. (TA+)

Plenary

• Recap the learning objectives.
• Talk Partners discuss each other's poems against the success criteria on ITP P2.9.
• Take feedback. *Who thinks their partner has created a particularly good layout for their shape poem? What is good about it?*
• Ask some of the children to show their drafts and encourage the class to use Two Stars and a Wish to evaluate the poems.

Assessment pointers

• AF1, 2, 3 (W): the children's poems show how far they are able to write imaginative poems appropriate to the task and organised effectively.

We are learning to ...
- use success criteria to give each other feedback
- edit writing to make it more effective
- revise and present our own play poems
  (PNS Strands 9.1, 12.2)

Assessment Focuses
AF (W): 1, 2, 3

Resources
Year 3 Poetry Collection
ITP: (P2.9)

Shared teaching

- Share the learning objectives and explain that the children will complete their draft shape poems ready for a class presentation. Remind the children that it is important to redraft their work to improve it, just like the poet Gina Douthwaite, who goes through several stages of drafts before she is happy with her poem.
- Recall 'Shape poems' (ITP P2.9) and recap the success criteria.
- Look back at the centre page of the *Year 3 Poetry Collection*: 'How I wrote my favourite poem: *Pheasant*' by Gina Douthwaite. *What problems did she have making her 'flat' poem into a shape?* (The words wouldn't fit and were hard to read; 'some got in a tangle'.) *Is anybody having similar problems with their poems?*
- Talk Partners discuss the layout problems they are having, focusing on whether the poems are easy to read.
- Take feedback and make a list of the different problems the children are having with layout.
- Look back at the different types of shape poems read in this unit from the *Year 3 Poetry Collection*. Discuss the things that make the poems easy to read, e.g. the poem broken into different sections (*Milking Time* and *Hair We Go Again*), clear space between the words and lines (*The Allivator* and *Downhill Racer / Uphill Climb*), the words clearly forming the animal shape (*Bathroom Bug*).
- Discuss how these features could help make the children's poems clearer. Ask for some of the children to show their poems from Session 9 and discuss these as a class. *What is good about the presentation of this poem? How could it be improved?*

Independent and Guided

- The children produce final versions of their shape poems, using ICT if possible and appropriate. Once the children have created their shape poems, pairs use ITP P2.9 to evaluate each other's work. The children then make final changes and illustrate the poems for display.

  ooo Write more than one type of shape poem if they have time.

  oo Add features outside and inside the shape of their poem. (TA)

  o Revise and edit their draft so that it fits inside the image well. (T)

Plenary

- Recap the learning objectives and hold a poetry presentation where all the children's shape poems are shown and read.
- Devise a display where the shape poems can be viewed and read by the children themselves and other audiences, e.g. through a slideshow, a display board, etc.
- Discuss the unit as a whole. *Which was your favourite type of shape poem? Would you like to read more of the poet's work?*

Assessment pointers

- S&L: pair work will show how sensitively the children can give and respond to opinions.
- AF1, 2, 3 (W): the children's finished poems show how far they are able to write imaginatively, with appropriate style and form.

Calligrams

Draw calligrams for the words.

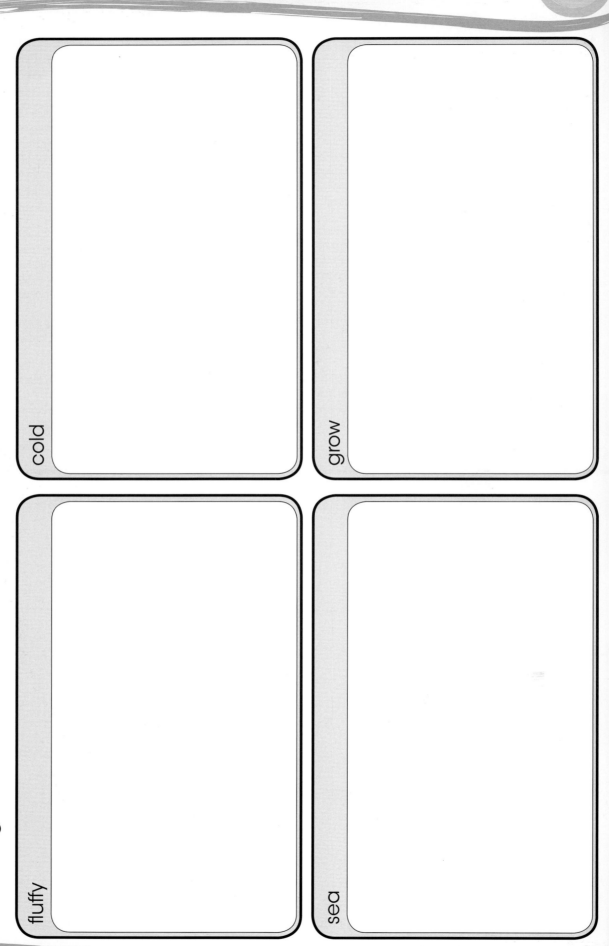

cold

grow

fluffy

sea

Butterfly

Write your poem inside the animal shape.

Elephant

Write your poem inside the animal shape.

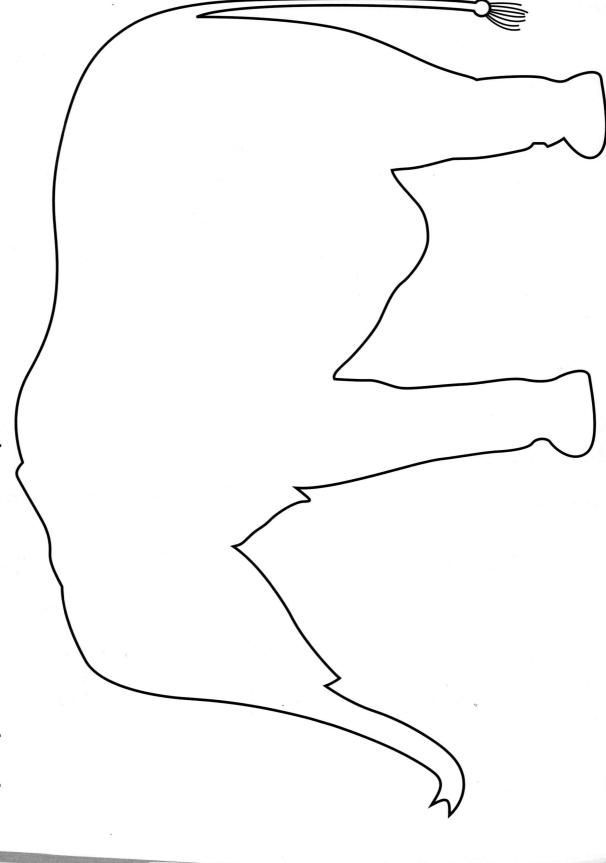

Word bank

Use the word bank to help you write an animal shape poem.

Adjectives

Nouns

Verbs

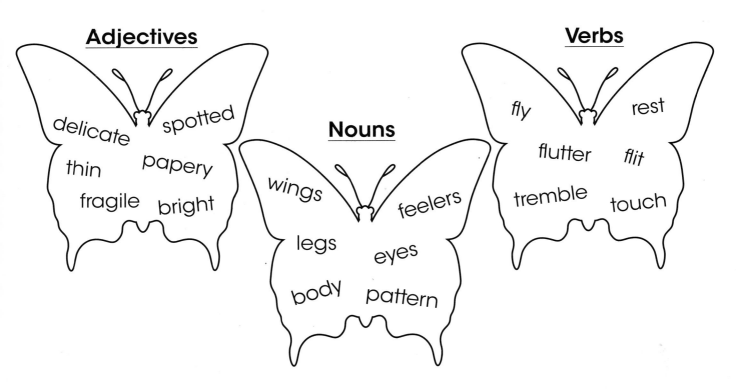

Adjectives: delicate, spotted, thin, papery, fragile, bright

Nouns: wings, feelers, legs, eyes, body, pattern

Verbs: fly, rest, flutter, flit, tremble, touch

Word bank

Use the word bank to help you write an animal shape poem.

Adjectives

Nouns

Verbs

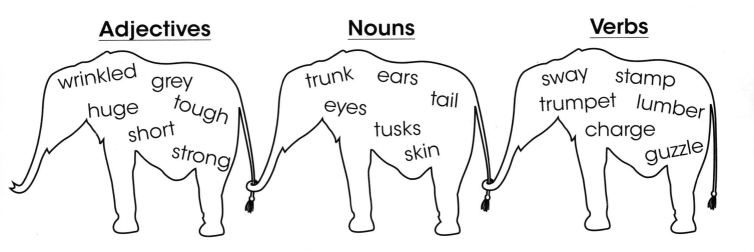

Adjectives: wrinkled, grey, huge, tough, short, strong

Nouns: trunk, ears, eyes, tail, tusks, skin

Verbs: sway, stamp, trumpet, lumber, charge, guzzle

Literacy Evolve Year 3 © Pearson Education 2009

Discussion checklist

1. Read *Fruit Salad* and use the checklist to discuss the poem.

Fruit Salad

a. What shape is the poem?	☐
b. How has the poet written the words into the shape?	☐
c. Would the poem be as good if it wasn't in a shape?	☐
d. What rhymes are in the poem?	☐
e. Which images do you particularly like?	☐
f. How has it made you think differently about fruit?	☐
g. What do you like about the poem?	☐
h. What do you dislike?	☐

2. Read *Handy to Have* and use the checklist to discuss the poem.

Handy to Have

a. What shape is the poem?	☐
b. How has the poet written the words into the shape?	☐
c. How would the poem be different if it wasn't in a shape?	☐
d. What rhymes are in the poem?	☐
e. Where does the poem start?	☐
f. How many ways can the words be read in a different order?	☐
g. What do you like about the poem?	☐
h. What do you dislike?	☐

Literacy Evolve Year 3 © Pearson Education 2009

Shape poem frame

Write a shape poem called 'Upstairs stomper / Downstairs slider'. Start writing at the bottom of the stairs.

Literacy Evolve Year 3 © Pearson Education 2009

Shape poem words

Make the text into a shape poem.

Upstairs stomper / Downstairs slider

When I have to go upstairs to bed
Instead of watching films on TV
I stomp up slower and slower
And the stairs seem to get
longer and longer, until
I find I've climbed all
the way to the top.
When, Yippee

I can
Slide
Back
Down
On
The
Ban-
-is-
-ter.
Splat!

Sense word banks

Use the word banks to write a poem about your creature. Add more adjectives.

See

bright	dark	_____
dazzling	colourful	_____
flickering	fiery	_____

Hear

noisy	squawking	_____
buzzing	quiet	_____
roaring	barking	_____

Smell

sweet	stinky	_____
perfumed	foul	_____
sweaty	fresh	_____

Touch

smooth	rough	_____
soft	slimy	_____
scaly	prickly	_____

Taste

bitter	tangy	_____
sweet	fruity	_____
spicy	sour	_____

ROGER MCGOUGH/GINA DOUTHWAITE (Language play)

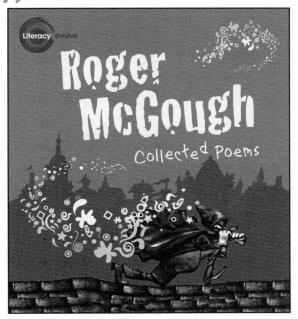
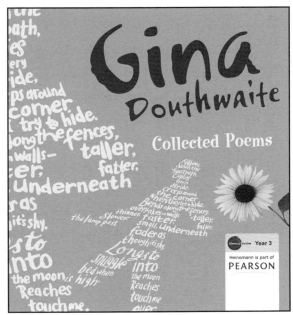

Medium term plan (2 weeks)	
Phase	**Learning Outcomes**
Phase 1: Familiarisation with the genre (5 days)	• Children can identify different types of language play and discuss the effect of poets' language choices on the reader. • Children can experiment with language play of their own.
Phase 2: Capturing ideas; shared composition (2 days)	• Children can contribute creative ideas and vocabulary for a shared poem. • Children can work together in pairs and/or groups to create a shared poem. • Children can use their understanding of performance poetry to reflect on the effectiveness of different language play poems.
Phase 3: Drafting and revising poems; independent composition (3 days)	• Children can identify success criteria for language play poems. • Children can draft their own poems, using poems already read as a model. • Children can work together to edit, redraft and finalise their poems. • Children can plan and conduct a performance of their poems.

ROGER MCGOUGH/GINA DOUTHWAITE

Big picture

The children explore the idea of language play and puns, drawing on real-life experiences and the poems of Roger McGough. They read a selection of poems, such as riddles and list poems, which include examples of alliteration, puns and similes. As a class and in groups, children suggest similes and other images to contribute to a class poem. Finally, they choose a type of language play to use as a model for their own poem. Together with a partner, children refine their poems and rehearse a performance of the final versions.

Prior learning

This unit assumes that the children can already:
• explore how words are used, including some understanding of puns, alliteration and similes
• discuss the effect of a poet's language choices on the reader
• view and comment on a performance of a poem
• create their own poems, with some experience of choosing words and phrases for particular effect.

Key aspects of learning

Creative thinking: Invent puns, alliterative sentences and other plays on words; use found language to spark creative ideas; use and reflect on poets' compositional methods.

Communication: Explore different ways of using language to convey meaning and impact the audience.
Self-awareness: Relate poems to personal experience; express preferences, likes and dislikes.
Social skills: Work together in pairs and small groups; listen to others and provide constructive criticism.

Progression in poetry

In this unit the children will:
• describe the effect a poem has on the reader
• discuss the choice of words and their impact, noticing how the poet creates 'sound effects' by using alliteration, rhythm or rhyme and creates imagery using similes
• invent new similes and experiment with word play; use powerful adjectives and verbs; experiment with alliteration.

Cross-curricular links

ICT: The children could film and review their poetry performances.

PHASE 1: FAMILIARISATION WITH THE GENRE (5 DAYS)

Session 1

We are learning to ...	Resources
• understand how riddles are written (PNS Strands 7.5) **Assessment Focuses** AF (R): 4	ITP: P3.1, P3.2, P3.3 PCM: P3.1

Shared teaching

• Share the learning objective and some favourite riddles, jokes or nonsense rhymes with the children, e.g. where do elephants get their clothes? A jungle sale!
• Discuss how playing with words is how we first experience what we call poetry. People have played with language for entertainment and pleasure ever since language began.
• The children Think-Pair-Share their favourite piece of language play, including puns, playground rhymes, nursery rhymes, etc. Pairs share with the class.
• Explain that the children are going to read and write some riddles. Read the poem 'What am I?' (ITP P3.1), revealing it line by line until the children guess the answer: the sun.
• Show 'Riddles' (ITP P3.2) and discuss the success criteria for writing this kind of poem. Add ideas the children suggest to the list.
• Read 'What am I now?' (ITP P3.3), revealing it line by line until the children guess the answer: the moon.
• Mind Map what would make good subjects for other riddles like these.
• Ask for feedback and list some of the children's ideas. Choose one and model how to write some comparisons starting with I'm a ... .

Independent and Guided

• The children work in small groups to draft a short riddle using ITP P3.1 as a model. Their riddles do not have to rhyme. Remind them of the success criteria for this kind of riddle.

   ⬤⬤⬤ Choose a subject and use rhyme if they wish. (TA)
   ⬤⬤ Use 'A green riddle' (PCM P3.1).
   ◉ Use 'What am I?' (PCM P3.1). (T+)

Plenary

• Recap the learning objectives.
• Ask the groups to read their riddles to another group from a different ability level. Emphasise reading the riddles at least twice, slowly and clearly. Encourage the children to guess what the riddles are about.
• Take feedback from the groups. *Could you guess what the riddles were about? Were they too hard or too easy?*
• Recap the success criteria. *Did your riddles meet the success criteria?*

Assessment pointers

• S&L: group work and poems will show how well the children collaborate and discuss ideas.
• AF4 (R): whole-class discussion and the group riddles show how far the children understand the features of riddle poems.

Session 2

<table>
<tr><td>We are learning to ...
• understand how authors use puns
(PNS Strands 8.3)
Assessment Focuses
AF (R): 5</td><td>Resources
Plague Around (film)
Year 3 Poetry Collection
ITP: P3.4</td></tr>
</table>

Shared teaching

• Share the learning objective and ask the children if they ever got words mixed up when they were little, e.g. saying mink instead of milk?
• Play Chinese Whispers to demonstrate how we sometimes mishear words.
• Explain that the children are going to read a poem called *Potato Clock* by Roger McGough. *Have you heard of a potato clock? What might it look like? What would it be used for?*
• Reveal the first four stanzas of '*Potato Clock*' (ITP P3.4). *Why does the speaker in the poem need a potato clock?*
• Click to reveal the last two stanzas. *Did anyone guess that a potato clock was a misunderstanding of 'up at eight o'clock'?*
• Explain that puns use words or phrases that sound the same but can mean more than one thing in order to play a trick on the reader or make them laugh. *Can you think of any puns?* (E.g. What is black and white and red all over? A newspaper!, How do you make a milkshake? Give it a fright!, Why did the apple go out with the orange? She couldn't get a date!)
• Explain the terms 'homophones' and 'homonyms' to the children. Homophones are words which sound the same but are spelt differently and mean different things, e.g. brake/break, pear/pair, sea/see. Homonyms are words which are spelt the same and sound the same,

but mean different things, e.g. 'fan' means something to cool you down, or a keen supporter.
• Watch the first four stanzas of *Plague Around* by Roger McGough until Marker 1. *There is another pun in the title of this poem. Can they guess what it is?*
• Continue to watch until Marker 2. *What will the next line be?* Continue watching to the end. *Did anyone guess what the word play was?*
• Watch the whole poem again.

Independent and Guided

• The children explore puns, homophones and homonyms.
- Complete 'Puns' (PCM P3.2). (T)
- Complete 'Homophones' (PCM P3.3). (TA)
- Complete 'What's the word?' (PCM P3.3).

Plenary

• Recap the learning objective.
• Ask groups to feed back. Ask the lower ability group to tell you some of their new sentences; collect examples of other homophones from the middle ability group and add to the Learning Wall; and ask the group who wrote their own joke puns to share some with the class. *Were they good jokes? Did they make you laugh?*

Assessment pointers

• AF5 (R): PCMs show how far the children understand the use of puns.

Session 3

<table>
<tr><td>We are learning to ...
• explore how authors use alliteration
• write sentences using alliteration
(PNS Strands 8.3, 11.2)
Assessment Focuses
AF (R): 5</td><td>Resources
Year 3 Poetry Collection
PCM: P3.4</td></tr>
</table>

Shared teaching

• Share the learning objectives.
• Play Grammar Poetry. In groups the children try to make up nonsense sentences consisting of an adjective, noun and verb all beginning with the same letter or sound, e.g. angry aardvarks amble, etc. The letters can be chosen in alphabetical order to make it harder.
• *What do you call it when all the words begin with the same sound or letter like this?* (alliteration) Ask for other examples of alliteration.
• Read *Sluggish* by Gina Douthwaite (page 7). *Did you like this poem? Out of all the words beginning with the letter 's', how many can you find that start with the blend 'sl'?* (E.g. 'sluggish', 'slob', 'slug', etc.) *Why has the poet chosen these words?* (Because they sound like a slug.) *What other words can you think of that start with 'sl' that could be used in this poem?* (E.g. sloppy, slippery, slow, etc.)
• Ask the children what other patterns they notice in the poem apart from the alliteration, e.g. the use of rhyme.
• Discuss it as a shape poem. *Which of the other shape poems is* Sluggish *most like?* The children look through the *Year 3 Poetry Collection* to find poems of a similar form, e.g. *The Ladybird Question* and *Bathroom Bug*.
• Read *Hair We Go Again* by Gina Douthwaite (page 8). *What is the pun in the title?* (Hair instead of here.) Compare *Hair We Go Again* with

Sluggish. Which poem did you prefer? How does Hair We Go Again *use alliteration?* (In pairs of words, e.g. 'Wet it' / 'Wash it'.)

Independent and Guided

• The children create their own alliterative sentences.
- Make up alliterative sentences which are tongue twisters.
- Use 'Word bank' (PCM P3.4) to make up alliterative sentences. (TA)
- Work in pairs to construct alliterative sentences using 'Repeat the letters' (PCM P3.4). (T+)

Plenary

• Recap the learning objectives.
• Ask groups to share the alliterative sentences they have created with other groups.
• Take feedback. *What are your favourite sentences?*
• Discuss how some alliterative sentences can be tongue twisters because they are very difficult to say. *Which of the sentences you've heard do you think could be tongue twisters?* Add these to the Learning Wall and have fun saying them as a class.
• Share some popular tongue twisters with the children, e.g. *She sells sea shells on the sea shore; Peter Piper picked a peck of pickled peppers*, etc. Encourage the children to try saying the tongue twisters.

Assessment pointers

• AF5 (R): whole-class discussion and the children's sentences show how far the children understand the use of alliteration.

Session 4

We are learning to ...	Resources
• understand how list poems are written (PNS Strands 7.5) **Assessment Focuses** AF (R): 4, 5	*Year 3 Poetry Collection* PCM: P3.5, P3.6

Shared teaching

- Share the learning objective.
- Write 'In Case of Fire Break Glass' on the whiteboard. *Have you seen these words anywhere? Are they displayed anywhere in school? What do they mean? Why are they found on fire safety equipment?*
- Explain that poets sometimes use 'found language' like this, words and phrases found around us in everyday life, and play around with it in poems.
- Talk Partners discuss predictions about the poem. *What do you think a poem called* In Case of Fire Break Glass *will be about? How do you think the poet might play with this language?*
- Read *In Case of Fire* by Roger McGough (page 11) *Did anyone guess correctly or was the poem a surprise?*
- The children Think-Pair-Share how Roger McGough plays around with the words he has found. *What patterns can you see in the poem?*
- Take feedback and discuss the features of the poem, e.g. the use of the same three words at the start of each line, the same line at the beginning and the end, and the word at the end of each line used in the middle of the next line.
- Explain that because each line starts with the same words it looks like a list, so these kinds of poems are sometimes called 'list poems'. Discuss ideas for other list poems.

Independent and Guided

- The children work in pairs to write simple list poems.
- 🔵 Create a list poem using 'List poems' (PCM P3.5).
- 🔵 As above. (T+)
- 🔵 Complete 'List poem framework' (PCM P3.6). (TA+)

Plenary

- Recap the learning objective.
- Ask pairs to share the list poems they have written with other pairs.
- Take feedback. *Who thinks another pair has written a good list poem? What makes it effective?*
- As an optional extra activity, the children could keep a record of any found language they see inside and outside the school. This could then be used to inspire new list poems in Session 8.

Assessment pointers

- S&L: pair work and poems will show how far the children can collaborate to explore and develop ideas.
- AF4, 5 (R): whole-class discussion and the children's own list poems show how far they understand how list poems are organised at text and word level.

Session 5

We are learning to ...	Resources
• understand how authors make up new similes • create similes (PNS Strands 8.3, 11.2) **Assessment Focuses** AF (R): 5; AF (W): 1, 7	*The Writer of this Poem* (film) *Year 3 Poetry Collection* ITP: P3.5 PCM: P3.7

Shared teaching

- Share the learning objectives.
- Show 'Comparisons' (ITP P3.5) and challenge the children to complete the well known comparisons. *Can you think of any other similar comparisons?* Add these to the Learning Wall.
- *What do we call words like 'sharp', 'strong', 'bold'?* Revisit the term 'adjective' and check that all of the children recognise this term.
- Encourage them to identify other adjectives in the comparisons on ITP P3.5.
- Explain that we call comparisons that use 'as something as ... ' similes and that authors use similes to create images in readers' minds by comparing something with something else.
- Write 'The Writer of this Poem' on the board. *What comparisons do you think the poet will make about himself?*
- Talk Partners discuss possible endings to the sentence 'The writer of this poem is as ... '. Take feedback and make a note of good ideas.
- Read *The Writer of this Poem* by Roger McGough (page 11). *Did you guess the comparisons the poet made? What did you think of the poem?*
- Discuss the way Roger McGough plays with language by changing the usual similes to new ones, e.g. 'as bold as a boxing-glove', 'as sharp

as a nib', 'as strong as scaffolding'. Check the children understand the comparisons in the poem.
- *Do you think the comparisons are true?* Draw attention to the last line. *What does this mean?*
- Watch *The Writer of this Poem*. *Which comparisons do you now think are true? Are there any you are not sure about?*
- The children Think-Pair-Share other similes for some of the adjectives in Stanzas 2 and 3. Ask for a few examples and add them to the Learning Wall.
- *What other ways does the poet play with language?* Draw out the use of a tick symbol instead of the word 'tick' in Stanza 3.

Independent and Guided

- The children explore adjectives and/or similes.
- 🔵 Make up some new similes using other adjectives. (TA+)
- 🔵 Use 'Similes 1' (PCM P3.7) to rewrite traditional similes.
- 🔵 Use 'Similes 2' (PCM P3.7) to create similes. (T+)

Plenary

- Recap the learning objectives.
- Talk Partners share their similes and discuss what they like about each other's ideas.
- Take feedback and add examples of good similes to the Learning Wall.

Assessment pointers

- S&L: pair work will show how far the children can listen and respond to others.
- AF5 (R): class discussion shows how far the children can respond to poetic language and understand similes.
- AF1, 7 (W): similes show how far the children can use language imaginatively.

Session 6

We are learning to ...	Resources
• work together effectively in groups, including all group members • write language play poems (PNS Strands 3.2, 9.4) **Assessment Focuses** AF (W): 1, 7	*Year 3 Poetry Collection* ITP: (P3.5), P3.6 PCM: (P3.7)

Shared teaching

- Share the learning objectives.
- Explain that the children are going to write some whole-class poems that use language play, using poems looked at in Sessions 4 and 5 as models.
- Explain that the children will be using *The Writer of this Poem* by Roger McGough to help them write their own poem.
- Read the poem again (page 11). Explain that the children will be keeping the first line and the last four lines of the original poem the same but adding two or three new stanzas in between. Their poem will not have to rhyme like the original.
- Roger McGough uses a 'tick' sign in the original poem. *Does anyone have an idea for something similar in our poem?* (E.g. a star, exclamation mark, question mark, ellipsis, etc.)
- Show '*The Writer of this Poem*' (ITP P3.6). Encourage the children to offer suggestions to add to the first stanza. Remind the children of the similes on the Learning Wall.
- Explain that the children are going to work in groups to create more similes. Remind them to actively listen and respond to all members of the group.

- Use Modelled Writing to demonstrate completing the first stanza of the whole-class poem, e.g. *The writer of this poem / Is taller than a mountain*, etc.

Independent and Guided

- The children work in groups to create more similes to use in their new stanzas, using different adjectives rather than the ones in the poem. Encourage them to use the Learning Wall, annotated 'Comparisons' (ITP P3.5) and 'Similes'(PCM P3.7) to help develop ideas.
- Write one or two stanzas and use rhyme as in the original.
- Write a new four-line stanza. (T)
- Write one or two new similes. (TA)

Plenary

- Recap the learning objectives.
- Recall ITP P3.6 and ask groups to offer suggestions to create the middle two stanzas, to add to the class poem. Save for reference.
- Discuss performance poetry. *How did Roger McGough perform the original poem? What did he do to make it interesting?*
- Use the class suggestions to perform the new whole-class version of *The Writer of this Poem. How does it compare to the original? What did you prefer about the original? What do you particularly like about the new version?*

Assessment pointers

- S&L: group work and poems will show how well the children collaborate to explore and discuss ideas.
- AF1, 7 (W): the whole-class composition and the children's group contributions will show how well they can make apt word choices to create interesting similes.

Session 7

We are learning to ...	Resources
• write language play poems (PNS Strands 9.4) **Assessment Focuses** AF (W): 1, 7	*Year 3 Poetry Collection*

Shared teaching

- Share the learning objective.
- Play Fortunately/Unfortunately where players take it in turn to tell a story in sentences which begin alternately with these words, e.g. *Unfortunately I lost my dinner money on the way to school. Fortunately I don't like school dinners! Unfortunately ....* .
- Explain that the children are going to use *In Case of Fire* by Roger McGough (page 11), which was read in Session 4, as a model. Read the poem again.
- Demonstrate how to create a different opening line using the same phrase, e.g. *In case of hunger buy chocolate* or *In case of maths use calculator*. Write this on the whiteboard and ask for suggestions for the next line, e.g. *In case of chocolate bake cake, In case of calculator press keys*.
- Talk Partners work together to think of more lines to continue the poem, e.g. *In case of cake have birthday, In case of keys open door*, etc.
- Take feedback and add the class's favourite lines to the poem.

Independent and Guided

- The children work in small groups to write more lines for the class poem.

- Extend the class poem further before returning to the original line in order to finish it as in Roger McGough's poem.
- Finish the class poem. (T)
- Write some more lines for the class poem. (TA+)

Plenary

- Recap the learning objective.
- Take suggestions from the groups and add lines to the class poem. Draw attention to the fact that some new lines may not make sense or follow on well from previous lines. Encourage the children to offer suggestions for adapting the lines so they progress clearly and eventually return to the beginning of the poem.
- Discuss performance poetry. *How do you think you could perform this poem? How can you divide up the lines? Should you use different voices: loud, soft, serious, etc?*
- Use the class suggestions to perform the new whole-class poem. *How does it compare to the original? What do you like about the new version?*

Assessment pointers

- S&L: group work will show how well the children can organise and sustain collaboration and discussion.
- AF1, 7 (W): the whole-class poem will show how far the children are able to write imaginatively, selecting relevant ideas and making apt word choices.

Session 8

<table>
<tr><td>

We are learning to ...
- use success criteria to give each other feedback
- write language play poems
  (PNS Strands 9.1, 9.4)

Assessment Focuses
AF (W): 7
</td><td>

Resources
Year 3 Poetry Collection
ITP: P3.7
</td></tr>
</table>

Shared teaching

- Share the learning objectives and explain that in Sessions 8, 9 and 10, the children will be writing their own poems that play with language and can choose which kind of poem to write from the different ones read so far.
- Reread some of the poems from earlier in this unit.
- Recap the kind of language play looked at in these poems, e.g. riddles like *What Am I?*, poems that use puns like *Potato Clock* (page 4) and *Plague Around* (page 10) by Roger McGough, alliterative poems like *Sluggish* (page 7) and *Hair We Go Again* (page 8) by Gina Douthwaite, list poems using 'found language' like *In Case of Fire* (page 11) and poems using new similes like *The Writer of this Poem* (page 11) by Roger McGough, etc. Make a note of the key features for the children to refer to during independent work.
- Explain that the children will be writing the first draft of their own poems in the rest of the session.
- Show 'Play with words' (ITP P3.7) and establish success criteria for the children's own poems. *Are there any you would like to add or change?*

Independent and Guided

- The children work independently to choose one or more types of poem from the *Year 3 Poetry Collection* as a model for their own poem(s). Remind the children to think about the types of language play their chosen poem includes and to try and use this in their own drafts.
- ∞ Draft more than one type of poem.
- ∞ Draft one type of poem. (T)
- ☉ As above. (TA+)

Plenary

- Recap the learning objectives.
- Talk Partners share and discuss each other's drafts. Encourage the children to use Two Stars and a Wish for their partner's poem, referring to the success criteria on ITP P3.7. *Do your poems match the criteria? Are there any points your partner has definitely covered? Are there any points your partner has missed?*
- Encourage some of the children to share their drafts, while the rest of the class comment on the poems. *What type of language play poems are they? Which of the poems looked at in this unit are they most like?*
- Save the drafts and the children's notes on their Talk Partner's feedback for use in Session 9.

Assessment pointers

- S&L: pair work will show how sensitively the children can express and respond to opinions.
- AF7 (W): the children's draft poems show how far they are able to choose appropriate vocabulary and make adventurous word choices.

Session 9

<table>
<tr><td>

We are learning to ...
- develop success criteria
- present poems using consistent handwriting
- revise and present our own play poems
  (PNS Strands 9.1, 12.1, 12.2)

Assessment Focuses
AF (W): 3
</td><td>

Resources
Year 3 Poetry Collection
ITP: (P3.7)
</td></tr>
</table>

Shared teaching

- Share the learning objectives. Explain that the children will revise their first drafts using the notes they made on their partner's feedback from Session 8. Talk Partners should support each other further as they make their revisions.
- Explain that they can illustrate their poems and, if possible, use ICT to present their finished poems. In Session 10, they will be performing their poems to the rest of the class.
- Recall 'Play with words' (ITP P3.7) and remind the children of the success criteria for their language play poems. *Are there any new success criteria you would like to add?*
- Talk Partners discuss which of the success criteria they think is most important for their poems. Take feedback and discuss ways in which the children can use the success criteria to develop their poems.
- Turn to the centre page of the *Year 3 Poetry Collection* and read Roger McGough's notes 'How I write'. *Where does Roger McGough get his ideas from?* (Usually staring at a blank page.) *What is his favourite poem?* (Whichever one he is working on.) *Why?* (Because he doesn't know how it will end.) *How does he write?* (With different pens and then on a computer.) *What does he do with his old drafts?* (He keeps them so that he can see how the poem has changed.)

- Explain that, like Roger McGough, the children are going to enjoy finding out how their poems are going to end.

Independent and Guided

- The children start again with a different pen, a new piece of paper and their old draft. Ask the children to spend a little time staring at the blank page, like Roger McGough, and thinking about the changes they want to make to their poem. Encourage them to use their partner's feedback and the success criteria on ITP P3.7 to help them write their new version.
- ∞ Create a final draft of more than one type of poem.
- ∞ Create a final draft of one type of poem. (T)
- ☉ As above. (TA+)

Plenary

- Recap the learning objectives.
- Talk Partners share their final drafts and explain the changes they have made, comparing their old and new drafts. They comment on how well the drafts have been improved, referring to the success criteria on ITP P3.7.
- Explain that the children will be performing their poems to the class in Session 10. *Have you got any ideas about how you would like to perform your poems?*
- Save the final draft poems for use in Session 10.

Assessment pointers

- S&L: pair work will show how well the children can express and explain relevant ideas.
- AF3 (W): the children's final draft poems will show how far they are able to sequence and present whole texts effectively.

We are learning to ...	Resources
• prepare and perform a poem • discuss and evaluate each other's performances (PNS Strands 1.1, 4.3) **Assessment Focuses** AF (W): 3, 7	*Plague Around* (film) *The Writer of this Poem* (film) ITP: (P3.4), P3.8

Shared teaching

- Share the learning objectives.
- Watch the performance poems from this unit, *Plague Around* and *The Writer of this Poem. What techniques does the poet use? How does he make his performance interesting? Does he change his voice, use actions or pauses, etc?*
- Show 'Performance poems' (ITP P3.8) and add any other suggested success criteria. *Are there other things you could do that the poet doesn't do?* (E.g. use sound effects, do a choral performance, etc.) *How can you stress the word play in your poems?*
- Refer back to the class suggestions made in Session 6 about performing the whole-class version of *The Writer of this Poem.*
- Look back at '*Potato Clock*' (ITP P3.4). Discuss ways to vary your voice when a poem is read aloud and any actions they could use. Add any further suggestions from the children to ITP P3.8.
- Perform the poem again and encourage the class to use Two Stars and a Wish to evaluate your performance.

Independent and Guided

- The children work in pairs to plan a performance of their poems using ITP P3.8 for ideas. They rehearse a performance of their poem and their partner offers suggestions for improvements. Encourage the children to speak slowly, clearly and fluently so that the audience can follow the words, and to vary their voices to make the reading more interesting for their audience.

- **∞∞** Choose which one of their poems to perform with an emphasis on the word play.

- **∞** Focus on a clear performance with dramatic pauses to surprise the listener. (TA)

- **●** Focus on speaking slowly, clearly and fluently. (T)

Plenary

- Recap the learning objectives.
- Organise a 'Poetry Show' where the children perform the final versions of their language play poems to the class. If possible, film or record the performance to review and play to other listeners.
- Encourage the children to evaluate their own performance. *What did you do well? What would you change next time?*
- Create a classroom display of the final poems or publish them for other audiences to read, e.g. as a book for other adults and children in the school to read or on the Internet for other schools to read.
- Recap the unit as a whole. *What did you enjoy most? What do you still find difficult? Do you want to read more of the poet's work?*

Assessment pointers

- S&L: poetry readings will show how far the children can shape their speech to engage listeners.
- AF3, 7 (W): the children's finished poems will show how far they are able to organise and sequence whole texts and make appropriate and adventurous word choices.

What am I?

Fill in gaps to complete the riddle:

I'm wider than a

I'm deeper than a

Sometimes I'm so calm that

Other times

Beneath the surface you will find

Children love to visit me to

(Answer: the sea)

A green riddle

1. Write answers to the questions to create a riddle about a tree:

a. What is the trunk like?

It feels rough when you touch it.

b. What are the branches like?

c. What are the roots like?

d. What are the leaves like?

e. How does the tree change through the year?

f. Who lives in the tree?

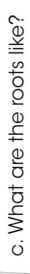

2. Now use your answers to write sentences.

My skin is rough when you touch me.

Puns

1. Match the two parts of the jokes . Discuss the meanings of each pun.

Did you hear about the man who was cut in half?

running late.

A small boy swallowed some coins and was taken to a hospital. When his grandmother telephoned to ask how he was, a nurse said,

A woolly jumper.

The jogger overslept and found himself

No change yet.

What do you call a sheep that can do the long jump?

He's all right now.

2. Make a list of other jokes that use puns. You can look in joke books for ideas.

_____

_____

_____

Homophones

1. Write the meanings of the pairs of homophones.

Remember: homophones sound the same but are written differently and mean different things.

Check _____   Cheque _____

_____   _____

Hare _____   Hair _____

_____   _____

Site _____   Sight _____

_____   _____

2. Write a list of other pairs of words that are homophones.

What's the word?

1. Complete the sentences with the homophones.

Remember: homophones sound the same but are written differently and mean different things.

too   pair   two   sea   week   pear   one   here   won   weak   see   hear

a. I'd like to paddle in the s _ _ . Then I can s _ _ the fish.

b. I'd like to eat a p _ _ _ . But not a p _ _ _ of socks!

c. Can you h _ _ _ me? What if I stand over h _ _ _ ?

d. We w _ _ the cup! We're number o _ _ !

e. I love chocolate t _ _ . That makes t _ _ of us.

f. I'm feeling very w _ _ _ . It must be the last day of the w _ _ _ .

2. Write more sentences using these homophones.

Word bank

1. Use the words from the lists to write your own alliterative sentences.

slithered	slippery	slowly	slime
dark	damp	dreary	drab
jerky	jump	jittery	jingle
flowing	fluffy	fly	float
growl	groan	grumble	grind

2. Give your partner three words that begin with the same sound and let your partner make up a sentence with them.

- ✂

Repeat the letters

1. Complete these sentences. Try to include another word that starts with the same sound.

a. The bossy bumblebee _____

b. Gus the greedy gorilla _____

c. A herd of hungry hippos _____

d. Six soggy sandwiches _____

e. Two terrible twins _____

f. My magic mirror _____

2. Make up some more alliterative sentences of your own.

Name: _____   Date: _____

List poems

1. Read the list poem.

When I'm Rich

When I'm rich, I'll live in a different house each year

When I'm rich, I'll have a different holiday each month

When I'm rich, I'll drive a different car each week

When I'm rich, I'll wear different clothes each day

When I'm rich, I'll eat different food each mealtime

When I'm rich, nothing will be the same.

2. Use one of the lines below to start your poem. Try to think of a slightly different line to end with.

If I was the strongest person alive ...

I dreamed I ...

When I'm grown up ...

When I'm prime minister ...

If I could see the future ...

I wish I was ...

List poem framework

Finish this list poem using your own words.

I Dreamed

I dreamed I scored the winning goal, but really I missed a penalty

I dreamed I won a gold medal, but really I came last

I dreamed I was top in the maths test, but really _____

I dreamed I won the lottery, but really _____

I dreamed I found some _____ , but really it was _____

I dreamed _____ , but really _____

I dreamed _____ , but really _____

I dreamed

Really!

Similes 1

Change the noun to make the traditional similes more modern.

Traditional simile	New simile

As bright as a button. ➤ As bright as a _____

As cool as a cucumber. ➤ As cool as a _____

As free as a bird. ➤ As free as a _____

As strong as an ox. ➤ As strong as _____

As old as the hills. ➤ As old as _____

As wise as an owl. ➤ As wise as _____

- -

Similes 2

Choose an adjective to complete the similes.

blue	wide	tall	huge	sparkling	mysterious
beautiful	colourful	noisy	strong	free	calm

a. As _____ as the wind.   d. As _____ as the moon.

b. As _____ as a mountain.   e. As _____ as a flower.

c. As _____ as the sea.   f. As _____ as a river.